FORWARD

This is a fascinating book, which helped me to understand the traditional Chinese medicine approach to attaining beauty, using acupressure, herbal remedies, breathing techniques and a positive mental attitude.

I was very impressed with the pre and post-treatment photos of women who had only finished a 30-day plan.

Although TCM is thousands of years old there is no method more current than the philosophy of taking control of one's life and health in order to achieve inner and outer beauty. I applause Ping for all of her efforts in bringing the knowledge to us and for her work in creating a superior skin care line which is free of harmful ingredients.

On a personal note, Ping is one of the most special people I have ever met and I feel privileged to have her as a personal doctor of TCM for my family.

Lisa A. Liberatore, MD,
FACS
Board Certified
Otolaryngology- Head & Neck Surgery
Facial Plastic & Reconstructive Surgery

D0369349

DEDICATION

To my husband, James Zhou for his
unconditional support and encouragement,
my son William and daughter Christina
for the support from their young hearts.
To all my patients and readers
of this book,
it is my sincere hope that you may gain
beauty, rejuvenation, enjoyment and
harmony in your life.

REVERSE THE AGING PROCESS
WITH TRADITIONAL CHINESE MEDICINE

ANTI-AGING THERAPY

Healing your skin with natural synergy
from body, mind and spirit

Ping Zhang

Nefeli™

TABLE OF CONTENTS

A Personal Message from Ping Zhang

As a practitioner of Traditional Chinese Medicine, I am often called upon to help people concerned about wrinkles. Many of my patients are surprised at the unusual way I go about rejuvenating their faces. But they are always pleased with the results.

I treat wrinkles according to the Chinese healing philosophy that health and beauty are intertwined. Inner health is the source of our beauty, and our face reflects our inner health. Wrinkles result from internal imbalances, so the best way to diminish them is to correct the inner body imbalances. In many cases, treating the face directly is a very low priority.

I have seen the same thing happen time and again in my practice. It doesn't matter how old or young a person is, how beautiful or plain, how strong or weak. Once an imbalance occurs inside the body, youth and vigor fades and the negative internal condition shows in the face.

I treat the internal condition and the face rejuvenates. Many patients who come to me for reasons that have nothing to do with wrinkles or other facial problems are amazed to see that as a result of their improved internal condition, their wrinkles have smoothed away, their facial complexion has improved, dark spots have disappeared, their hair looks and feels more nourished, and their eyes are brighter than ever.

This ancient theory that external beauty results from inner health is basic to Chinese medicine, but played down in conventional Western medicine. So Traditional Chinese Medicine offers an entirely new approach to smoothing wrinkles for almost every person in the Western world.

I come from a long line of Chinese medicine practitioners. I have inherited a great passion for what I can offer my patients. What I give them is a new understanding of how their bodies' own natural healing capacity holds the key to their health, longevity and facial beauty.

Chinese medicine stimulates and assists that natural healing power. By doing that, the techniques that I offer help your body correct internal imbalances that are causing wrinkles, eye bags, dark eye circles, discoloration and other facial beauty problems.

They have worked for countless Chinese for several centuries. With this book, they will work for you as well.

Your At-Home Anti-Wrinkle Program

I have written this book so that you can use Traditional Chinese Medicine in your own home to diminish the wrinkles on your face and prevent new ones from occurring. You will be taking advantage of many of the same techniques that I use in my practice to cure wrinkles. They are safe, simple and inexpensive (often free, in fact). But they are powerful. There are four kinds of Chinese treatments you will be using:

The first is Chinese herbs, which are now easily available in the United States and elsewhere in the Western world.

The second is acupressure, a self-applied version of acupuncture without the needles.

The third is called Qi Gong (pronounced Chee Gong). It is a time-horned form of mind/body exercise with emphasis on breathing techniques.

The fourth is Chinese food therapy. This is exactly what it sounds like - choosing and eating specific foods for their therapeutic benefits.

A fifth "treatment" that will be very important in your anti-wrinkle program comes under the heading of "lifestyle." I'll give you tips on leading a healthy and stress-free life that will do wonders for your facial complexion, and help the other treatments work better.

As you practice my methods you will also be learning a more natural and holistic approach to health, beauty and rejuvenation. The kind of beauty you will be achieving is based on an improved overall well-being of your body, mind, spirit, and what the Chinese call life energy. All of that holistic health is reflected in smoother and more supple skin, a firmer chin, brighter eyes, nourished lips, and lustrous hair.

East and West

You may have picked up this book because you've already tried one or more of the ultra-modern techniques that address wrinkles, skin sagging, dark spots, etc. Those techniques include facelift surgery, Botox shots, laser treatment and other mechanical procedures. Some people are disappointed with the results of these modern techniques, others are quite happy.

My approach to facial beauty is very different than what those procedures represent. I have already mentioned that the Chinese approach to facial beauty treats the inner cause of wrinkles and other skin problems. As I like to say, we rejuvenate faces from the inside out. And everyone, no matter what their experience with Western-style treatments, can benefit from natural approaches that will take their anti-aging efforts to another level and improve their health along the way.

The Western method is quite the opposite of my inside-out approach. Plastic surgery, for example, deals with the face superficially by tightening the skin. I'm not saying that's a bad thing, but it's very different than anything I would do. And it certainly isn't an approach that lends itself to home treatment.

Laser treatments and Botox shots also approach the problem at skin level rather than treating the internal imbalances that cause wrinkles and other facial skin problems. They often do successfully erase signs of skin aging - for a period of time. But Traditional Chinese Medicine believes that nothing can compare with nourishing and healing the skin from the inside out.

Changing Times

In my more than 10 years of practice, I've seen that the ideas behind Traditional Chinese Medicine have become more widely accepted in the West. In the last decade or so, more and more people have expanded their concept of health and understand that it means something more than just being free of disease.

Chinese medicine's focus on prevention, its holistic integration of body, mind, spirit and vital energy, and its link between internal balance and external beauty have become accepted notions for a large and expanding segment of the Western population

Baby boomers reached their 50's healthy, active and fit. They still want their faces to reflect their overall well-being. They have long been attracted to the idea of "going back to nature," and they're willing and eager to explore Chinese medicine's natural approach to facial rejuvenation.

Fashion and lifestyles have also changed across the board. The idea of putting on heavy cosmetics has lost its appeal. Achieving beauty naturally through improved inner health is an idea whose time has come in the West.

That's why I wrote this book. I'm convinced that there are literally millions of women and men outside Asia who are ready and willing to reap the benefits that Traditional Chinese Medicine offers.

What Lies Ahead

In the pages ahead you'll find a comprehensive do-it-yourself guide to use simple Chinese medicine techniques to smooth out existing wrinkles and prevent new ones. You will also find Chinese treatments that improve a dull or discolored complexion, eye bags and puffiness in the eye area, dark circles around your eyes, and spotting.

The treatments will do more than rejuvenate your face. They will correct the internal body imbalances that are causing your facial beauty problems. They will make you healthier and happier. And they will introduce you to a fascinating field of traditional medicine that has helped people like you for thousands of years.

Here's how I'll be presenting the information and instructions you'll be following:

In Part 1, I'll explain briefly what Traditional Chinese Medicine is and how you'll use it to treat your wrinkles and rejuvenate your face. You certainly don't need to understand the theoretical underpinnings of Chinese medicine in order to benefit from it. But you'll be glad to have an idea of how it differs from Western medicine. And it will definitely help to know the context in which you'll be doing your at-home self-treatments.

Part 2 will describe and explain the do-it-yourself Chinese medicine techniques for preventing and getting rid of wrinkles. You will be told what Chinese herbs to take and what healing whole foods to eat. At-home anti-wrinkle acupressure and Qi Gong routines will be clearly explained and illustrated.

Parts 3 and 4 will give you the best at-home treatments for beautifying your eyes and clearing up other complexion problems such as dullness, discoloration and spotting.

Part 5 offers three more chapters. One helps you to personalize your own facial beauty program, based on your age category. Another chapter takes the self-treatment program to a higher level, incorporating some more advanced TCM concepts such as treatment modifications based on seasonal changes.

In the last chapter, I share with you my experience of creating a line of holistic natural herbal nutritional supplements for taking internally, as well as natural skin-healing products. Both the supplements and the topical skin healing products are based on my years of clinical experience, as well as centuries of TCM practice.

These herbal nutritional supplements and natural herbal skin healing products are geared toward balancing your inner system, which is the ultimate source of health and beauty. They strictly adhere to the ancient Chinese philosophy of using the healing powers of nature. Anything that is unnatural or harmful to the skin is not used.

As I stressed throughout this whole book that all the acupressure, Qi Gonq methods, herbals/herbal formulas, food therapies recommended here are being practiced and used for thousands of years, they are safe and non-toxic, most importantly, they work. If you have time to follow through them and if you happen to have an experienced TCM practitioner at your foot steps to assist you through the process, then that's great , you can then recieve the first hand and first rated results for your anti-aging program. However, I do understand that living in a modern society like this, you may not have enough time to shop around and prepare the food recipes mentioned in the book, or even to find an experienced TCM practitioner to help you for your anti-aging concerns. If that is your case, then I can assure you not to worry about it. Because there is an alternaltive way for you to consider: I have already developed a ready

–to-use program for your concerns. It is called Nefeli line. It includes all you need for your anti-aging concerns, namely, 1.An all natural herbal supplement line with all the anti-aging herbal and food in the formulas, 2. A 100% natural herbal-based paraben free skin care line, This special made-for-you Nefeli anti-aging line covers all you need for your anti-aging concerns including you wrinkle concerns, eye concerns as well as facial discoloration and dark/age spots.

Throughout the book, "Tips From Ping" gives you related information that you'll find helpful. My goal has been to help you benefit not just from Chinese wisdom, but also from my experience in helping people just like you achieve their ultimate facial beauty.

I designed the book so that you can go directly to the chapters that interest you the most. If your main problem is eye puffiness, for example, rather than wrinkles, you can skip from Part 1 straight to Part 3.

The treatments I'll be giving you are simple and effective. Practice them daily and you'll soon notice the positive difference in your face. You will be delighted.

See Your Doctor First

I have one more important message before you start in on your Chinese anti-aging protocols. Please see your doctor or other health care professional before trying any of these self-treatments.

The herbs, foods and exercises in this book are proven safe. However, you may have allergic reaction to any herbs or foods listed in this book, or a pre-existing condition that would contra-indicate one or more of them. Or you may be taking a medication that is incompatible with a certain herb or food. Your doctor can help you avoid any problems. Take this book into the office with you and tell your doctor that you're planning to use the treatments it describes. Get the go-ahead before proceeding.

Then get started. If you have patience and stick with the treatments, you will be happier, healthier and more beautiful.

Important

You must never exceed the recommended dosages of any herb or herbal supplement listed in this book. If any allergic reaction and/or discomfort occur after taking or appling the herbs/herbal formula or any foods listed in the book, discontinue use immediately and consult with your health care professionals. You also must follow any cautions and contraindications for taking herbs/foods mentioned in this book, and for practicing any Qi Gong or acupressure exercises listed in this book.

PART ONE

THE NATURAL PATH TO FACIAL BEAUTY

CHAPTER 1

The Spiritual Basis of Youth and Beauty

The at-home beauty treatments that I will show you to clear your face of wrinkles, eye bags and complexion problems come directly from Traditional Chinese Medicine. This healing discipline is thousands of years old, and it is still practiced successfully today throughout the world. It is very different than the conventional Western-style medicine you may be used to.

Traditional Chinese Medicine is a holistic healing method that treats the body and spirit as one. It is a natural medicine that uses herbs, foods, mind-body exercises, acupuncture and special self-massage routines to stimulate your body's self-healing capacity.

The reason the herbs and the other Chinese treatments in this book will work for you is because they treat the true causes of your facial skin problems. These causes are seldom located in the face itself. The causes are internal health conditions that are reflected in your face.

Traditional Chinese Medicine (which I'll often abbreviate as TCM) beautifies your face by improving these internal conditions. TCM theory holds that these unwanted conditions are the results of imbalance. The treatments in this book will help your body's natural healing powers restore balance. That balance will in turn restore smoothness, clarity and youthfulness to your face.

In other words, beauty and health are intertwined. You can't have one without the other. The information in this book will help you have both.

This system has worked for millions of people for thousands of years. It will work for you too. The Chinese people are famous for their healthy facial complexions. A big reason for that is the traditional use of the same beauty techniques you'll be learning in this book.

The Three Treasures

What do I mean by "balance"? What exactly is being put back into balance with TCM medicine? The answer goes straight to the core of Chinese healing philosophy.

Ancient Chinese sages based their healing philosophy on a concept with a beautiful name — the Three Treasures. The Three Treasures are what make a human being. They are essence, energy and spirit. The Chinese names for them are Jing, Qi (pronounced "chee") and Shen.

Health is the result of these three things being in balance. Disease (and wrinkles) results from an imbalance of the Three Treasures.

When one of the Treasures is out of balance — a low spirit, for example, or stagnant energy — you are out of balance. The intricacies of balance and imbalance can of course be very involved. But your body seeks balance; that's what self-healing is. TCM helps your body in that effort.

The treatments you'll be using to restore luster to your face are not medicines, per se. They are gifts of nature. They come from nature to help your natural self-healing powers restore the natural harmony to your Three Treasures,

The very notion of the Three Treasures came from observing nature. The ancient sages saw three treasures in the heavens — the sun, moon and stars. They found this same trinity in the human being — essence, energy and spirit. The synergistic interplay of these Three Treasures is the basis of Chinese medicine.

None of these three words — energy, essence and spirit — have precisely the same meaning in Chinese medicine as they do in common English usage. But it helps to use familiar concepts to begin to understand what these treasures actually are.

Essence, for example, can be thought of as the physical component, the basic material that forms the human body. It's the part of you that reproduces, which regenerates. "Pre-natal" essence is what you were born with. "Post-natal" essence comes from what you eat and drink (and breathe) after you're born. In Chinese medicine, the most important organ for essence is the kidney; deficiency in kidney essence is definitely to be avoided.

Energy as a Treasure is more accurately thought of as "vital energy" or "life force" than what the word "energy" usually denotes in English. That's why I prefer to use the Chinese word Qi and will do so often in the pages ahead. If you think of essence as the physical, you can think of Qi as the physiological. It is the body's power to function, the source of all movement.

Qi, your life force, moves through your body in known patterns through channels, also called meridians. The acupressure routines you'll be doing and the acupuncture protocols a trained professional will use are designed to improve this flow of Qi through the channels. There are many kinds of Qi, and each organ system has its own Qi.

When TCM talks about spirit, or Shen, it's expressing everything about you as an individual that is not material. That includes consciousness, thinking, all your cognitive functions, and your emotions. It's also a way of describing your vitality, the manifestation of your essence and energy that make you alive and not just an accumulation of physical and chemical phenomena.

The Treasure of spirit is not independent of the other two Treasures. All three Treasures interrelate. Qi comes from essence, but at the same time essence formation can't happen without Qi. Vitality comes from both.

Therefore, if your essence and Qi are abundant, your spirit will be healthy. If your spirit is weak, then there is not enough essence and Qi in your body, since your spirit (vitality) is the external manifestation of your essence and Qi.

Though the Three Treasures are equal in importance, the role of the spirit in Chinese medicine in general — and for facial beauty treatments in particular — is the most intriguing for many people, as well as the most difficult to understand. Let's take a little bit closer look at this thing called Shen.

What TCM Means by Spirit

Traditional Chinese Medicine gives a broad meaning and a narrow meaning to Shen, or spirit. The broad meaning is the outward manifestation of everything that makes up the vitality of a human being, the nonphysical expression of essence and Qi. In the narrow sense, Shen refers to consciousness, cognition, and thinking.

Mind and spirit are not separated in TCM thinking. When it is mentioned that an individual is treated "holistically," the Western interpretation would usually be that the body, mind and soul are included in the term "holistic." TCM says the body, spirit and energy (Qi) are what combine to make a "holistic" entity.

That difference aside, the holistic approach is the only way to be truly healthy. Achieving a balance of the Three Treasures is the highest level of life preservation and rejuvenation.

The spirit, however, is first among equals. A balanced spirit is a TCM healing priority.

You can see why if you think of your body as a production plant, well equipped with machines (your organs) and a power and communication system (Qi). No matter how well each individual unit is functioning, the plant won't produce unless there is a central command system coordinating the action. That's your spirit, through your thinking processes, both conscious and unconscious.

When your spirit is out of balance, you can't think clearly. The command center is inefficient. That's why, for example, destructive emotions can weaken the spirit, leading to blocked energy flow, organ imbalance, and disease. This is reflected in your face.

That's why the spiritual aspect, sometimes ignored in Western medicine, is so central to Chinese medicine. How we deal with stress, how we adapt to change, the way we see what's going on in the world around us, the appropriateness of the lifestyle we adopt, the way we control our emotions — all of these are spiritual matters that affect our health and beauty.

It's no exaggeration to say that spiritual healing is the most important part of your facial beauty program. Your spirit must be strong and healthy before any improvement is made. Only through a strong spirit can you achieve the results and make smart decisions that will guide your progress.

You've been aware of this in daily life. When you're calm internally, the muscles in your face feel more relaxed, more natural. Anger disturbs your face. Accumulated negative emotions, such as feelings of hopelessness, dull the eyes.

A balanced, uplifted spirit is not just achieved by praying, as Western religion might advocate. TCM relies on natural, not just supernatural, methods. TCM uses herbs, food and exercises to treat spiritual imbalances directly. You will be introduced to many of them in the pages to come.

Taoism, Buddhism, Confucianism and Healing

Taoism, Buddhism and Confucianism all deal with the spirit, but they aren't really religions as the term is usually thought of in the Western world. They are three systems of philosophical thinking that arose at different periods in China's 5,000-year history. We are interested in them here because all three have contributed greatly to the development of Traditional Chinese Medicine. They also apply directly to your quest for clearer, smoother, healthier facial skin.

One of many points these three disciplines have in common is a stress on spiritual healing. They recognize that spiritual strength and calmness underlie physical health, allowing the body to heal from the inside out.

At the same time, they place great emphasis on physical health, since the spiritual (Shen) is nourished by the physical (essence). They also teach what I will be repeating often — that a smooth, radiant youthful-looking face is a reflection of internal balance, which in turn is made possible by a strong, healthy spirit.

So in a sense, you are practicing philosophies of Taoism-Buddhism-Confucianism each time you use any of the at-home facial beauty treatments in this book. That doesn't mean you need to "convert" to any of these philosophies, or even understand them completely. But I've found that my students and patients get more out of their Traditional Chinese Medicine treatments when they have some understanding of the great spiritual wisdom at the heart of these healing techniques.

So let's take a look at how Taoism, Buddhism and Confucianism have influenced Chinese medicine over the centuries.

Taoism

Taoism is the oldest of the Chinese philosophical systems and the one that has influenced TCM the most. Not only did Taoism contribute much theory to TCM, it also contributed specific modalities, such as the herbal medicine, food therapy and Qi Gong (mind/body) exercises you'll be using.

You could correctly say that TCM grew out of Taoist teaching. Taoism teaches the integration of essence, Qi and spirit, as does TCM. Taoism encourages calming of the mind, as does TCM. Taoism practices adjusting to seasonal changes, balancing the seven emotions, and all-natural healing. So does TCM.

Taoism's ultimate prescription for mankind is to seek and attain one's true place in the universe. Only by accepting nature and living in harmony can one achieve happiness. Through its teachings, Taoism shows the "Way" to this harmony. The word for the Way is "Tao." (It is sometimes spelled in English translation as "Dao" and "Daoism," which is really closer to its Chinese pronunciation.)

Taoism sees the goal of healing as not just to attain health and balance but also to achieve longevity — a long life. Spiritual healing is strongly stressed as a means to that end. Spiritual exercise — as practiced in the Qi Gong routines you'll learn — is considered the highest level of the healing arts. The aim of these exercises is to clear and calm the heart (the ruler of emotions), clearing it of self-desire.

Taoism's approach to stress management is to use such exercises to learn to be happy and grateful for what you already have. This is a particularly important point for your facial beauty goals.

Our modern lives are goal-oriented, fostering frustration. We let things bother us — health, family, career, and children. This invites what we call "sub-health conditions," that might include depression, unmanaged stress, an irregular lifestyle. Organ systems are impaired as a result, balance is disturbed, and the aging process is speeded up. Wrinkles, eye puffiness, facial discoloration and hair loss are some results. As I will be repeating often, your face reflects your internal body health.

These things are avoidable if we practice living right. Taoism tells us, for example, that we decide ourselves whether to be happy or not. We also choose our own lifestyles — healthy or harmful. I will stress throughout this book the importance of making the right lifestyle decisions. And I will tell you what they are.

Tips From Ping
To attain ultimate internal balance, you need to learn to eat well, play well, and rest well.

Buddhism

Buddhism entered China almost 2,000 years ago, but was a relative latecomer compared to the much older and homegrown Taoism. Buddhism teaches that suffering in life is due to attachment, which can be overcome by achieving enlightenment and wisdom via certain behaviors and practices. It is a challenging and rewarding philosophical system, but we'll focus here only on its contributions to Traditional Chinese Medicine.

Buddhism stresses internal calmness and self-discipline. It uses meditation to purify the mind through adjusting the breath. The practice of Buddhist meditation in China is called Zen. From the TCM point of view, Zen benefits life preservation and disease prevention, the two primary goals of TCM.

Buddhism strongly influenced the development of Qi Gong exercises in TCM. The ultimate purpose of Zen meditation is to enlighten the mind. But the meditation aspects of Qi Gong become a higher-level treatment for mental and spiritual imbalances.

Giving up negative thoughts, for example, is a powerful means to foment spiritual health in the TCM sense. The Zen techniques as adapted to Qi Gong exercises heal the heart, which in TCM means clearing out negative emotions. We've already talked about the importance of that for achieving the internal health that helps get rid of wrinkles and eye puffiness, as well as facial spotting and discoloration.

Tips From Ping
Keep the following in mind for your entire beauty program: Sleep is a pill for beauty. Happiness is another pill for beauty. Learn to let go of things that bother your mind.

Confucianism

The Chinese philosopher Confucious (551 B.C.- 479 B.C.) stressed the importance of ethical behavior over antisocial behavior. He advocated treating others kindly, practicing moderation in all things, and cultivating your own mind.

Those concepts are also a key to TCM. Wisdom and kindness bring happiness and health. Moderation is at the center of TCM, which is always seeking balance. Moderation also governs TCM treatments. A certain food may be good for a certain organ system; too much of it can cause damage.

Moderation is also adopted by TCM in its approach to emotions. Even positive emotions are considered harmful in excess. TCM's lifestyle guidelines also emphasize moderation, and even encourage adopting a "regular" lifestyle.

Confucious thought of ethical behavior, moderation, pursuit of wisdom, and healing not as several goals but as all part of one idea. His teachings consisted of ways to reach this one goal.

Confucious also taught that the inner peace that comes from attaining this ideal strengthens the spirit and therefore overall health — just as TCM does.

Only when the spirit is calm and balanced, he said, can "the skin be enriched and relaxed, the eyes brightened, the extremities strong, and the body's Palace of Essence replenished."

His prescription for nourishing the spirit is to adjust your emotions. Try not to act on instinct, don't be stubborn or selfish. Practice what he called "forget-me," a state where the body and mind are unaffected by destructive emotions. Much of what this book will show you how to do will help you achieve that health-inducing state.

Confucious considered physical activity to be an important element of a rejuvenating life. Life, he said, depends on movement. He also saw the connection between a regular lifestyle and internal health.

Tips From Ping
You don't need to be a follower of Confucianism, Taoism or Buddhism to enjoy the beauty benefits of Traditional Chinese Medicine. But your efforts will benefit tremendously if you practice positive thinking. A positive attitude generates a very real power that complements and enhances your body's healing power. Try it. Think positive!

CHAPTER 2

Beauty's Just Another Word For Balance

Many of my patients and students wonder why Traditional Chinese Medicine techniques give them better results in terms of improving overall well being than what the more economically powerful conventional Western medicine seems to offer.

The answer is that TCM goes about smoothing wrinkles and clearing up complexion problems in a completely different way. Not only are most of the actual treatments different, the entire approach is different.

The TCM methods you'll be using distinguish themselves from conventional Western medicine in four key ways:

TCM treats the individual, not the disease. In this case, you won't be concerned with "wrinkles" in the abstract (or "eye bags, or "discoloration"). Rather, you'll be concerned with you , with what's going on in your being that creates your wrinkles (or eye bags or discoloration).

TCM's strongest stress is on prevention. What's considered "superior" treatment is prevention. Treating a person who is already sick is considered an unwise approach to medicine.

TCM treats the whole person holistically. The herbs and exercises you'll be using address all aspects of your existence — the physical, the spiritual and the life energy.

TCM treats the root causes, not the symptoms. This is what I call healing from the inside out. Much of the root cause of wrinkles is not in the face, but in internal body imbalances that can be improved with natural herbs, foods and exercises.

Another equally important difference is the unique way TCM looks at the person being treated. TCM theory sees anatomy and physiology very differently than Western practitioners.

It's not that the Chinese body works any differently than a non-Chinese body. But the way Chinese sages and physicians understand it and describe it is thoroughly different. This system of understanding is extremely complex and uses a metaphorical language far removed from what Western doctors are used to.

But it has worked well for thousands of years. And in my experience, it is the best approach to explaining and treating facial beauty concerns.

Your facial beauty program will introduce you to this fascinating world of the Chinese theory of health and healing. Of course you don't need to master it to reap the benefits of my anti-wrinkle program. But you'll get more out of the treatments if you know a little bit about why you're taking this herb or that herb, or why you're doing a certain acupressure routine.

You've already been introduced to the most important concept — the Three Treasures of essence, energy, and spirit (Jing, Qi and Shen). Let's take a brief look at the rest of the picture.

Yin and Yang

You've surely had occasion to see the sign of Yin and Yang, the black Yin figure and the identical but white Yang figure forming a circle and divided by a flowing curved line. Look again and notice how the position of the figures puts the Yang inside the Yin and vice versa.

The Yin/Yang sign explains the structure of all phenomena in the world, including the human body and its functions. There are two sides to everything in the physical world, polar opposites but integrated. Something cannot exist with just one of these. Without Yin, there isn't a half a thing with just Yang. There's nothing.

Hence night and day, male and female, black and white, and so on.

Yin and Yang are at the core of Chinese medicine as well. The body has Yin and Yang, and that's reflected in its structures and operations. There are Yang organs and organ functions, and Yin organs and organ functions.

Essence and blood are Yin, but they rely on Yang organ function and Yang energy flow.

TCM works to keep body Yin and Yang in balance. If any part of Yin or Yang is weakened, the balance will be thrown off and problems will arise, problems that show up on your face.

For example, young people tend to have too much Yang, which manifests itself in the face as acne.

Menopausal women, on the other hand, tend to have less Yin. Diminished Yin itself can ultimately result in dry and easily wrinkled skin. At the same time, less Yin means a relative overabundance of Yang, a reason for hot flashes.

When Yang is underrepresented in the body, the Qi function (a Yang function) will be weak. That creates conditions (such as phlegm obstruction) that can cause all sorts of facial problems, including sagging and puffy eye bags.

As I'll be pointing out to you as they come up, many of the foods, herbs and exercises you'll be learning about work specifically to increase weakened Yin or Yang, as well as balancing the two.

Energy Channels and Points

Your life energy "Qi" flows through channels that we often call meridians. These aren't tubes or any other physical structure, but energy pathways that connect the body.

Centuries of detailed study and observation enabled the Chinese sages to trace the meridians' paths and understand exactly where they go. Even more amazing, they have been able to identify and locate hundreds of special points along those channels where the energy can be influenced positively for health benefits. That's the basis of acupuncture, and of the acupressure routines so important to your facial beauty program.

I know that Qi flowing through channels is a difficult concept to picture. TCM also recognizes a more familiar action — blood flowing from organs through vessels to other organs. Qi flow is similar, but with energy instead of a fluid. As a matter of fact, what is true is that Qi resides in the blood and pushes blood to flow. By the same token, it pushes lymph flow. But Qi is not limited to push liquid flow, it performs other bigger functions. Organs generate much Qi, and the meridians deliver that energy to nourish the whole body, including the extremities and the face.

There are 14 principle meridians, and dozens of secondary channels. Twelve of the 14 are associated with and pertain to specific organ systems. That is why we talk about the lung channel or the gallbladder meridian. ("Meridian" and "channel" are interchangeable words). These organ channels are actually symmetrical pairs of channels.

Two other special channels run in a single line up the center of the front and back of the body. They are not connected with specific organs. They are called the Du meridian or channel and the Ren meridian or channel, also known as the Governing channel and the Conception channel.

Here are 14 principle channels. Several are key to your facial beauty program, and they'll be popping up quite often as we describe the home treatments you'll use. For convenience, we abbreviate most of

Channel Abbreviations

Lung	LU	Large Intestine	LI
Kidney	KI	Urinary Bladder	UB
Spleen	SP	Gall Bladder	GB
Heart	HT	Sanjiao	SJ
Liver	LIV	Pericardium	PC
Stomach	ST	Du	DU
Small Intestine	SI	Ren	REN

the channels with two- or three-letter initials.

The Sanjiao is often called the Triple Burner or Triple Energizer. It pertains to the upper, middle and lower parts of the trunk of the body (the mid-torsal area). It is not associated with a specific organ as we know it.

The specific energy points along the meridians also have names, but we usually refer to them with numbers. Thus one point along the kidney meridian is KI3. Of course, there are actually two of them, as all but two of the channels are symmetrically paired.

I'll be mentioning the points' names in Chinese and English as they come up, because they're often fascinating in their description of the point's location or function. For example, KI 3 is called the Great Canyon because it's found in a depression near your Achilles tendon.

Energy flow through the meridians is key to your facial beauty program. It is how the organs' energy reaches your face. Since you'll be treating organs more than your face directly, this is important. Note also that all of the Yang meridians actually meet in the face, and all the yin meridians stop in the truck, but internally merge with Yang meridians in the upper part of the body and eventually go to the face.

The Chinese Way of Organizing Organs

Traditional Chinese Medicine sees the same organs as Western medicine, but organizes them differently and describes their functions in a more complex fashion. For example, you may know that the kidneys collect and discharge urine. In TCM, they also store essence and therefore govern reproduction.

TCM thinks of the organs as systems instead of just individual body parts. We've seen how organs operate as systems via the channels through which they disperse the Qi they generate. That's one of the reasons that seemingly distant organs like the liver can have such an important effect on your facial beauty.

The Chinese recognize five of the organs as broadly related in the type of function they carry out. They are considered Yin organs because they retain essence, a Yin Treasure. They are called Zang organs. They are the heart, liver, kidney, spleen and lungs.

The Yang organs are called the Fu organs. They don't retain essence, but rather process it. The Fu organs also perform the function of excreting toxins from the body. Not surprisingly, they are related to digestion. The six Fu organs are: the stomach, the large intestine, the gall bladder, the urinary bladder, the small intestine, and the triple burner or Sanjiao (which performs the function of water metabolism in the body).

A seventh, the pericardium, is also thought of as a Yang organ. With that one included, you can see how the Zang and Fu organs combine to include the 12 main meridians that are based on organs.

The five Zang organs are the most important, especially for anti-wrinkle treatments. Each of the five is paired with a Fu organ in function, creating a Yin/Yang balance that your home treatments will seek to maintain.

We'll of course be dealing with the organ systems in a very limited way for the purpose of this book, concentrating on how they affect your facial beauty. Since the five Zang organs enter into the picture the most, let's review just a bit how TCM looks at their functions.

The Heart

According to TCM theory, the heart rules not just the blood and blood vessels, but also the spirit. Thus the Chinese call the heart "the king of emotions." You'll see time and again how important controlled emotions are for getting rid of wrinkles, so many of your treatments will serve to calm the heart.

The Fu organ that the heart pairs with is the small intestine, which is in charge of transforming pure food into nutrients and unpure food into waste. The heart is directly involved with the blood flow, which is why weakened heart function can lead to pale face, facial swelling and puffiness.

The Lungs

"The life energy of the heavens connects to the lungs," according to the Yellow Emperor's Inner Classic. That's because the lung system controls respiration, a Qi function. But TCM also holds that the lung system rules the Qi of the body, forming what we call "chest Qi" by combining the air breathed in with food essence and spreading it to the body as a whole. That includes the skin and face, of course, so many of your herbs and other treatments will be directed to your lung system.

The organ paired with the lung is the large intestine, which discharges body waste. Function impairment in the lung will lead to undernourishment of the skin, causing dryness, wrinkles and a withered-looking complexion.

The Liver

The liver system is key to your anti-wrinkle efforts. It is a blood container and flow regulator. At the same time, it plays a role in the Qi flow of all the other organ systems. As such the liver is closely linked to all the body's organ systems.

Liver function imbalance will therefore interrupt QI and blood flow everywhere, including to the face. So stagnant liver Qi can mean wrinkles, dark spots, and a dark complexion.

The liver's Fu partner is the gall bladder, which relates to your mental state, and can affect decision-making abilities if out of balance.

The Spleen

The spleen is also strongly related to facial beauty. Because it dominates the functions of converting food into Qi and blood, it's where your face ultimately gets its nourishment. Its transportation and transformation functions for converting what we eat and drink into body's essential nutrients play a vital role in facial beauty and total body health because the digestive system, the spleen, the stomach and the "post-natal sea of energy" are all related. We aren't what we eat. We are what we digest. It doesn't matter how well you eat if you don't convert and absorb the nutrients.

The paired organ of the spleen is the stomach, which receives and decomposes food. If spleen Qi is deficient, the skin will be undernourished, resulting in a loss of skin tone, as well as sagging and looseness. Also, if the spleen's ability to control the transportation of fluids is diminished, the face will look puffy and eye bags can appear.

Tips From Ping

Nothing is more important for your health than making sure your digestive system is working at its best. Toxins result from poor digestion, and toxins can cause facial problems. Nutrition is paramount. Remember, you aren't what you eat. You are what you digest.

The Kidneys

The Kidney system regulates the fluid balance in the body in many ways. The one we're most familiar with is its role in extracting excess fluid from the body. It works with its paired Fu organ, the urinary bladder, to discharge the fluid.

TCM also sees the kidneys as the storage center for essence. That means it is involved with growth and even reproduction.

If your kidney Yin is deficient, you're at risk for dark eye circles and age spots. If kidney Yang is low, puffiness around the eyes can occur. If kidney essence is insufficient, aging is accelerated. That can affect your skin and cause wrinkles as well as thinning of the hair.

Risks and Benefits

TCM recognizes a huge number of factors that affect your body's functioning and could lead to wrinkles and other facial beauty problems if out of balance. One category of these risk factors is environmental conditions, such as wind, cold, summer heat, dampness, dryness and fire. These are called the "Six Evils.". Here, I will add another one --- environmental pollutions. Living in an industrial environment, our bodies are always stressed by the air we breathe in (exhaust from the air), the water we drink (put in plastic bottles for too long) and the things we put on our skin (heavy preservatives, for example).

The potential damage to your facial skin from those conditions is easy to see. What's interesting, though, is that TCM sees those same conditions as *internal* factors as well as external factors. For example, there is external wind and internal wind. There can be too much heat in your body, or not enough fluids. Chinese herbs and other treatments can deal with such problems.

Another category of health risks is the Seven Emotions. They are anger, joy, worry, pensiveness, sadness, fear and shock. Does it surprise you to see "joy" on the list? The health danger of emotions isn't that they are "good" or "bad" emotions but that they can reach excess. Again, TCM treatments help control facial beauty problems stemming from emotions by treating imbalances in the organ systems that control them.

Other categories involved in your body's functioning include color, taste and even the seasons. One of the most fundamental categories in TCM, though, is known as the "Five Elements." It deserves a closer look.

The Five Elements

The Chinese sages of ancient times were keen observers of natural phenomena, just as scientists are today. Their observations led them to believe that the physical world was a process of change, and that all that exists is the result of transformation based on five basic elements. Those basic elements are wood, fire, earth, metal and water.

TCM practitioners saw the same five basic elements in the human body. What's more, they were able to connect each element to a Zang organ, and then connect that pair to all the factors that determine health or disease — color, taste, emotions, and so on.

Of course, when TCM relates the five elements to the human body and it's functioning, it shouldn't be interpreted as saying that the body is made out of earth, and fire and metal, etc. TCM language is usually not that literal, and of course it loses a lot in the translation from Chinese to English.

Rather, TCM is dealing with properties, using an "as if" kind of metaphor to explain what's going on in the body and to be able to talk about the complex interactions involved.

By finding relationships between organs and elements, and then seeing how they interact with other categories of health factors, TCM was able to construct an intricate and useful system for explaining how the body works. As a basis for medicine, it has served us very well for very long.

So let's take a quick look at how all these elements are grouped together. The following groupings tell how each element is connected with organ pairs, tastes, colors, emotion, environmental factors and seasons, as well as which sensory organ it is related to (or "opens to" in TCM parlance).

Wood
Organs: Liver and gallbladder. Environmental factor: Wind. Direction: East. Season: Spring. Rules: Tendons and ligaments. Emotion:Anger. Color: Green. Taste: Sour. Opens to: The eyes.

Fire
Organs: Heart and small intestine. Environmental factor: Heat. Direction: South. Season: Summer. Rules: Facial complexion. Emotion: Joy Color: Red. Taste: Bitter. Opens to: The tongue.

Earth
Organs: Spleen and stomach. Environmental factor: Dampness. Direction: Center. Season: Late summer. Rules: Four limbs and the flesh. Emotion: Pensiveness, worry. Color: Yellow. Taste: Sweet. Opens: to the mouth.

Metal
Organs: Lung and large intestine. Environmental factor: Dryness. Direction: West. Season: Autumn. Rules: Skin and hair. Emotion: Grief, sadness. Color: White. Taste: Pungent. Opens to: The nose.

Water
Organs: Kidney and urinary bladder. Environmental factor: Cold. Direction: North. Season: Winter. Rules: Bones, marrow, and brain. Emotion: Fear. Color: Black/blue. Taste: Salty. Opens to: The ears

From these associations TCM over the centuries has been able to identify and confirm certain treatments for certain conditions. For example, if your complexion is yellowish with puffiness and eye bags, you probably tend to worry a lot. According to the five-element theory, the earth element is causing your problem. Dampness may be blocking nutrient and Qi flow. All of this is taken into consideration when recommending herbs for you to take and food for you to eat.

The good news for you is that the countless TCM practitioners who came before me and I have already done all that work for you. Follow my instructions and you'll reap benefits thousands of years in the making.

CHAPTER 3

Your Facial Beauty Kit

The Chinese wrinkle cure you'll be using to rejuvenate your face uses four time-honored techniques for restoring youth and glow. They happen to be the four major tools of Traditional Chinese Method that have been healing and beautifying for thousands of years.

They are:
Chinese herbs
Mind/body/breathing exercises called Qi Gong,
Food therapy
Acupuncture/Acupressure. (Acupressure is a needle-less version of acupuncture that you can easily perform yourself at home.)

I'll add a fifth modality to that list — lifestyle improvements. That refers to healthy behavior such as exercise, stress management, no smoking, and adequate sleep. This is a key component to your beauty program that I will be emphasizing time and again in the pages to come.

Except for an occasional herbal-based facial cream, the Western approach to treating wrinkles rarely includes any of those four (or five) treatment methods. That's one reason you will find results with my anti-wrinkle program even after having tried and failed other methods.

How these treatments work also set them apart from other approaches to facial beauty care. Traditional Chinese Medicine does not fight wrinkles by covering them up or trying to "straighten them out" directly. It treats the root problem of imbalance in your internal organ systems. That is what the herbs and other techniques accomplish that Western medicine doesn't even attempt to do.

Think of your body as a tree, full of energy and essence taken in through the roots. If the leaves are suffering, what is the best approach to realign them? Clearly it's the tree that has a problem that's manifesting itself in the leaves. So healing energy should first fill the trunk and then channel out to the branches and leaves.

The same applies to your own health. Only when the inner body is abundant with Qi and essence, with the organs in balance, can the healing energy spread to your extremities, including your face. Real healing, of wrinkles or anything else, starts with inner health and then spreads to where the problem is reflected.

Herbal treatments, Qi Gong, acupressure and food therapy do exactly that. They have been helping the Chinese and others rejuvenate their faces for thousands of years. They will be part of your life from now on.

Let me now introduce them to you.

Individually, herbal therapy, food therapy, Qi Gong and acupressure are very effective treatments for facial beauty. But this Chinese wrinkle program will only give you the results you want if you practice all of them, along with a healthy lifestyle. This is not a pick-and-choose program. It's a package deal.

Chinese Herbs

Herbal treatment is at the core of Traditional Chinese Medicine. It counts for more than 75 percent of TCM practice, and will also be the major emphasis in your facial beauty program. Chinese herbs are a rich and potent source of healing energy, and their use has been perfected and refined over the last 3,000 years.

In China, herbs are considered gifts of nature. Individuals unable to "fight" a disease directly but to enhance the body's natural healing ability consume them. Taken internally, their purpose is to balance and regulate internal body functions as a whole system. By doing that, they eliminate the conditions that lead to complexion problems, wrinkles and eye puffiness.

They can also be applied externally in the form of masks, washes and other topical treatments to work directly on the face to restore glow and smoothness.

Tips From Ping

You'll find Chinese herbs in a number of presentations — as pills, capsules, teas, tinctures, fresh cut or dried. Some are roots, some flowers, some leaves, and some the whole plant. Some are powdered minerals, and others are even dried animal parts. I will usually indicate to you as I introduce each herb which form is best to take. Often any form is fine. More important than the presentation is the quality. Buy from reputable dealers.

Unlike in Western herbology, where the very word "herb" means plants. Chinese herbs also include minerals and even animal parts. The instructions I'll be giving you for choosing and taking herbs will be simple and easy to follow. But you should know that the science behind these herbs functioning is complex and sophisticated. A large number of factors determine an herb's actions. Centuries of observation and fine-tuning are behind the herb choices that I have made for your facial beauty program.

Herbs can be taken individually or in formulas that mix several herbs that interact synergistically for a more potent effect. Chinese herbalism stresses formulas, and there are a number of them that work wonders for your facial rejuvenation. However, I emphasize individual herbs in this book for the simple reason that formulas are usually hard to deal with on your own without personal professional help. Some formulas are suitable for self-treatment and I will be describing them for you later in the book, including some that are available commercially as supplements.

Tips From Ping

Most of the Chinese herbs I'll be recommending to you are readily available in health food stores. Some you'll be more likely to find in the Chinese and other Asian markets that can be found in medium or large cities across North America. Chinese herb stores are rare, but of course they are your best bet. If you have difficulty finding an herb you want to take for facial beauty, use the Internet. Every herb I recommend can be found somewhere online.

The most important thing to remember is that most of the herbs you'll be taking don't "fight" wrinkles. They help your body's self-healing capacity correct the conditions that cause the wrinkles in the first place. That's much more effective.

How Chinese Herbs Work

Chinese herbs don't work like Western pharmaceuticals do. Though the "active" ingredients in an herb can and have been isolated, an herb's effectiveness is not based on its ingredients, per se. All the properties of an herb work together in ways that Western science usually cannot explain.

True, many Chinese herbs contain amino acids, proteins, vitamins, anti-oxidants, and other phytochemicals (plant-based nutrients) that Western medicine recognizes as helpful for the skin. There's certainly overlap between East and West. But that doesn't mean that those "known" factors are the only reasons those herbs containing them help the skin.

It also doesn't mean that herbs not containing such "known" factors can't beautify skin. They most demonstrably do.

In short, TCM doesn't analyze herbs by their chemical ingredients.

It categorizes herbs by their properties and observed effects. That includes everything from taste and temperature to the organ channel that it affects or "enters."

Let's look at some of the major ways of looking at Chinese herbs.

Herbs by Levels

The oldest Chinese medical literature divides herbals into three levels: superior, middle and inferior.

- **Inferior:** Herbs are used on individuals with special ailments. They can only be taken safely in small doses. They are often quite toxic.

- **Middle:** Herbs are nourishing and are used for short periods only and in small doses. They are sometimes toxic, and often used in formulas with other herbs that offset their toxicity.

- **Superior:** Herbs are not toxic and are used for long periods of time to treat many different conditions. They are associated with longevity and rejuvenation and are best for general balancing.

Most of the herbs I recommend in this book are superior herbs. And the few that aren't superior are not toxic. They are put in the middle level for other reasons.

Herbs by Taste

TCM practitioners have known for a long time that the taste of an herb tells a lot about the kind of action it will have inside the body. There are seven categories of taste:

- **Sweet:** Sweet tasting herbs nourish the body and skin, therefore help rectify a number of deficiency conditions that cause drying or wrinkled skin.

- **Pungent:** Pungent-tasting herbs help energy and blood circulation, clearing up Qi or phlegm blockage that causes skin rashes and dark spots.

- **Bitter:** Bitter-tasting herbs clear heat and toxin from the body and skin. They are mostly used for skin rashes and acne.

- **Sour and Astringent:** Both these tastes indicate the herb's function of stopping fluid leakage in the body. They can help stop the excessive secretion of sweat and oil in the skin.

- **Bland:** Herbs with a bland taste tend to help the body leach out excessive dampness and end water retention in the body. Combined with other herbs, they're helpful in clearing away puffiness and eye bags.

- **Salty:** Salty-tasting herbs can dissipate nodules and calm spirit. They are often used in herbal formulas for acne conditions.

Herbs by Channel

Herbs usually benefit one or more specific organ systems by "entering" those organs' channels. For skin rejuvenation, five of those channels are most important:

- **Kidney:** Herbs entering the kidney channel generally nourish body essence. (Remember that the kidneys are the storage bins for body essence). You'll see them in herbal formulas for nourishing the skin. Many of the herbs I'll be recommending for wrinkles and age spots work through the kidney channel.

- **Liver:** Herbs that enter the liver channel nourish blood and soothe emotions. They are commonly used for facial discoloration and weakened vision.

- **Stomach and Spleen:** Herbs entering either or both of these paired channels tonify Qi (energy) and help the body transform dampness. If the digestive system is weak, qi will be deficient and the dampness obstruction often accompanies it. These have important functions for skin rejuvenation. Spleen and stomach herbs are especially effective for aging skin such as wrinkles, sagging of the face and eye puffiness, including eye bags.

- **Large Intestine:** Herbs that enter the large intestine channel are usually used to treat skin conditions like acne and eczema.

Herbs by Function

Chinese herbs are also categorized by what they actually do inside the body. There are 20 categories of herb function. These are the most important for herbal beauty treatments:

- **Herbs that release the exterior**
  They are usually pungent tasting and enter the lung channel. Many induce sweating, a good example of "releasing the exterior." Many herbs in this category are used for treating facial discoloration, skin rashes and acne, especially if external wind is a factor in the condition.

- **Herbs that clear away heat**
  By eliminating excess internal heat, these herbs clean the blood and detoxify the body. Many of them are bitter and cold in nature and enter the stomach, liver or lung channel. They may have anti-bacteria and anti-inflammatory properties and help your body fight

infection. For facial beauty, they are used for acne, skin rashes, dark facial spots and redness of skin.

■ **Herbs that drain downward**

These herbs are used to promote bowel movements in conditions of constipation brought on by heat stagnation, food stagnation or low energy. Most of them enter the large intestine channel. They are often bitter and cold in nature. Caution is needed with herbs in this category because some are very harsh and can weaken the body. Others, though, are safe and are used for heat-induced skin conditions such as acne.

■ **Aromatic herbs that expel dampness**

Warm and aromatic herbs that enter the stomach and spleen channel revive spleen function. Their action can penetrate skin and muscle layers, so they are often used externally as herbal creams. Internally they address any skin conditions coming from weak digestion including sagging of face, puffiness of eyes.

■ **Herbs that tonify the body**

Herbal tonics replenish essence, help to support healthy body's immune function, increase energy and regulate internal body balance. Their tonifying (replenishing) action also helps the body's Qi, blood, Yin and Yang. Most tonifying herbs enter the lung, liver or kidney channels. They tend to be sweet in nature. They are excellent herbs for facial beauty and rejuvenation, and they are used for dull complexions, wrinkles, sagging of face, eye bags and dark circles.

■ **Herbs that regulate Qi**

Harmonizing Qi movement is of tremendous benefit in treating dark spots, facial discoloration, dark eye circles, and eye bags. Most of the herbs that treat Qi stagnation are warm and dry in nature and enter the lung, liver, spleen or stomach channel.

■ **Herbs that warm the interior**

By nature, these herbs are warm, pungent and enter the spleen or kidney channels. They are used to treat sagging skin and drooping eyelids due to Yang deficiency with internal cold. Some can also be used externally to brighten dull complexions.

■ **Herbs that invigorate the blood**

These mostly enter the liver and heart channels and vary widely in taste and temperature. They work to promote blood flow and opening channel systems to move Qi. As herbal beauty treatments, they're used for treating skin discoloration and roughness, wrinkles, dark eye circles. No herb in this category should be taken by anybody on blood thinners.

- **Herbs that calm the spirit**

  They enter the liver and heart channels, often anchoring the spirit by nourishing heart blood. In TCM theory, the heart is the house of the spirit, and the liver the house of the soul. Some herbs in this category are actually minerals. Calming the mind and spirit, as I've mentioned, is extremely beneficial for skin beauty.

Herbal Regimen for Internal Taking and External Application

When you start with any single herb, take it daily from 10 days to two weeks. Then rest for several days and repeat the 10-14 day regimen. Keep that on-again, off-again regimen going for a month or two, and then decide if you want to stay with that herb.

Herbal/Food masks and wash follow this regimen: use mask or wash once a day or once every 2 days per one week, see how you feel and see. If you want to start again, you can rest for several days and restart the regimen on and off for one week to 10 days.

An Important Caution Before Taking Herbal Supplements

Always be careful about what you take into your mouth. The herbs I recommend are safe in normal circumstances for healthy body conditions, but you must consult your health care practitioner before using any herb/herbs/herbal formulas. This is especially important if you have any existing medical conditions, or pregnant, or nursing, or taking any medications. For example, herbs that move the blood can be a problem if you are on blood-thinning medication.

As I will repeat later in this book, if you feel any discomfort or if any allergic reaction occurs after you take any herb, herbs or herbal formula, stop immediately and consult with your health care professional.

Also, make sure you use only pure, high-quality herbs that meet or surpass FDA safety requirements. If there is no indication on the label that they do so, talk to the store manager. If he or she doesn't know, go someplace else.

Caution for Using Herbs or Food for External Skin Care

Sometimes your body can easily get an allergic reaction to something applied externally for skin care. Because of that possibility, please test any herbal or food used externally, including washes and masks, by first applying it to a small area on your inner wrist or the inner part of your upper arm. Leave it on for 24 hours. If any allergic reaction results (such as a rash, redness, swelling, or itching), do not use that herb or food or formula. If there is no reaction, feel free to use it. But remember not to over-use it. Follow my suggestions throughout the book.

Acupressure: Do-it-Yourself Facial Beauty Massages

Acupuncture is probably the best known, most accepted and easiest-to-find Chinese treatment method in the world today. It can work wonders to rid your face of wrinkles. Acupressure uses the same principles as acupuncture, except pressure from the fingers or hands replaces the needles.

Acupuncture can't work as a self-treatment. It requires a trained practitioner and a very involved diagnosis. That's why you'll be using exclusively acupressure routines in your program.

Over the millennia, acupressure techniques have been refined and perfected to the point that we know precisely how to apply them to facial beauty concerns. I will be giving you easy-to-follow acupressure protocols that are specifically designed to correct the internal imbalances that are creating your wrinkles, discoloration, dark circles or eye bags.

What Acupressure Does For Your Face

Like acupuncture, acupressure heals by manipulating the flow of Qi in beneficial ways. It does this by pressing (and therefore activating) certain energy points along the meridians.

Acupressure's power for facial rejuvenation works in many different ways internally. Here are some of them:

- It soothes and vents the channel system.
- It regulates the free flow of Qi and blood.
- It harmonizes Yin and Yang.
- It encourages lymph drainage.
- It facilitates nutrient absorption.
- It enhances the skin's ability to "breathe."
- It promotes normal secretion from the sweat and oil glands.
- It stimulates the skin's own ability for collagen production. softens the skin and smoothes wrinkles.
- It regulates and stimulates internal organ system functioning.
- It promotes muscle contraction.

Acupressure's stimulation of the internal organs, is key to its beauty benefits. By restoring organ balance, it eliminates the root cause of your facial skin problems.

More specifically, it promotes blood flow to the skin surface so more nutrients can reach skin cells.

Its effect on muscle contraction reduces muscle fatigue and increases elasticity, which in turn helps prevent sagging skin and wrinkle formation.

Acupressure and the Channels

You've met the energy channels (or meridians), which are where acupressure's action takes place. Here, in order, are the channels that are most important for acupressure's use as a facial beauty treatment. For your convenience and easy understanding, the following simplified figure shows the parts of the channels that run through the extremities. *(See Fig. 3.1)*

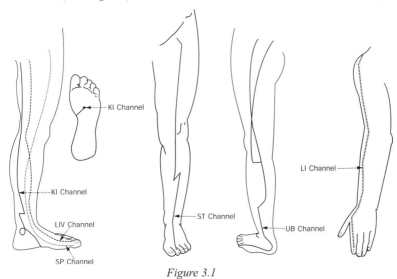

Figure 3.1

- **Stomach** (ST): It starts under the eye and ends on the outside corner of the second toe. It has 45 energy points.

- **Liver** (LIV): It starts from the lateral corner of the big toe and ends at the sixth intercostal (between-ribs) space directly below the nipple. It has 14 energy points.

- **Spleen** (SP): It starts at the big toe and ends at the side of the trunk. It has 21 energy points.

- **Kidney** (KI): It starts at the sole of the foot and ends right below the clavicle. It has 27 energy points

- **Urinary Bladder** (UB): It starts at the inner side of the eye and ends at the small toe. It has 67 energy points.

- **Large Intestine** (LI): It starts at the tip of the index finger and ends at the side of the nose. It has 20 energy points.

Getting to the Points

Most of the points you'll be "pressing" or massaging in your face-beautifying acupressure routines are on one of these six channels.

Some are on others. A few points, by the way, are not on any channel. They are called "extra" points. And some have no specific location; rather, they are wherever the problem is — a facial discoloration spot, for example. These are called "ashi" points.

I'll help you find and understand each point as it comes up in the descriptions of the acupressure routines. But while you're looking at the charts now, why not pinpoint some key spots in advance? Not all of them are on your face, of course. The idea of acupressure is to move Qi for facial benefits, and the best points for doing that can be anywhere along the meridians.

Here are the main facial-beauty acupressure points that are on your face *(See Fig.3.2)*: Yang Bai (GB 14), Tong Zi Liao (GB 1), Feng Chi (GB 20), Si Zhu Kong (SJ 23), Cheng Qi (ST 1), Si Bai (ST 2), Ju Liao (ST 3), Di Cang (ST 4), Ying Xiang (LI 20), Xia Guan (ST 7), Jia Che (ST 6), Quan Liao (SI 18), Jing Ming (UB 1), Zan Zhu (UB 2), Shang Xing (Du 23), Bai Hui (Du 20), Tai Yang (extra point), Yin Tang (extra point), Qiu Hou (extra point), Yu Yao (extra point).

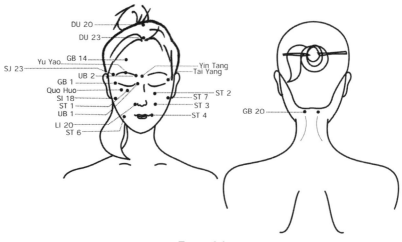

Figure 3.2

Here are the main facial-beauty acupressure points on the body *(See Fig 3.3):* Zu San Li (ST 36), Feng Long (ST 40), San Yin Jiao (SP 6), Yin Ling Quan (SP 9), Xue Hai (SP 10), Guang Ming (GB 37), Qu Chi (LI 11), Yang Xi (LI 5), He Gu (LI 4), Tai Chong (LIV 3), Chi Ze (LU 5), Yang Liao (SI 6), Fei Shu (UB 13), Xin Shu (UB 15), Ge Shu (UB 17), Gan Shu (UB 18), San Jiao Shu (UB 22), Da Zhui (DU 14), Ming Men (Du 4), Tai Xi (KI 3)

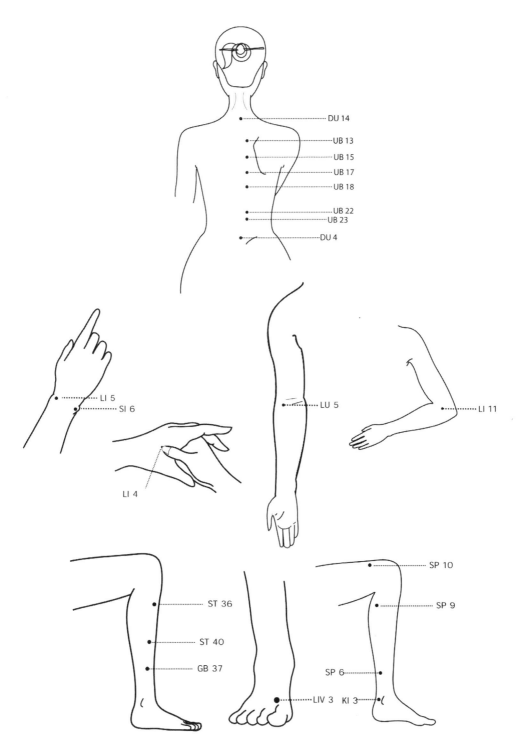

Figure 3.3

How To Do the Acupressure Routines

With acupressure, you use your hand or fingertips to activate points along the meridians. But how do you actually "press" or "rub" or massage a point?

There are many different hand techniques for performing acupressure. The simplest one that you'll be using almost exclusively in your home routines is pressing and kneading. These are one-finger acupressure techniques *(See Fig 3.4)*, usually using the pads of the index finger or thumb to press on the chosen point or knead it in a to-and-fro motion or you can simply call it digital pressing motion. The force should start lightly and gradually increase; the overall effect should be soft, yet penetrating.

You can press rather quickly, at a rate up to 100 pressings per minute, less than a second each. You'll only press each point up to 60 times, though; the number of presses will be given in each routine's instructions.

Acupuncture and acupressure use a special measurement to indicate distance when locating a point. It's called a "cun" and it's roughly equivalent to your thumb width, a little less than an inch. So to move two cuns up your arm from your wrist line is a little less than two inches. I'll usually give the distances in inches, since that will be more familiar. *(See Fig.3.5)*

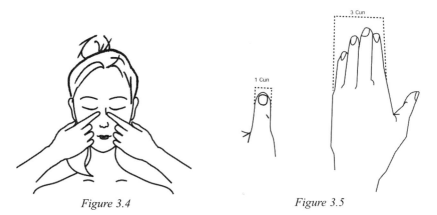

Figure 3.4   *Figure 3.5*

Tips From Ping

All the acupressure strokes should be done with light force gradually increasing to moderate force. Also, move from the surface to the deeper layers as you press. Start slowly and gradually increase the speed to up to 100 circles or presses per minute. The routines should be followed by relaxation. For the best effect, apply an herbal facial cream before you start the acupressure routine.

Caution: Do not use acupressure if you have any cardiovascular, brain or lung condition. Do not use it if you have a contagious skin condition or bleeding problems. Postpone your routine if you feel full, hungry, or have just exercised. If you are pregnant, use caution and consult your doctor first. Pregnant women should always avoid working the following energy points: GB 21, LI 4, SP 6, SP 10, UB60, UB 67, LIV 3, or any point on the lower and upper abdomen and lower back. (See Fig.3.6)

Getting Started: A 15-Minute Acupressure Technique

You'll probably want to choose acupuncture routines based on your personal beauty problem (wrinkles, eye bags, etc). To get you started, here's a multi-purpose, everyday routine that works on balancing the Three Treasures. This routine (or "protocol") will replenish body essence, Qi, restore emotional calmness, happiness, and to help beautify your face.

Step 1: Sit in a comfortable position, close your eyes, and relax your face. Rub both your hands together nine times until they feel warm, and then apply your warm hands to your face. Massage nine times as shown here in the figure. *(See Fig.3.7)*

Step 2: Use all 10 fingers to massage your scalp, starting from the front hairline and working backwards. *(See Fig.3.8)*

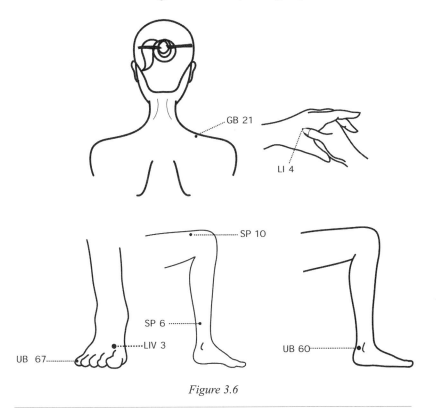

Figure 3.6

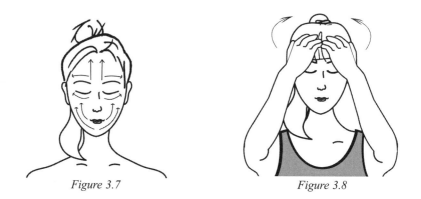

| *Figure 3.7* | *Figure 3.8* |

Step 3: Now, using the pads of each thumb, press the following points 50 times each (using the chart for location). *(See Fig.3.9)*

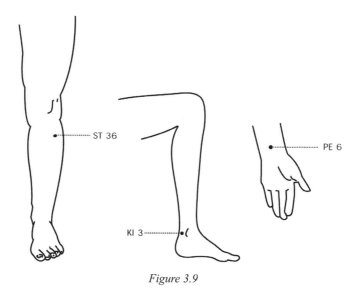

Figure 3.9

- **PE 6:** Nei Guan, or Inner pass, located to thumb-width about the mid-point of your inner wrist line. It is a special point for calm spirit and regulates digestion.

- **KI 3:** Between the medial malleolus (the inside ankle bone) and the Achilles tendon is a "great ravine" where lies the Tai Xi (or KI 3) energy point. The name, indeed, means "great ravine" or "canyon." It is called a "yuan" source point, meaning it contains vital kidney energy. It strongly nourishes the kidney organ system, tonifying dry wrinkled skin due to Yin deficiency.

- **ST 36:** Called Zu San Li, this is a point along the stomach meridian just below each knee. Activating these symmetrical points gives you the strength to go for three miles, which is what the Chinese name means. Find it by locating the mushy point just below your kneecap and then moving 3 cun (3 thumb widths) down along the shinbone, then one thumb-width toward the outer side. This is one of the most important points that tonify Qi and blood, support the body's healthy immune system, and improves overall skin condition.

Qi Gong: Mind, Body and Breathing

You may be less familiar with Qi (remember, it's pronounced "chee") Gong than herbs or acupressure, but it's actually considered the highest level of self-healing for facial beauty. It is actually an older practice than herbal medicine, a unique treasure of Traditional Chinese Medicine.

The purpose of Qi Gong is to assist your body's natural self-balancing capacity by manipulating internal energy with your mind and breathing. Like acupressure, it involves no introduction of outside elements (such as herbs or food). But it is even more self-sufficient than acupressure because you don't even need to press anything. All the "work" is done with the mind, the breath, and some gentle movement.

Qi Gong uses the body by moving it. It uses the breath by concentrating it and directing it in specific ways. And it uses the mind by focusing it to achieve relaxation and to move energy.

Using Qi Gong to promote beauty and slow down aging is not a new variation. It has been a beauty treatment for thousands of years. Of course, it is a whole body exercise that helps essence, Qi and spirit. It incorporates TCM concepts of Yin/Yang, the five elements, channel theory and the organ systems.

As I mentioned in the first chapter, Qi Gong has been influenced by Zen meditation, enriched and heavily practiced by Daoism. It regulates the heart (which rules the emotions), purifies the spirit, and promotes the free flow of Qi.

Principles for Successful Qi Gong

Qi Gong is not physically difficult. But it is probably unlike anything you have tried before. Much of it involves using your imagination to move energy around in your body.

It can take some practice to feel comfortable doing that. That's fine. I'll be giving you specific instructions with each exercise. Just stick with it and do the best you can; before long, it will come easy.

Here are some suggestions for doing the exercises. You'll want to refer back to these when you get to the actual exercise instructions.

■ **Your body position:** There are many different body positions involved in Qi Gong. But almost all the exercises I'll be giving you simply require sitting comfortably in a chair. A hard chair is best. Keep your body upright, relax the shoulders, let both hands rest loosely on your lap, set your feet at shoulder-width on the floor, and let them just relax.

- **Your breath:** You want your breath to be, above all, natural and even. Even breathing is best achieved by keeping it softer than your normal breath. Easy does it. Sometimes you might find yourself short of breath or even "forgetting to breathe" because you're focusing so much on something else. If that happens, stop everything and relax. Figure out what caused the problem and start over. After some practice, soft even breathing will come naturally.

- **Your mind:** Qi Gong exercises are mind exercises. You will be using your mind to concentrate on your body or a part of it. You will be using your mind to create energy as well. Imagining energy balls or energy movement is a big part of Qi Gong. The secret, as you might have guessed, is relaxation. Focusing first on soft, even breathing helps you relax. So does repeating a relaxation word of your choice, like "calm" or "relax."

Sometimes you will be asked to focus your mind on an actual channel point, as in acupressure. Most of these are on the middle or lower parts of your body. An important such point is called the Dan Tian. It's located 2 cuns or 2 thumb widths directly below your navel.

Getting Started: A Simple Qi Gong Exercise

The best way to familiarize yourself with Qi Gong exercises is to try one. Here's a beginner's "exhale-inhale" type of Qi Gong that benefits the Three Treasures — the Qi, essence and spirit.

Step1: Stand with your feet shoulder-width apart. Relax your face, shoulders and knees. Breathe in slowly through your nose and feel the breath going to the Dan Tian area. Breathe out slowly through the mouth. Keep this relaxing breathing going to about 1 minute. You should feel slight warmth in the Dan Tian area by this time. If you don't, that's okay. *(See Fig. 3.10)*

Step 2: Slowly, gently, rotate your waist first clockwise and then counter clockwise, 9 times each. Imagine that this movement spreads energy to your kidneys, which are under your ribcage toward your back. You might feel a light warm sensation in this area after a while. This is where the "gate of life" is energized and where the Qi and blood meet. It's where the life energy is preserved. Then stop your waist movement, keep breathing slowly, and finish. *(See Fig. 3.11)*

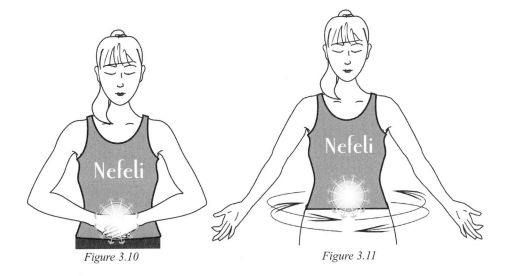

Figure 3.10   *Figure 3.11*

Staying Calm and Comfortable During Gi Gong

Do not get too uptight when concentrating your mind. Pushing too hard to achieve relaxation is counterproductive. If you can't relax, that's fine. You will eventually.

Qi Gong is a process of continual self-adjustment. Because of that, you can experience physiological reactions while doing an exercise, even the one you've done many times before. Those reactions can include feeling excess warmth in your body or a general discomfort. On rare occasions, especially if you're rushing, you might experience a shortness of breath, palpatations, or a spiritual unrest.

If anything like that happens while you're practicing a Qi Gong exercise, stop right away. Relax. Rest for several days before trying the routine again. When you do start up again, relax your entire body before doing the first step.

Caution For Practicing Qi Gong

Do not practice any Qi Gong exercise if you are pregnant or have any kind of heart condition including high blood pressure. If you're sick in any way, put off Qi Gong until you're better. If discomfort occurs during or after Qi Gong exercise, you should stop practicing Qi Gong. Qi Gong is only appropriate when your body is in a healthy, normal condition.

Also, do not try to rush a Qi Gong exercise in an attempt to see results sooner. Practice each exercise in a slow and calm manner. If you do not feel any change I mention during or after a Qi Gong exercise, do not worry. It does not mean that it does not work for you. You can still benefit from these Qi Gong exercises.

Chinese Food Therapy

At least 1,800 years ago, and probably much earlier, Chinese texts lauded the beautifying effects of many foods. Just as Chinese herbs promote healing in concentrated form, certain foods are applied to the same principles to benefit the Three Treasures in addition to their nutritional benefits. Food therapy, as much as the other three TCM techniques in your facial-beauty program, is a powerful tool for smoothing wrinkles and diminishing dark eye circles, eye bags and facial discoloration.

Throughout this book, I will be suggesting the best foods to eat to treat the facial beauty conditions that affect you.

> **Tips From Ping**
> The major advantage of Chinese dietary therapy is that it is safe, taste great, and can be used every day for the rest of your life. Best of all, it really works!

Food Types, Chinese Style

Like Chinese herbs, each food has its own properties. Each has a distinguishing flavor, a temperature, a channel that it enters, and a therapeutic function.

- **The flavor of the food** (sweet, pungent, sour, bitter, or salty) has very important application to its healing effects. Sweet foods, for example, tonify Qi and blood, nourish Yin and moisten dryness. I don't mean artificially added sugar food; I mean the foods that have naturally sweet flavor. Those benefits smooth and refresh the skin and have an anti-aging effect that improves dry, wrinkly skin.Pungent food has a dispersing effect, which is good for superficial skin conditions. Bitter food detoxifies the skin. Sour or astringent food improves oily skin. Salty food expels skin nodules.

- **Temperature** is another important food property for facial beauty. Cold food, for example, clears heat from the skin, cools the blood, and detoxifies. It can thus be very helpful for treating heat-induced skin conditions like acne, rashes, and spotting, Remember, though, that "cold" food isn't necessarily literally cold as though it just came out of the freezer. It is cold "in nature." We say, "cold" as a descriptive property.

- **Color** is another way of categorizing food for targeted facial beauty benefits. There are five colors for food:

  Red - According to TCM's five-element theory, red goes with the heart. Red foods help to improve the skin's complexion. They usually enter the heart channel, and have an anti-aging effect. Good red foods include tomatoes, red rice, carrots, strawberries, and watermelons.

White - White foods enter the lung channel, white being the color of the lungs. They nourish the skin, and are best if you have fair skin prone to dryness. Good white foods include tremella, coconuts, bamboo, pears, water chestnuts, and lotus root.

Green - Green foods are associated with the liver, which governs the free flow of emotions. Green foods relax the body, and moisten the skin. They also cleanse the skin and are often anti-inflammatory and anti-infection. Recommended green foods include cilantro, field mint, bitter melon, kiwi, dandelion, green apples, fresh luffa, asparagus, and all kinds of bitter greens.

Black - Black foods belong to the kidneys. They delay the aging process and rejuvenate the skin by tonifying the kidney system and the blood. Good black foods include black beans, black sesame seeds, black fungus (Chinese name is Hei Mu Er), black mushrooms, black Chinese dates, blackberries, mulberry fruit, seaweed and other sea plants

Yellow - Yellow foods enter the spleen channel and nourish the entire body and its energy. That includes the skin and face. Good yellow foods include yellow soybeans, millet, ginger, papaya, banana, and pineapples.

One of your food goals will be to include foods in your daily meal plan of different colors and flavors. That will ensure beneficial foods entering different channels and boosting different organ systems. Some foods work best for certain facial conditions. I'll be telling you what those are in the appropriate chapters.

Tips From Ping
Remember that the benefits from these foods are based on their healing properties. They're all healthy foods that fit into any diet, but they don't comprise a diet themselves. It will still be up to you to maintain a balanced, healthy diet for overall weight control and nutrition. As a diet strategy, I suggest as wide a variety as possible in your intake of plant and animal food. Both are very important to your body, though of course you will eat much more fruits and vegetables that meat. An old Chinese saying puts it best: "Green vegetables guarantee peace and health."

Foods have specific healing actions. You will want to include enough variety in your food choices to include all of the following. Depending on your condition, however, you will emphasize one or more of them.

- **Expel wind.** This helps treat itchy skin, red rashes, acne, and facial discoloration.

- **Tonify the Body.** By which we mean tonify Yin and Yang, Qi and blood. This action is beneficial for treating wrinkles, dry skin, withered and dull complexion, dark eye circles, puffy eyes, eye bags, and sagging.

- **Drain the dampness.** This action is good for a puffy face, eye bags and dark eye circles, as well as skin discoloration, dull complexion, and acne.

- **Transform phlegm.** Beneficial for eye bags, eye puffiness, a red swelling nose (especially the tip of the nose), rough skin, dull complexion, and facial dark spots.

- **Expel stasis.** Helps dark spots, age spots, rough skin, a dull and dark complexion, and dark eye circles.

- **Regulate Qi.** By regulating energy, certain foods can improve dark spots, aging spots, dark eye circles and eye bags.

> **Tips From Ping**
> Fresh is best, for vegetables and fruits. Canned or prepared fruits and vegetables lose much of their healing powers. From a Western point of view, they lose some phytonutrients (beneficial plant chemicals) if they're not fresh. Note that Western medicine recognizes the healing power of most of the Chinese foods I'll be recommending. But rather than acknowledging their properties, as TCM does, Western medicine points to their chemical components such as their vitamin and mineral content, amino acids, and antioxidant phytochemicals.

Getting Started: Healing Food Recipe

According to Traditional Chinese Medicine, foods with different healing properties — such as different tastes or colors — enter different organ systems. So, to balance and nourish the organ systems of our body, we should include a variety of foods in our diet to keep our body balanced.

Here's a mixed "five-element vegetable salad" remedy using different characteristics and properties of different vegetables for a healthy and balanced body system.

Simply mix a salad with the following vegetables and fruits: Cooked black beans and red beans (cooled), 1/4 cup of cooked lily bulb, 1/4 lotus root (Chapped), seaweed, red peppers, cucumber, celery, mushrooms (any kind), tomatoes, carrots, broccoli, walnuts, beets, spinach, and brussels sprouts, 1/2 green apple, 1/2 cup of strawberry. Use enough to almost fill a salad bowl. Add one hard-boiled egg. As a dressing, use the juice squeezed-out of seven thin slices of ginger, sesame oil or olive oil, vinegar, and lemon juice.

Caution: As I mentioned before, if you happen to use food as your mask or wash, please do a test in your wrist for 24 hours to make sure you are not allergic to them. It holds true, if any discomfort or allergic reactions happen after taking the foods recommended in this book, then stop it and use a different food in the same category.

PART TWO

USING CHINESE WISDOM TO SMOOTH AWAY
WRINKLES FROM THE INSIDE OUT

CHAPTER 4

Your Wrinkle Free Life Style

Nobody likes wrinkles. That was just as true in ancient China as it is today in modern America.

But for those of us who practice Traditional Chinese Medicine, facial wrinkles aren't simply a cosmetic concern. We know that the condition of the facial skin reflects the health of the entire body. The expression "You can see it in her face" is taken quite literally by Chinese healers.

"Yellow Emperor Inner Classics," a 2,000-year-old Chinese medical text, notes that "all the Yang energy converges in the face," and that "all the meridians' Qi and blood flourish up to the face." The text also demonstrates direct correspondences between areas of the face and the inner organs. *(See Fig.4.1)*

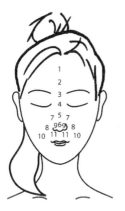

1. Face and Head
2. Throat
3. Lung
4. Heart
5. Gall Bladder
6. Liver
7. Small Intestine
8. Large Instetine
9. Stomach
10. Kidney
11. Urinary, Bladder and Reproduction System

Figure 4.1

These aren't vague notions. They're based on centuries of close observation by first-rate medical minds.

As a result of this view, Traditional Chinese Medicine (TCM) has developed a large number of facial beauty and rejuvenation treatments that are completely different than what Western medicine has to offer. These unique techniques include, of course, wrinkle-reducing and wrinkle-preventing treatments

No two of these treatments are alike. Yet they all have helped countless women and men achieve a smoother, brighter, more youthful-looking face.

In this chapter, you'll learn dozens of those wrinkle-reducing treatments — from herbs and herbal masks to Qi Gong and acupressure techniques. All of them are self-treatments easily done at home. As you put them to use, you'll soon notice not only fewer wrinkles, but also vibrancy in your entire body that is reflected in your face.

Beyond Botox: The Difference Between East and West

Why choose TCM over modern Western techniques? After all, there's certainly no shortage of wrinkle-reducing options in Western medicine.

Besides commercial cosmetic beauty products, there are non-surgical procedures such as chemical peels, collagen injections, fillers, Botox injections, laser resurfacing and micro-dermabrasion. There are surgical treatments such as micro suction, belepharoplaty and the ever-popular facelifts.

Most of the non-surgical techniques work by destroying surface skin cells so that fresher, healthier cells waiting underneath can move up and take over. Some, like Botox and fillers, artificially firm the muscle tissue just under the surface.

A few of these procedures are reasonably priced. Many are very expensive. Some work for many; many work for some. Each has its pros and cons.

But there's one thing all the modern Western techniques have in common: They focus exclusively on a symptom — the actual wrinkles — rather than the imbalances in the body that are causing the symptom. Western medicine sees wrinkles on the face, so it treats the face and only the face. Such treatment is superficial, in the literal sense of the word.

Traditional Chinese Medicine takes an entirely different approach to wrinkle reduction. It treats you, not your wrinkles. Following nature's laws, it seeks to balance the body by treating underlying conditions that lead to wrinkling. It does this by acting on the processes we discussed in the first three chapters — by strengthening the internal organs, by freeing Qi and blood to move smoothly to your face, by distributing essence and fluids evenly through the body. All this nourishes your face, promoting youthful, supple, wrinkle-free skin — naturally.

Yes, plastic surgery and many non-surgical treatments can diminish your wrinkles (for a while at least). But you'll still lack that beautiful, natural skin tone that can only come from the inside out. That's what you really want, and that's what TCM offers.

Getting to the True Cause of Wrinkles

You may be wondering about the idea of "underlying causes" of wrinkling. Isn't age the true culprit?

Well, yes. But it's not the end-all and be-all of wrinkles.

Like our entire body, our skin is constantly aging. Around age 25 to 30 the changes begin to become noticeable. Those thin little wrinkles creeping in at the side of your eye reflect the aging going on in your internal organs.

But it's not like some alarm goes off at a certain age and wrinkles automatically appear. At its most basic, the problem is skin cell "turnover." Young faces stay smooth and vibrant because new, healthy cells quickly replace old cells on the surface of your skin. As you get older, the pace of this replacement slows down, you're left with older superficial skin cells, and it shows.

That's not the whole story, though. There are reasons — both external and internal — that the cell turnover rate slows down. TCM identifies more such reasons than Western medicine does, and treating them is the basis for TCM's anti-wrinkle treatment.

But let's look at those causes from the Western point of view first.

Beneath the outer layer of the skin that you see (the "epidermis") lays the dermis, a thicker layer of connective tissue. The dermis contains collagen and elastic fibers, which work together to give the skin its strength, extensibility and elasticity. Also embedded in this deeper layer are blood vessels, nerves, glands and hair follicles.

With ageing, blood flow to the dermis decreases, damaging the collagen, and taking the elasticity out of the elastic fibers. The skin-strengthening team is weakened, healthy new cells are fewer, and wrinkles occur. As you'll see, many TCM anti-wrinkle treatments boost the flow of fresh blood to your dermis.

Another wrinkle factor is facial muscle deterioration. Strong, elastic muscles encourage firm, supple skin. Years of facial expressions ultimately weaken the facial muscles, encouraging wrinkling. Some of the TCM techniques you'll be practicing help re-vitalize those muscles.

Your Face's External Enemies

As I mentioned, TCM recognizes many more age-related factors than slowed blood flow. And it knows how to smooth or prevent wrinkles by reversing aging's effect on those factors. The best way to understand what those internal factors are, however, is to first look at some factors that TCM and Western medicine basically agree on. These are the external factors, which roughly correspond to TCM's Six Exterior Evils of wind, cold, heat, dampness, dryness, and fire.

■ **Too much sun**

The sun's ultraviolet rays penetrate the skin and damage skin cells. The list of undesirable results of this is a long one, including leathery skin texture, discoloration, premature aging, skin cancer — and facial wrinkles.

■ **Too much wind**

Long-term exposure to the wind upsets the natural harmony of the skin layers, causing your facial skin to become dry, rough and peeling.

■ **Dryness**

Extreme dry air or ongoing inadequate hydration withers the skin, causing cracking and wrinkles.

■ **Smoking**

Nicotine constricts the blood vessels, further obstructing blood flow to the dermis. That reduces the nutrient supply, accelerating wrinkle formation and other aging symptoms, such as a yellow-gray or pale-gray facial discoloration.

■ **Too much alcohol**

Among other things, over-imbibing increases the formation of cell-damaging free radicals.

■ **Poor diet**

Eating processed food, sweets and saturated fats at the expense of fresh green vegetables, fruits, proteins, soy products and fish oils creates an overall unhealthy state that shows in your face. It also encourages the formation of free radicals as side products, promoting wrinkle formation.

■ **Too-rapid weight loss**

The skin layer is unable to "bounce back" from the lost fat if it happens too quickly.

■ **Inappropriate exercise**

No exercise at all will slow down your metabolism, restricting nutrient flow to the skin. Over-exertion, on the other hand, jeopardizes the immune system, delaying the skin repair process. As we'll see in later chapters, certain forms of exercise are better than others for your face. Those that include a lot of bouncing or impact — by requiring running with heavy pounding, for example, or jumping — will actually loosen the facial skin, which you don't want. (For similar reasons, incidentally, an ancient Chinese beauty trick advises women not to laugh hard, since too much muscle movement around the mouth causes smile lines.)

- **Lack of sleep**

  Too little sleep slows skin repair by weakening the immune system.

- **Stress**

  It makes all the other external factors worse, and also weakens on your immune system.

- **Soap**

  When used as facial cleansers, soap and soap-based products, which are alkaline in nature, change the skin's environment, upsetting the skin's all-important PH balance — that is, the balance between acid/alkaline.

The Chinese Approach to Clearing Away Wrinkles

As I said, Chinese and Western medicine both recognize, in their own way, the external factors we just went through. Now let's see what TCM tells us about the internal factors that cause wrinkles. One already mentioned is weakened blood circulation. And if you already read the first part of this book, you may have guessed some of the others: Qi strength, Qi balance, internal organ function, and essence distribution.

Take bad diet, for instance. In TCM, eating and drinking are directly related to the two digestive organs that relate to the so-called "middle burner" — the spleen and stomach. Now, the spleen and stomach (with help from the small intestine) transform food and water into essence, and transport that essence to nourish and replenish all parts of the body, including the facial skin. So poor nutrition isn't the only problem caused by a bad diet; it also compromises stomach and spleen function, creating toxicity and inadequate essence supply.

That's why many of the TCM herbs and dietary suggestions you'll be putting into practice in your anti-wrinkle strategy focus on the spleen and stomach. They are crucial organs for a smooth face. A Western cosmetic surgeon may not talk to you about these organs.

Another example. Aside from the vessel-restricting problem we mentioned, we also know smoking damages the lungs. But what do your lungs have to do with wrinkles? Everything! Remember that in the paper-covers-rock-breaks-scissors-cut-paper analogy we used to describe TCM organ theory, the lungs "rule" the skin and hair by regulating the skin's metabolism and bringing "breath" to the skin. So lung tonics will be a major emphasis in your herbal menu.

Smoking sheds light on a few other TCM anti-wrinkle methods. In the long term, smoking creates an imbalance of Yin and Yang. This imbalance (whether it's caused by smoking or age-related factors) leads to dysfunctions in the flow of Qi in the body. Qi dysfunction and Yin-Yang imbalance lead to wrinkles. Most of the herbs and exercises I'll be recommending to you specifically address these two factors.

Another insight: From the TCM viewpoint, the problem with over consumption of alcohol is more than just free-radical creation. It causes "damp heat" accumulation in the spleen and stomach, injures the liver, and weakens the kidney Yin. These conditions in turn cause Qi and blood stagnation, blocking the nutrient supply to the skin and causing wrinkles. Again, whether you drink or not, your TCM self-treatments specifically address damp heat, liver function and kidney Yin.

Examples abound of TCM pathways to wrinkle prevention that Western medicine won't touch. I'll just give you one more. In TCM organ theory, the heart rules the blood and the spirit. Heart tonics, then, will be part of your anti-wrinkle treatment plan, because abundant heart energy creates a lustrous and healthy facial glow. If you don't take care of your heart system — that is, if you don't compensate for aging with tonifiers — a lusterless and wrinkled face is likely.

Checklist for Your Wrinkle-Free Lifestyle

Chinese medicine recognizes that aging is natural and some facial wrinkling goes along with it. But TCM also has a long tradition of longevity-enhancing and youth-restoring treatments that can delay the onset of wrinkling in people in their 30s and significantly help reduce wrinkling in older women and men.

Now it's time for you to take advantage of that knowledge by using a variety of herbs, herbal formulas, acupressure techniques, Qi Gong exercises and nutritional strategies to realize your dream of a smoother and more radiant face. That's what the coming chapters will deal with.

The first important step to do is to start making the lifestyle changes that will serve as a sort of launching point for your TCM treatment program. I know it's hard to change some lifelong habits, but it's worth it. If you can follow my suggestions, you'll notice the results in your face even before you take a single TCM herb or do your first Qi Gong exercise. If you don't, your TCM program will be much less effective.

■ **Protect your skin from the sun.** Even today in China, you'll see women carrying umbrellas on hot and sunny summer days. They're protecting their skin. I'd like to see parasols make a comeback in Europe and North America, but broad-spectrum sunscreen products (SPF of 30 or more) will provide protection. Make sure you choose a product containing zinc oxide, which protects against UVB radiation as well as short and long UVA radiation.

- **Protect your skin from windy and dry conditions.** You can't control the weather, but you can make sure you drink plenty of water   and use a good moisturizer regularly. There's even some extra-credit Yin tonic herbs for skin hydration that will help, as you'll see in future chapters.

- **Limit caffeine and alcohol.** Some green tea is beneficial, and an occasional drink won't be a problem. But over consumption of either sabotages your anti-wrinkle quest.

- **Stop smoking.** Completely. Today.

- **Get enough sleep.** Sleep is good medicine for your skin. Get to bed before 11 p.m. According to TCM, the hours between 11:00 p.m. and 1:00 a.m. are prime liver detoxification time.

- **Lose weight if you need to.** The health problems that accompany being overweight accelerate skin aging. But you should avoid sudden weight loss since it will cause the skin to sag, resulting in wrinkles. Lose weight moderately, not rapidly.

- **Choose natural soft soaps or cleansers.** Keeping your face clean is essential for battling wrinkles, but commercial soaps damage your facial skin. Avoid alkaline hash soap. Suggestion: Try crushed rice germ from a health food store and soak it in clean water, then use the soaked water to clean your face. It not only cleans thoroughly, but also nourishes. Or, use several drops of natural vinegar mixed with water as a facial wash. It brings a surprising glow to your skin.

- **Eat right.** I'll be giving you ideas for beneficial anti-wrinkle foods. Eat them instead of greasy, spicy and, especially, processed foods. Remember, to keep a young and supple skin, you will have to have balanced intake of adequate fat (from a good source), protein(amino acid), and hydration supplying food (these do not just refer to pure water, remember the experience that you feel dry, but it doesn't matter how much you drink, you still feel dry. The water comes from one end and out from the other end), you need yin tonic food. Also, eat your meals at regular intervals.

- **Get a handle on stress.** Prolonged stress jeopardizes your health, which shows in your face. The Qi Gong exercises you'll be doing will help. Your best start, though, is to forget negative thoughts. That is, simply learn to let them go and move on. That may sound simplistic, but try it.

■ **Stay even-keeled.** Emotional reactions are healthy, but exaggerated emotions are not. TCM theory says that even joy needs to be kept at a reasonable level. At the same time, over constrained emotions (working to hard to keep them bottled up) is also unhealthy. Emotional balance is a basic precept of Chinese medicine. Unbalanced emotions mean unbalanced internal organs, and in very specific ways. For example, too much joy saps the heart's energy, which we've seen is detrimental to your facial skin. Similarly, wallowing in melancholy disrupts lung function, which is so key to a smooth face.

About Sagging of The Face

According to Traditional Chinese Medicine theory, sagging of the face comes from the same cause as wrinkles. Many treatment modalities for wrinkles mentioned in this chapter are suitable for sagging of the face, especially the modalities for tonifying and boosting qi (energy). You can follow the same food and herbal recommendations, acupressure routines and Qi Gong exercise for healing the sagging of the face.

CHAPTER 5

Herbal Wrinkle Treatments, Chinese Style

When it comes to using nature's bounty to prevent or eliminate facial wrinkles, Traditional Chinese Medicine offers tremendous riches. Herbal medicine is the most abundant and best-documented modality in Traditional Chinese Medicine, especially for skin rejuvenation.

There are hundreds of different herbs or foods that the Chinese use to treat skin conditions, many of them specifically for wrinkles. There are even more anti-wrinkle herbal formulas.

Not all of these Chinese herbs are found only in China, of course. Many grow in the Western Hemisphere and all of the herbs I'll be recommending to you are available in the United States. But all of these herbs work according to TCM principles to address the underling causes of your wrinkles and treat them from the inside out.

Western medicine tends to think of an herb's healing effect as the result of its chemical constituents — the phytochemical (plant molecules) and other nutrients that are its "ingredients." But that's only part of the picture. More important from the TCM point of view are the "non-scientific" factors we learned about in the first three chapters — that is, an herb's temperature, smell, taste, and the channels (meridian) it enters. This is the point of view with which you'll be taking the herbs.

Let's take an example. Fu Ling (or "poria," not one of the herbs you'll be taking specifically for wrinkles) leaches excess dampness out of the body and calms the spirit. As far as anybody knows, this isn't because of any ingredient in Fu Ling that Western science can identify. In fact, Western science doesn't recognize the TCM concept of "dampness," or the idea of "calming the spirit."

Rather, Fu Ling does these things because its taste is bland. In TCM bland-tasting herbs leech out dampness. Also, since it enters the heart channel, it calms the spirit. This special TCM way of explaining an herb's healing action is even more pronounced with herbal formulas, where it's believed that, with boiling, the energies from the various ingredients synergize to create a united effect.

Most of the anti-wrinkle herbs I'm about to recommend do indeed contain a wide range of amino acids, vitamins, and minerals. Other antioxidants, as well as polysaccharides — all essential to skin's health and are considered as super skin nutrients according to modern science. But that doesn't mean herbs must contain a significant amount of these nutrients in order to beautify your skin. Nor does it mean that those herbs that do contain the "right" ingredients necessarily work in TCM because of those ingredients — although in many cases it's true that they do.

In a sense, an herb's chemical content is beside the point, though it's useful to know about it. Huang Qi, for example, has been used to beautify skin for thousands of years by Chinese healers who had no knowledge of its polysaccharide and saponins content. It didn't work any the less for that lack of knowledge.

Most Chinese herbs don't work directly on your face, because Chinese medical philosophy doesn't separate your face from the rest of your body. Like any Chinese medicinal method, herbs benefit your facial skin through their effect on the five-element system, the energy channels, and the organ systems.

Most anti-wrinkle herbs take one or more of the following routes to beautify your skin. They moisten the lungs, they nourish the liver, they benefit kidney essence, they regulate Qi, they tonify Yin and they improve blood flow.

All of these actions rejuvenate facial skin, many at the cellular level. Some moisten the skin for a smoother, more supple look, and some strengthen the skin's ability to fight off external evils (environmental factors).

Your Line-Up of Herbs For A Youthful, Wrinkle-Free Face

An experienced herbalist would be able to select the best herbs for your individual condition. But there are a number of anti-wrinkle herbs that have been proven valuable for anybody. From my TCM training and clinical experience, I've found that the following array of individual Chinese herbs are ideal for home use and astonishingly effective in helping the healthy body delay aging process, smooth wrinkles and preventing new ones.

There are a few things you should know about them first:

- Almost all the herbs I recommended are from the "superior" category, according to traditional Chinese herbal texts. That means they all have anti-aging effect and are considered to be longevity herbs. They can be taken as herbal supplements if you have a healthy body condition. It also means they're useful for other conditions besides wrinkles. You'll be meeting many of them again in future chapters.

- Most of these herbs are available either as an extract, as the powdered whole herb, or the raw herb itself (dried or fresh). In general, I recommend finding the raw, dried, whole herb and making a tea (steeped) or decoction (boiled or simmered for a longer time) according to my instructions. But they will work in any form.

- Don't feel you need to take all the herbs I recommend. (You wouldn't have time for much else if you tried!) Pick a few for starters and add on till you reach a daily "menu" that you're comfortable with. Often you can choose herbs that fit your individual condition, including your particular skin type, based on information I provide with each herb's description. For example, if you tend to suffer frequent colds, and tend to have sagging and wrinkle skin, Huang Qi is a good anti-wrinkle herb for you. If you have dry mouth, or hot flashes with a dry and wrinkle skin, then Sheng Di Huang is a good choice.

- Take an herb daily for 10 days to one month. Then stop and evaluate your condition and the herb's effect to see if you want to continue. Remember, aging is a continuous process, so take these herbs periodically to tone up the body. You do not have to take the herbs everyday for long time. I recommend taking them periodically and only when your body in is a healthy condition.

- There are three ways to determine dosage — that is, how much of an herb you take at a time. The best way is to follow the advice of a TCM or other health care practitioner. Another is to follow the instructions on the label, if you're buying prepared products. The third is to use the recommendations I give you with each herb — but only if you know you're clear of any health conditions. The only way to know that for sure is to consult with your health care practitioner before starting any herbal program.

- Pay special attention to the cautions and contraindications given with each herb in terms of traditional Chinese medicine. These are all safe herbs according to TCM texts, but some of them are strong tonics and are very rich in nature. They can cause indigestion and/or loose stools in some cases, which is why you need to avoid them if you have diarrhea or weak digestion.

- Last and most importantly, if you are currently taking medicine, have a medical condition, or pregnant or nursing, you should check with your health care provider before starting to take these herbs.

Now let's walk into the fascinating world of Chinese anti-wrinkle herbs. I will usually give the Chinese name first, followed by the common name in English. When appropriate, I'll include the botanical (Latin) name, which often helps you be sure you're buying the right herb.

HUANG Qi *(Astragalus Root)*

The word "Qi" in the Chinese name doesn't refer to life energy in this case, but to "senior." To the Chinese, Huang Qi is the senior or top herb in its category of energy tonics. ("Huang" means yellow, this fibrous root being a yellowish-brown color). So Huang Qi's very name is a tribute to its superior tonic function.

Under the name astragalus root, this is one of the better-known Chinese herbs in the West, where it's mainly used to enhance the healthy immune system. But not everybody is aware of its powerful anti-wrinkle action. I have two patients older than 80, and both have taken Huang Qi for many years. Not only are they active and independent, but their skin is healthier and noticeably less wrinkled than you usually see at that age. They are truly beautiful octogenarians.

- **How Huang Qi cures wrinkles.** Huang Qi is a sweet, slightly warm herb that enters the lung and spleen channels. It's one of the most prominent Qi tonifiers in Chinese medicine, with a special function of protecting the body from the "Six External Evils (or, in Western terms, of helping support the healthy immune system). That same Qi energizing action — especially of lung Qi — combines with its blood -nourishing qualities to make Huang Qi a powerful preventer of wrinkles.

  This herb also helps smooth existing wrinkles by raising the Yang Qi of the "postnatal sea of energy" to lift and firm muscles, including those below the facial skin surface. (If a phrase like "raising the Yang Qi of the postnatal sea of energy" leaves you baffled, take a look back at Chapter 1 and 3, where this and other TCM healing energy concepts are explained).

  Astragalus/Huang Qi is rich in antioxidant plant chemicals, such as flavonoids, which help the body to delay aging. It also contains saponins and polysaccharides, which help soften and hydrate the skin. Also in Astragalus are 21 amino acids and 14 different minerals.

  Huang Qi is especially recommended if in addition to your wrinkle concerns you suffer from low energy, frequent colds, poor digestion or low appetite.

- **Finding and taking Huang Qi.** Huang Qi roots are harvested in the northeastern and Inner Mongolian regions of China. Because it's a root, you'll need to decoct it by simmering 6 grams of the root in 16 ounces of water for 25 minutes. That will yield two cups of tea for two day's dose. Drink one cup per day for two days.

Making a root decoction has the most immune-enhancing and anti-aging effectiveness, but you can also find Huang Qi as a powdered extract in capsule form. Make sure you see the botanical name Astragalus membranaceus on the package, or the pharmaceutical name Radix astragalim, which simply means root of the Astragalus. The amount in each capsule will vary, depending on the product. Take 1 gram worth once a day.

- *Cautions concerning Huang Qi.* Astragalus, a "superior" herb in the Chinese herbal tradition, is considered very safe. But because of its Qi-raising properties, it's not recommended while you're suffering from an "exterior excess" (that is, a cold or upper respiratory infection), or from digestion problems from overeating or a weak stomach, or from skin lesions. Also stay away form Aastragalus if you've been diagnosed by a TCM practitioner as having Yin deficiency with heat signs or if you have high blood pressure.

SHA YUAN JI LI *(Astragalus Seed)*

You get a pretty good idea of the intricacy of Chinese naming when you realize that this is simply the seed of the same plant we just discussed (astragalus), yet the Chinese name is completely different. The seed was a favorite beautifying herb of the early Taoists some 2,500 years ago.

It is said that during the Tang dynasty between the years 618 and 907 (A.D.), political turmoil forced an emperor to flee his kingdom. He found refuge in a distant village where he noticed that all the women looked young and beautiful. Naturally, he asked what their secret was, and was told that all the women in the village drank a tea made from Sha Yuan Ji Li regularly.

Not convinced, the emperor asked his own daughter, a weak and sickly princess with dry and wrinkly skin, to drink such a tea daily. With the possibility of becoming beautiful, the princess, for once in her life, obeyed her father. Within three years, her face had rejuvenated itself and "looked as smooth and nourished as jade." Even her figure improved!

- **How Sha Yuan Ji Li smoothes wrinkles.** Like the root of the same plant, Astragalus seed is a sweet, warm herb that serves as a Yang tonic. And it includes the same antioxidant ingredients. But it enters the kidney and liver channels, tonifying those organ systems to nourish liver blood and kidney essence which nourishes facial skin.

The seed is the best form of Astragalus for your wrinkle-fighting strategy if you also suffer from such kidney Yang deficiency signs as chronic low back pain, tinnitus (low pitch ringing in your ears), vaginal discharge, or (for men) impotence or premature ejaculation as well as low libido (for both men and women).

- **Finding and taking Sha Yuan Ji Li.** Look for the actual seeds in bulk at well-stocked herb stores or Chinese markets. Measure out 3 grams of seeds and wrap them in cheesecloth so they won't escape. Drop the package in 16 ounces of water and keep it at a low boil for 20 minutes. Strain the liquid out and drink a cup of the resulting tea twice a day. Or you can buy the powdered seeds in capsule form. Take 1 gram a day.

- *Cautions concerning Sha Yuan Ji Li.* Again, Astragalus seed is a safe herb. But don't take this herb if you've been diagnosed with a Yin deficiency with heat signs, or if you have difficulty urinating or a hyperactive libido, since this herb is used for reducing urinary frequency and raising the libido.

DANG GUI *(Chinese Angelica Root)*

In Chinese, the name "Dang Gui" refers to a wife praying for the return of her far-away husband. In English, it's the herb of angels. Angelica has a rich supply of phytochemicals, including significant amounts of vitamin B-12, vitamin E; ferulic acid (an antioxidant), carotene (another antioxidant).

- **How Dang Gui smoothes wrinkles.** TCM recognizes Dang Gui's ability to invigorate and harmonize circulation as it enters the heart, liver and spleen channels. Improved blood flow to your facial skin means faster replenishment of nutrients needed to prevent and clear wrinkles. It also carries toxins away from the skin.

  As a blood tonic, Dang Gui is an important herb in Traditional Chinese Medicine for treating gynecological conditions, alleviating PMS symptoms and regulating periods. It's especially recommended if your wrinkles are accompanied by a pale, ashen complexion, which are signs of a blood deficiency.

- **Finding and taking Dang Gui.** Look for the botanical name Angelica sinensis. It has becoming more and more popular in recent years for its soothing properties for PMS and menopause. You can easily get the dried raw herb from quality herbal stores. The capsule form is readily available in health food stores or even supermarkets, It's best to get the raw form and make a decoction by low-boiling 3 grams of it in 10 ounces of water for 15 minutes, straining and drinking. (If it's too bitter for you, add honey). If taking in capsule form, 1 gram per day is a good dosage.

- *Cautions concerning Dang Gui.* Consult with your doctor first if you're on blood thinners or other medication. Don't take it if you suffer from diarrhea, or if you've been diagnosed by a TCM practitioner as having an excess heat condition.

HUANG JING *(Solomon's Seal)*

Its Chinese name means "essence of the yellow earth," which is exactly what the ancient Taoists considered it. It's also been called the "food of the immortals," and it's been highly lauded in China over the centuries as an anti-aging and beautifying herb. As one medical text puts it, "This herb harmonizes the internal organs so the face will be beautiful, grey hair will turn black again, and fallen teeth will regrow."

A slight exaggeration? Well, perhaps not as much as the following story from another text: A rich family's servant escaped deep into the mountains, where she saw the lovely Huang Jing growing and dared to eat it. She found that by so doing, she could remain full of energy without feeling hungry. She could sleep soundly beneath tall trees, climbing easily to the treetop when threatened by animals and leaping from tree to tree. When she was finally found by her master, they almost didn't recognize her because of her new healthy and youthful appearance. And all she'd eaten was Huang Jing and water!

- **How Huang Jing smoothes wrinkles.** You may not fly through the trees by taking Huang Jing, but you'll definitely smooth your wrinkles. This herb is a beautiful example of TCM theory in action. It works on all five-organ systems, especially benefiting the Qi of the heart and lungs. Heart energy manifests itself on the facial complexion, and the lungs rule the skin. It also tonifies the Qi and Yin of the spleen, stomach and kidney. Remember that the spleen and stomach form that postnatal sea of energy that supplies abundant Qi and blood to nourish the face.

Li Shi Zhen, author of the authoritative TCM herbal text "Ben Cao Gong Mu," (or "Grand Companion of Materia Medica") puts it another way: "This herb receives all the essence from heaven and earth and nourishes the mother [that is, the "earth" element of the five elements]. When the mother is nourished, then the water and fire elements can interact in harmony, allowing in turn for wood and metal to work. So all the evils in the body will go away by themselves and disease cannot come."

From the point of view of modern medicine, Solomon's seal (the English name for Huang Jing) includes the active ingredients azetidine-2-carboxylic acid, aspartic acid, homoserine, diaminobutyric acid, digitalis glycoside, and 11 amino acids. It helps to support the cells' healthy immune function, improve digestion and delay the aging process of the internal organs and the skin.

Huang Jing is an excellent anti-wrinkle herb for older people, and anybody with wrinkles accompanied by low energy and diabetic conditions.

- **Finding and taking Huang Jing.** Huang Jing is specifically Siberian Solomon's seal, or Polygonatum sibiricum. Other Polygonatum species, such as Polygonatum multiflorum, are not quite the same, though easier to find. Either way, it's the rootstalk that you want. If you find raw Huang Jing rootstalk, low-boil 6 grams in 16 ounces of water for 20 minutes, strain and drink twice a day. If you buy the herb in dry powdered form or capsule form, take 1 gram per day with warm water.

- *Cautions concerning Huang Jing.* Huang Jing is a very safe herb that can be taken daily for long periods. But it's very rich and tends to be claying, so avoid it if you have weak digestion or diarrhea.

E JIAO *(Donkey-Hide Gelatin)*

You know that Traditional Chinese Medicine is different than what you're used to when a hard, dry "glue piece" made from soaking donkey skin is used as a powerful skin beautifying "herb." But it's for good reason that E Jiao is a tremendously popular treatment. I myself took it for three months after giving birth to each of my two children, and I was thrilled (as most women are) with the healthy, wrinkle-less glow it brought to my face.

- **How E Jiao smoothes wrinkles.** Remember that in TCM, whatever performs the action of an herbal — that is, providing what we lack — is considered herbal. It can be vegetable, animal or mineral. E Jiao fits the bill perfectly.

  Our skin relies on protein to rebuild, and donkey skin gelatin delivers exactly the right kind. When hydrolyzed in water, the amino acids released by E Jiao are very easy for our body to absorb. The result is not only tonified blood, but also an improved calcium balance and an enriched nutrient supply that retards aging and wrinkles.

  Also, the best treatments for skin beauty are those that nourish the blood, tonify Yin and moisten the skin and the internal environment. E Jiao, a sweet, neutral herb that enters the kidney, liver and lung, does all three of those things. More blood circulating replenishes facial skin cells, and the hydration effect helps fight off wrinkle causing "evils" in the external environment.

Over the centuries, E Jiao has gained a reputation as a "woman's herb," especially useful after giving birth or in response to any kind of blood deficiency. It will work extremely well as an anti-wrinkle herb for those with any blood weakness that results in frequent dizziness, pale complexion, anemia, irritability or insomnia.

■ **Finding and taking E Jiao.** Mail order or Chinese markets are your most likely sources. If possible, choose a product that originates from China's Shangong province, known for high quality E Jiao. Also, make sure you're getting donkey skin gelatin (Gelatinum corii asini or Equus asinus), and not the less effective cow's skin.

What you'll get are hard little pieces that you crush and then dissolve in hot water or (more of a treat) warm wine. The dosage you want is 1.5 grams, once per day. If you buy it in powdered form, take 1 gram in warm water once per day.

■ *Cautions concerning E Jiao.* It's a safe herb, but discontinue use if you catch any kind of cold or flu, have an upset stomach, or suffer from any other temporary condition. Also, E Jiao counteracts Da Huang (rhubarb root), so don't take the two together.

REN SHEN *(Chinese Ginseng Root)*

As you've surely noticed, Ren Shen, or Ginseng Root or Ginseng, as it is commonly called here in US, has been quite the rage in the West for several decades now. It's been the rage in Asia for several millennia. The root of the ginseng plant is probably the most precious herb in China, where it has strong spiritual as well as medicinal associations.

One of its ancient names is "Di Jing", meaning "a gathering of essence from the earth." Another is "Shen Cao", or "spirit plant." That combination of names recognizes the ginseng root as human in shape and plant in spirit. The names also reflect TCM's belief that ginseng anchors the human soul spirit, expelling bad energy, boosting brain power, "enlightening" the body, improving overall well being, and extending the lifespan.

But the old name that fits our purpose best is "Zhou Mian Huan Dan" — meaning "a magic recovery from a wrinkled face."

■ **How Ginseng smoothes wrinkles.** Ginseng's special ingredients are usually called ginsenosides (or more properly tripterpenoid saponins). Not only are these molecules powerful stress-reducers and fatigue-reducers, they're also antioxidants that neutralize the free radicals that accelerate aging. Another ginseng component — panaxtriol — is a natural steroid that aids in tissue formation.

Another way ginseng protects your skin is by supporting your immune system's ability to fend off infection.

In TCM terms, ginseng is simply a superb Qi tonifier of the entire five-organ (Zang) system — the heart, lung, spleen, kidney and liver. It also nourishes the stomach, restores the pulse, calms the spirit and generates fluids throughout the body. It boosts the skin's metabolism and replenishes nutrients the skin needs. All this leads to a slowdown in the aging process, and a decrease in wrinkle formation.

Because Ginseng is beneficial in so many ways, it makes sense for anybody to include it in any anti-wrinkle strategy. It's especially useful if you're also bothered by such complaints as chronic fatigue, weak digestion, and shortness of breath, chronic diarrhea, insomnia, anxiety, or forgetfulness.

■ **Finding and taking Ginseng.**   There are so many sub-par Ginseng products on the market that your wisest strategy is to look for and buy the whole root at well-supplied herb stores or Chinese markets. Ideally, you'd like ginseng roots harvested after the plant is seven years old from the wild in the Chong Bai Mountains of the Ji Ling province in northeast part of China. Those are the Ginseng roots of highest quality, neither too hot nor too cold in nature. But they're rare, expensive, and hard to find. You'll probably have to settle for cultivated roots, which can be very good.

Choose the Asian species (Panax ginseng or Panax schin-seng), which can be Chinese but will more likely be Korean. (Siberian ginseng, or Eleutherococcus senticosus, is a completely different herb.) The Korean ginseng is also known as red Ginseng and tends to be slightly stronger and warmer than Chinese Ginseng. The American Ginseng (Panax quinquefolium) is a cooling herb, and should be selected instead of other Asian Ginseng if you have heat signs.

There are many ways to get ginseng into your body, but I recommend decocting the dried root, which is what you'll usually find in herbal stores. Take a 2-gram piece of the root and soak it in 4 ounces of fresh water for half an hour. Then steam in a double boiler for an hour. Drink half the resulting strong liquid in the morning before breakfast, and finish the other half the next day.

You can buy the powdered root, but make sure it's from a reputable dealer you trust to provide pure ginseng. Simply stir 1/2 gram of the powder   into warm water and dink it in the morning. Don't mix it with any tea or take with turnip; it will decrease the ginseng's effectiveness.

■ *Cautions concerning Ginseng.* Avoid taking Asian ginseng, which is warm in nature, if you have high blood pressure. If you are taking medication, consult with your doctor or health care practitioner before taking any kind of ginseng.

DI HUANG *(Rehmannia)*

Here's another major herb that Chinese women have used throughout the centuries for wrinkle care. The early Taoists, whose philosophy was so influential in the development of Chinese medicine, relied heavily on the tuberous root of Rehmannia as a beauty herb.

An interesting feature of this herb is that it's used in a cooked (or "prepared") form as well as fresh or dried. Typical of the Chinese way of seeing things, each form belongs to a different category, acts differently, and even has a different name — Sheng Di Huang is the raw version, Shu Di Huang is cooked.

- **How Di Huang smoothes wrinkles.** Raw or cooked, Rehmannia enters the heart, kidney and liver to generate internal fluid. It strengthens the Yin, nourishes the skin and ultimately beautifies the face. The prepared (cooked) version is more of a blood tonifier, while the fresh version clears away heat and tonifies the five internal organs. Both nourish dry and wrinkled skin.

  A more Western view would credit Rehmannia's polysaccharides, alkaloids, 15 amino acids and 29 minerals for its wrinkle prevention effect with long-term use. It's rich in vitamin A, a known anti-wrinkle agent. Its antibacterial and anti-inflammatory activity also plays a role in stabilizing the skin. And because it's traditionally used for menopause conditions, it's double useful for menopausal women with wrinkle concerns.

- **Finding and taking Di Huang.** Both Sheng Di Huang and Shu Di Huang can be fund in local Chinese herbal stores. Look for the Latin name Radix rehmanniae glutinosae or Rehmannia glutinosa . Low-boil 6 grams of the dried or cooked root in 10 ounces of water for 20 minutes. Strain and drink half early in the day, the rest later in the day.

  If you buy the powdered root, stir 2 grams in warm water and drink it down once a day.

- *Cautions concerning Di Huang.* Sheng Di Huang and Shu Di Huang are safe but very rich herbs. Stop taking either one if you experience digestion problems.

LING ZHI *(Reishi Mushroom)*

In olden times, miraculous spiritual and physical healing powers were attributed to this mushroom. Ingesting Ling Zhi was nothing short of taking in the pure essence of mountain clouds, rain and the four seasons.

It wasn't an easy matter to obtain such a marvelous mushroom, which grew in six different colors high up on certain mountains in the Guongdong, Shangdong, and Hainan provinces of China. A seeker of Ling Zhi could only look for them at certain times of the year, and not without praying first and bringing gifts to the god of the mountain.

An ancient poem tells of a reishi-seeker who was led up the mountain by "immortals riding a white deer, with short hair and long ears." The seeker filled a beautiful jade box with Ling Zhi, which he gave to his master. The Ling Zhi turned the master's gray hair black, made him look young and handsome, and prolonged his life.

- **How Ling Zhi smoothes wrinkles.** These days, reishi mushrooms are cultivated and found in health food stores. But they are no less miraculous as herbs that calm the spirit, open chest congestion, strengthen the heart energy, improve memory and cognition, nourish the liver and enlighten the body. Reishi enters the heart, lung and kidney channels, nourishing essence and Qi.

  Ling Zhi's anti-aging and skin-beautifying functions are well documented in Chinese medical literature. I use it in my practice. One patient, who suffered from different illnesses at different times, came to me with a very dull and wrinkled facial complexion. After several months of taking Ling Zhi in powder form, her dizziness and weakness were gone, and her illnesses were less frequent. Also, though, her skin condition was noticeably improved. Ling Zhi is an excellent herb choice for you if you have wrinkles with overall sub-health conditions.

  Reishi's beautifying function comes from its especially powerful long chain of polysaccharides, and an antioxidant plant chemical category called triterpenoids, in particular one called ganoderic acid (the botanical name of reishi mushrooms is Ganoderma lucidum).

- **Finding and taking Ling Zhi.** Reishi mushrooms are hard, woody, but edible with certain amount of preparation. As an herb, it's best to low-boil 3 grams of the mushrooms in 16 ounces of water for 30 minutes, then strain and drink the decoction on an empty stomach in the morning.

  In powdered form, take 1 gram in warm water on an empty stomach in the morning. There's also a concentrated extract in capsule form derived from the spores. If that's your choice, take 1 gram per day.

- *Cautions concerning Ling Zhi.* Ling Zhi is a very safe herb and can be taken for long time, but avoid to take it if you are on any heart medication and blood thinners, including aspirin. Check with your doctor before taking it.

TIAN MEN DONG *(Chinese Asparagus)*

The Chinese Tian Men Dong is not the same asparagus you know as a side dish. It's a potent herb that the "Divine Husbandman's Classic of the Materia Medica" (the ancient Chinese herbal bible) calls an "all-purpose beauty herb." Its roots are used as a Yin tonic.

For the ancient Taoists, Tian Men Dong was a key herb in secret formulas. One text, for example, called for making little balls out of a mixture of about a pound of Tian Men Dong, a half-pound of Shu Di Huang (see above) and some honey. Those who would eat three of those balls three times a day with warm liquor for 20 days "would be free of disease", with a face "as beautiful as a flower."

- **How Tian Men Dong smoothes wrinkles.** Tian Men Dong is considered a cold Yin nourisher that enters the kidney and lung channels. It clears the heat to attain pure blood and strong, healthy lungs — two paths to smooth and supple skin. (Remember, skin is part of the lung function.) It also moistens the skin and the internal organs, which is another reason for its anti-wrinkle effect.

Tian Men Dong is a good choice for those with wrinkling dry skin.

- **Finding and taking Tian Men Dong.** Make sure you're getting Tian Men Dong, Chinese asparagus. The dried wild root can usually be found at Chinese herb shops. You can simmer about 6 grams of the raw root in 16 ounces of water for 30 minutes, then strain and drink half the potent liquid. Drink the other half later in the day.

If you chose to take the granules, then take 1 gram in warm water once a day.

- **Cautions concerning Tian Men Dong.** This is a safe, non-toxic herb. But because it has such a cold property, it's best to avoid it when you have a cold with cough, low appetite, or diarrhea.

More Wrinkle-Fighting Chinese Herbs

I've just described for you nine superb Chinese herbs that have been used for many centuries to keep Chinese faces free of wrinkles. Whether you choose to use one or two, or all, you will be pleased with the results if you stick with your herbal treatments over the months and years — and especially if you combine them with the acupressure, Qi Gong and dietary strategies to follow.

But there are plenty more anti-wrinkle herbs in the Chinese medicine cabinet — literally hundreds more. Once you become familiar with the above herbs and incorporate some of them into your daily routine, you'll soon want to try more. At some point, you'll need to use the services of a qualified TCM herbalist to guide you through the bewildering array of available herbs, and to choose the ones that best address your underlying wrinkle-causing conditions.

Meanwhile, though, there's still much to explore on your own. Here are some more very effective and readily available Chinese anti-wrinkle herbs for the next stage of your herbal adventure:

■ **Gou Qi Zi** *(Chinese Wolfberry)*
Another top beautifying herb with a millennia-old history as an anti-aging agent, this Chinese fruit (Fructus Lycii) smoothes wrinkles by nourishing kidney and liver Yin, as well as the blood. Noting its rich phytochemical content (including antioxidants like zeaxanthin, beta-carotene, and B vitamins, the anti-inflammatory B-sitosterol, linoleic acid and polysaccharides), modern study recognizes its supportive function for a healthy immune system.

■ **Ju Hua** *(Wild Chrysanthemum)*
The Chinese decoct their own unique variety of the well-known flower to clear the liver and gallbladder channels and bring beauty to the face. It's a cooling herb best taken in summertime to relieve eye irritation and other symptoms caused by heat and smog. It clears the liver and lung channels, detoxifying and cleaning the skin. It helps clear your skin of furuncles (boils), carbuncles and sores. It is an excellent detoxifying and beautifying herb.

■ **Du Zhong** *(Encommia)*
Another kidney Yang tonic that nourishes essence and Qi, this herb is a bark of a tree (Eucommia ulmoides) that prevents facial sagging and wrinkles, as well as fatigue.

■ **Sang Shen** *(Mulberry Fruit)*
Rich in carotene, vitamins, minerals and linoleic acid, this fruit is celebrated in traditional Chinese herbal texts as a skin beautifier and eye brightener. Sang Shen improves blood circulation to the skin and scalp as it nourishes Yin.

■ **Shan Yao** *(Chinese Yam)*
This Chinese herb's skin-nourishing qualities are so well recognized in the West that you'll find it in many beauty cream products. Chinese medical texts credit long term use of Shan Yao with sharper hearing, brighter eyes, appetite control and prolonged life — as well as more supple, glowing and wrinkle-free skin.

■ **Wu Wei Zi** *(Schisandra Fruit)*
A berry-like fruit that protects and detoxifies the liver and nourishes the lungs and kidneys. It's a strong antioxidant. It is considered a women's precious herb for beauty through out centuries in China.

Anti-Wrinkle Herbal Formulas:
Yesterday's Wisdom Today

All the anti-wrinkle herbs I've given you are individual, and safe for home use. And yet I've also told you that much of Chinese herbal medicine consists of formulas — that is, mixtures of many different herbs. So shouldn't herbal formulas be part of your do-it--yourself strategy?

The answer is yes for topical herbal blends you apply directly to your face. But for those you take internally, make-it-yourself formulas are probably not a good idea for typical home treatment. This is because of one thing, you have more than enough single-herb options to treat your facial wrinkles. When and if you feel it necessary to take it to the next level, I recommend you don't do it alone.

The main reason for this is simple. A trained and experienced herbalist must make an informed diagnosis of the underlying conditions contributing to your wrinkles — and then derive a specific, personalized treatment formula based on the eight principles, the five element system, internal organ theory and all the other tenants of Chinese medicine.

Even once the diagnosis is made, a good effective herbal formula for facial beauty isn't a matter of putting in a little of this and a little of that. The formula has to be the ideal combination of not only the right herbs but also the right amount of each herb to create the perfect dosage ratio.

And there's another reason I don't recommend homemade formulas. While all the individual herbs I've given you are smooth to the body and safe, chances are a personalized formula will need to include some harsh herbs. That's fine in the hands of a professional, because he or she knows how to combine ingredients to offset the harshness. For you to be able to do that, you'd need enough instruction to fill another book...at least.

Still, there are many Chinese herbal formulas with wrinkle-smoothing properties that you'll find as products in markets. They're usually safe, but I strongly recommend that you discuss any formula with a TCM practitioner or other health care professional before indulging. To give you an idea of the kinds of fascinating formulas used in TCM, here's a sampling of what's out there.

- **Ming Dynasty Emperor's Secret**
  During the Ming Dynasty (1368-1644), the emperor told a team of the best healers in the kingdom to come up with a formula that would rejuvenate his face and prolong his life. After much hard work, they created one that pleased the emperor. It consisted of the

following herbs, most of which you'll recognize from earlier in this chapter: Xian Shen Di Huang (fresh rehmannia), Korean Ginseng, Go Qi Zi (lycium fruits), Tian Men Dong (Chinese asparagus), Mai Men Dong (ophiopogon tuber), Bai Fu Ling (white poria), white wild honey.

■ **Forever Young**

The ancient Chinese wrote poems about (and to) this formula, lauded its power to prevent wrinkles and rejuvenate the face. Instead of nourishing the kidney and liver, the usual herbal beauty pathway, this one concentrates on harmonizing the entire body to facilitate abundant Qi and blood flow. It's ingredients: Shen Jian (fresh ginger), Da Zhao (Chinese date), Salt , Gan Cao (licorice root), Ding Xiang (clove), Chen Xiong (aloeswood), Hui Xiang (fennel).

■ **Eight Treasures**

This is one of the most famous traditional Chinese herbal formulas. Its uses are wide and varied, and include facial beauty. Ingredients: Ginseng, Bai Zhou (Atractylodes rhizome), Bai Fu Ling (White Poria), Dang Gui (Chinese angelica root), Chuang Xiong (Szechuan lovage root), Bai Shao (white peony), Shu Di Huang (Rehmannia root), Zhi Gan Cao (honey fried licorice). Usually added to this formula are two Chinese dates and three thin slices of fresh ginger.

> **Tips From Ping**
>
> I do not usually recommend making your own formulas for internal use, here's one you can safely try using familiar herbs if you are really interested. Mix 25 grams of Huang Jing (Solomon's seal) with 10 grams of dried Sheng Di Huang, (rehmannia), boil in 24 oz of water with low simmer for 40 minutes, then take the two herbs out, and add 5 teaspoonfuls of wild honey, continue simmer until it's all of one sticky consistency. Let it cool down, and make small balls of it, each about 6 grams. Put it in a glass jar, keep in refrigerator, and take one ball each day.

Your Alternatives

It will be your first choice and it will work absolutely great if you have the time to find all the herbs suggested in this chapter and prepare them the way it is suggested. In time, your face will tell the difference. However, for some reason, if you find it hard to look for these herbs (normally it will not be the case) or it is not possible for you to have the time to prepare them, here is your alternative: Use Nefeli "Wrinkle Smoother" – an all natural herbal supplements that combines all the superior anti-wrinkle herbs together to help your healthy body's ability rejuvenate the skin cells and promote a radiant and wrinkles free complexion from inside out.

After years of helping patients with their wrinkles, I was able to refine this formula for internal use. Based on the TCM principles of balancing Yin and Yang, tonifying yin energy, nourishing and promoting blood circulation, supporting the body's healthy immune system, and delaying the aging process. As the mirror of inner health, your face will reflect the resulting inner harmony with a young,healthy, wrinkle-free glow. The ingredients: ginseng root, pearl, Go Qi Zi (lycium fruit), Dang Gui (Chinese angelica root), Tian Men Dong (Chinese asparagus root), Da Zhao (Chinese dates), Ling Zhi (reishi mushroom), Huang Jing (polygonati root), Shu Di Huang (rehmannia root), Fu Ling (poria), To Si Zi (cuscutae seed), E Jiao (Gelatinum Corii Asini) Chrysanthemum Flower (Flos chrysanthemi morifolii).

Topical Treatments:
Make-Them-Yourself Herbal Masks

Taking herbs internally — that is, swallowing them in one form or another — is vital to your anti-wrinkle program. But it's not the only way to use these potent plants. Chinese herbal skin care also calls for topical treatment using herbs made into masks that you can put on to your face for direct wrinkle-fighting action.

Herbs are used in a number of Chinese topical formulas available in stores or by mail order. But there are plenty you can make and apply yourself, simply and easily, in the comfort of your own home.

Homemade herbal masks give you the best of both worlds. They're safe and natural, full of precise skin nutrients that are readily absorbed by the skin, sparing your face the chemicals and toxins that are found in many commercial products. At the same time, these natural external treatments help protect your skin from the effects of air pollution, sun exposure and radiation. Some fight off viral and bacterial infections, helping your skin "breathe" better and calming irritation that might exist, of course, they help eliminate existing wrinkles.

Even through these herbs used for musk are safe, your skin may have allergic reaction to them. So do your allergy test first. Put a little of the mask or wash on a small area of your wrist. Wait a day to see if you have a reaction. If not, try some or all of the following.

Here are four do-it-yourself herbal topicals that will smooth and beautify your skin quickly:

■ **Pearl Powder Mask**
The Chinese ruler Chi Xi was famous for her beautiful and wrinkle-free skin even at an old age. One of her secrets was the frequent use

of pearl powder, both internally and externally as a facial mask. This is actually powder from real pearls that serves as a treasure to our skin due to its unique amino acid and trace elements contents.

Traditionally, if you wanted to use pearl powder internally, you'd need to steam it with rice and water for hours, strain, and drink the liquid. Nowadays, water processed pearl powder is available at Chinese herb stores (and not as expensive as you might believe).

As a topical, you simply mix together in your palm a teaspoon of processed pearl powder with an egg white and half teaspoon of honey (add a little water if needed) and apply the mask to your face. After 20 minutes, wash it out. For best results, massage your face and apply a warm wet face cloth before and after you apply the mask to help your skin absorb the nutrients.

- **Xin Ren** *(Apricot Seed)* **Mask**
  Xin Ren is the pit or kernel of southern sweet apricots. Rich in vitamin A, it's a commonly used herb in Chinese facial masks. Soak 15 grams of Xin Ren in hot water for 2 hours. Get rid of the excess water and blend the soaked apricot kernel with 1/2 cup of milk, a raw egg and 5 grams of pearl powder. Wash your face thoroughly and apply the mask. Leave it on for at least 25 minutes before washing it out.

- **Fruit Flowers Mask**
  The seasonal flowers of fruit-bearing trees make for pleasant and very effective skin-saving herbal masks. You face can truly enjoy from the real fresh essence of the flowers. In TCM terms, your skin readily absorbs the essential nutrients from natural's fresh flowers and uses it as a powerful healing remedy.

  Pick the flowers yourself from peach, pear, cherry, apricot, plum, papaya, rose or camellia trees. Two or three different kinds — or even just one — will suffice for a great healing mask. Wash the flowers thoroughly. Then make a paste by crushing the petals with water and flour (oat, whole wheat or soybean). Apply the mask for 20 minutes and wash off.

- **Beautifying Skin Wash**
  This is a ancient do-it-yourself blend of 9 grams of Wang Gua, (a kind of melon also known as Chinese snake gourd), 9 grams of Huang Bai (amur cork-tree bark) and 7 pieces of Chinese dates. Purchase the herbs at a Chinese store and blend them together. Mix a teaspoon of the blend with water to wash your face, neck and hands each morning. Snake Gourd (Trichosanthes cucumeroide), may not sound pleasant, but one ancient Chinese text noted that "after using it for 100 days, the wife became so beautiful that the husband couldn't even recognize her."

Your Alternatives

Making your at home masks is fun to do and it really works for your skin. However, if at times it becomes overwhelming for you to do, remember you always have an alternative choice - Simply use Nefeli Anti-Wrinkle/Sagging Natural Herbal Skin Care Collections. This includes:

- Nefeli **"Skin Brightening Facial Wash"**. Made with Ginkgo Biloba and Papaya that removes make-up and cleans the skin at the same time, initiating the skins healing process from the start. Use mornings and evenings.

- Nefeli **"Intensive Wrinkle Care Mask"**. Made with Astragalus, Angelica, Coix Seed, Papaya and Luffa, this herbal mask helps distress and detoxify, at the same time, nourish, hydrate and firm the skin from inside out.

- Nefeli **"Intensive Wrinkle Care Day Cream"**. The combination of Ginseng, Pearls, Tremella, Rhodiola, Ginkgo Biloba and Green tea helps to protect the skin from environmental factors and energizes the skin to restore it's firmness and radiance. Use in mornings. It also serves as an ideal make-up base.

- Nefeli **"Intensive Wrinkle Care Night Cream"**. Made under the guidelines from TCM's healing principles with Reishi Mushroom, Ginseng, Pearls, Astraglus, Phellodendron Bark, Trichosanthes Fruit and Luffa, this herbal combination helps to support the skin's healthy natural healing process to reduce the inflammitary process from the toxins, and to increase skin's natural oxygen uptaking for cell renewal. It also calms the skin so the skin's healing process can be maximixzed during sleep. Use at night time.

- Nefeli **"Facial Rejuvenating Mask"**. Infused with potent Chinese herbal essence, this mask brings to the face an instant result for a more firmer, smoother and radiant complexion. Chinese herbs used for this multilevel skin healing mask are: Winter Melon, Tremella, Atractyylodis, Pearl, Ginseng, Rhodiola, and Angelica.

This mask is suggested to be used at night time, 2 to 3 times a week followed by Intensive Wrinkle Care Night Cream. Also use it as your skin's rescue remedy for immediate skin repair, including sun damaged skin, and instant "face lift" before you go to any important occassions, followed by Nefeli day cream because it will simply make you look your best.

CHAPTER 6

Massage Away Your Wrinkles, Chinese Style

Before we get to the anti-wrinkle acupressure treatment you'll be taking advantage of at home, let's take a look at the differences and similarities of anti-wrinkle acupuncture and anti-wrinkle acupressure.

Acupuncture as an anti-aging treatment has become so popular in recent years that even people who have never heard of Traditional Chinese Medicine are considering acupuncture for facial beauty. The relatively new concept of the "acupuncture facelift" has received lots of recent attention within the field of Chinese medicine, as well as among non-TCM cosmetic surgeons. The general public is streaming into clinics to take advantage of this unique procedure's wrinkle-removing powers.

This "new" technique is based on very old TCM theory and procedures. Chinese textbooks clearly document that acupuncture for facial rejuvenation has been performed for many centuries in China. The new surge of interest in facial acupuncture confirms what TCM has always known — that acupuncture works both to prevent wrinkles and diminish those that already exist.

The insertion of needles at acupuncture points on your face and elsewhere clears wrinkles in two ways. It stimulates local energy (Qi) flow and blood circulation based on channel theory. It also tightens the muscles in the deep layer of the facial skin, providing the "lift" you hear so much about.

By moving that Qi and blood, acupuncture triggers many other beneficial processes that help rejuvenate your face. It balances Yin and Yang, as well as your internal organ system. It strengthens your entire body and improves your skin's metabolism. In other words, it corrects the age-related imbalances throughout the body that are causing your wrinkles.

What You Should Know About Acupuncture Facelifts

I do suggest professional acupuncture treatment as part of your anti-wrinkle program. But I do not recommend acupuncture as a substitute for the various home-treatments in this book. It's absolutely essential that you follow a well-rounded plan that includes herbal remedies, Qi Gong and diet therapy, as well as acupuncture and/or acupressure.

Herbs and foods provide the material basis for your healing, while acupressure and acupuncture deal with channels and flow. By analogy, if you want your plumbing to work well, you want clean pipes and a smooth flow (acupuncture/ acupressure) but you also need water in them (herbs/food) so there's something to do the flowing. And Qi Gong, though not material-providing, works in an entirely different way than acupressure or acupuncture.

If you are able to complement the home treatments in this book with professional acupuncture treatments, that's ideal. If you can't, make sure you include the acupressure protocols below, and you will still see amazing results.

If you seek acupuncture treatment to reduce wrinkles, only consider a licensed acupuncturist (L.Ac) who is well trained in Traditional Chinese Medicine, especially in the fields of facial rejuvenation. There's no one-size-fits-all acupuncture protocol for facial wrinkles. The treatment must be based on your own unique condition, and only a TCM practitioner knows how to discover that condition using Chinese principles.

For example, diagnosis is crucial. Is your condition Yin or Yang? Is it from a deficiency or excess? Is it hot or cold? What is the condition of your Qi, blood, essence and body fluids? And so on. None of this means anything to a non-TCM physician. But getting the correct acupuncture treatment without such a diagnosis is impossible.

How Acupressure Smoothes Your Wrinkles

Since acupressure is based on the same TCM principles as acupuncture, it's also a very effective natural way to smooth your facial wrinkles and prevent new ones from forming. Acupressure accomplishes these worthy goals the same way acupuncture does — by working on specific points of your body to activate and regulate the flow of Qi along energy channels.

But there are two major differences. One, of course, is that with acupressure the points are stimulated by massaging rather than inserting needles. That makes it a more relaxing and less invasive experience.

The other difference? Unlike acupuncture, you can take advantage of acupressure's wrinkle-smoothing powers in your own home, with your own hands, and without spending a nickel.

The Chinese people have used acupressure to smooth wrinkles longer than they've used acupuncture for that purpose. Especially when combined with the herbal facial masks you're now familiar with. Chinese healers have documented acupressure's ability to increase energy and blood flow to the face, relax facial muscles, increase the skin's elasticity, and induce lymph drainage from the face area. All of those acupressure effects — and many more — add up to a smoother, more lustrous face.

Tips From Ping
Clinical experience suggests that loosening up tight muscles and adhesions in the neck and facial area may help smooth wrinkles in the face. Make sure you do your facial acupressure routines every day to get this benefit.

Most anti-wrinkle acupressure techniques — including those I'm about to describe for you — emphasize points along the stomach channel, one of the 12 principle meridians (or channels). Called Yang Ming by the Chinese, the stomach channel is especially rich in Qi and blood. Activating it sends abundant nourishment to your face.

You'll focus on several other principle meridians (channels) in your anti-wrinkle acupressure routines. Three important ones are the liver, spleen and kidney channels. All three are Yin meridians, as opposed to the Yang of the stomach channel. Their activation at certain points further nourishes your facial skin while improving your entire body's hormonal balance, another important factor for wrinkle-free skin.

One channel involved in your anti-wrinkle acupressure is a special one. You may recall from Part 1 of this book that the Du meridian (channel), or Du Mai, is the "governing channel" where the body's Yang energy gathers. It runs from the bottom of your spine straight up to the top of your head, then down your face to the upper lip. Parallel to the Du runs the urinary bladder (UB) channel.

Safe and Easy At-Home Acupressure Routines

Here are three simple and relaxing but very effective massage routines (more accurately called facial acupressure protocols) that you can do yourself. One is quick and basic, the other more comprehensive. If you use either one (or both) of these protocols consistently, you will be amazed at how quickly the results come — especially when you combine acupressure with herbal treatments and the other anti-wrinkle strategies in this book.

It shouldn't surprise you that many of the points you'll be massaging or pressing are nowhere near your face. Remember, you're activating specially selected points along channels that send energy to your face. (The shorter routine, however, concentrates on points on the face).

The acupressure channel points you'll be working on in the first protocol include important motor points on your face — that is, acupressure points within muscles that will activate more qi and blood flow to the skin. Activating these points (labeled ST-7 and SI-18)

(See Fig.6.1) stimulates muscles underneath the wrinkles, deepening the effectiveness of the procedure.

There are more key points that are going to be used in these protocols. I'll describe them briefly, and you can also find them on the accompanying illustrations. *(See Fig.6.1)*

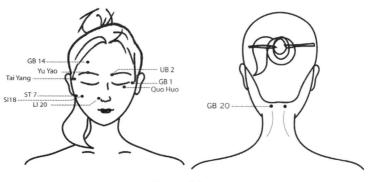

Figure 6.1

- **GB 20**: Known as Feng Chi and occupying the pool-like depression under the occipital bone at either side of the base of your skull located by bending your head forward and run your fingers up the muscled part of the back of your neck to the points just before hitting the skull bone.This point releases all the wind from the head. According to Traditional Chinese Medicine, "wind" is a disease evil that can cause muscle twitches. "Wind" comes and goes, which can cause a lot of skin problems like skin rashes, dry skin etc. So, activating this point can release the tension of the facial muscles; relieve headache, sinus conditions, and the common cold. Massaging it increases the face's resistance to external environmental factors, relax and beautify the skin.

- **GB 14:** Called Yang Bai, it's another facial point along the gallbladder channel. Activating it benefits the whole eye area and helps smooth forehead wrinkles.

- **LI 20:** It refers to points on either side of your nose. It's called Ying Xiang, which means, "meeting fragrance" or "welcome fragrance." As the last point in the large intestine channel, it clears the blockage from the facial area and helps clear smile lines.

- **ST 7:** Or Xia Guan. It's a motor point along the stomach channel just below the zygomatic bone. It is a powerful motor point. By massaging on ST 7, abundant flow of qi and blood in the facial area can be activated since it belongs to the stomach or Yang Ming channel which is full of Qi and blood. It's also an excellent point for lifting chin wrinkles that have resulted fro mmuscle "prolapse" or "falling down."

- **UB 2:** This point on the urinary bladder meridian is found right where each eyebrow begins above the nose. The Chinese name, Zhan Zhu, means "an assembly of bamboo," which is a pretty good way of describing the first hairs of your eyebrows. Like all facial points above the nose, this one clears away wind (an external evil), smoothing frown lines and forehead wrinkles.

- **GB 1:** This is right in a "hole" in the bone about a half cun from the outer canthus, the outer corner where your eyelids meet. This is great for smoothing crow's feet.

- **SI 18**: Called Quan Liao, it's another motor point on the face along the small intestine channel directly below the outer canthus, in the hole-like depression on the lower border of your cheekbone. Another powerful motor point which when massage correctly can improve blood circulation and smooth wrinkles, lift up sagging of the chin.

- **Yu Yao:** This means the "waistline of a fish" and you'll find it at the very center of each eyebrow. It's an "extra point," meaning it doesn't belong to any meridian. This is good for forehead lines and wrinkles around the eyes.

- **Quo Huo:** "Quo" is pronounced "Cho" and means eyeball. "Huo" means "at the back." You'll find it along the ridge bone under your eyes two thirds away from inner corner. Massaging it gently brings blood flow to the eye area and helps local drainage.

- **Tai Yang:** This refers in this case to a point at either temple, not the urinary bladder channel. It's a special point, not belonging to any meridian. It is a powerful point for pulling the Yang energy together. Gently massaging it helps smooth wrinkles around out side of the eyes.

- **Ashi points**: These points can be anywhere a wrinkle is. Pronounced like "ashy", the Ashi is the "ouch" point, the point where the problem is.

  In the second routine given below, the spleen, liver, kidney and stomach meridians are the key channels to work on.

- **Spleen and Stomach:** Full of Qi and blood, these Yin/Yang paired meridians are considered to be our digestive system, controlling ingestion of what we eat and drink as well as transforming and transporting the water and food that create the post-natal sea of energy. Activating the normal flow of Qi (energy) and blood in this paired channel will guarantee an abundant nutrient supply to the face. It also promotes healthy metabolism, which serves as the basis for a wrinkle-free and radiant face.

- **Liver Meridian:** This meridian contains more blood and less Qi according to Traditional Chinese Medicine. Activating this channel addresses a dull wrinkled face that's due to a lack of blood nourishment and to liver Qi stagnation.

- **Kidney Meridian:** This meridian contains more Qi and less blood. Activating this meridian helps the body replenish the essence, nourishes kidney Yin and Yang, improves dry and withered skin, and smoothes wrinkles.

The points you'll be working along those channels in the second routine: *(See Fig.6.2)*

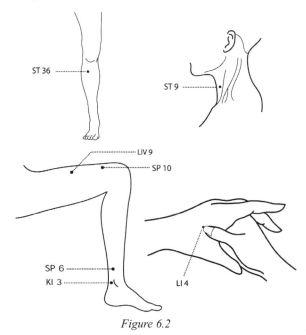

Figure 6.2

- **ST 36:** Called Zu San Li, this is a point along the stomach meridian just below each knee. Activating these symmetrical points gives you the strength to go for three miles, which is what the Chinese name means. Find it by locating the mushy point just below your kneecap and then moving 3 cun (3 thumb widths) down along the shinbone, then one thumb-width toward the outer side. This is one of the most important points that tonifies Qi and blood, increases your body's immune system, and improves your overall skin condition.

- **SP 6:** This is a key point on the inside of the leg between the knee and ankle where the liver, spleen and kidney channels meet. Its name is San Yin Jiao, which literally means the crossroads of the three Yin meridians. Feel for the big bone protruding from the inside of your ankle (the medial malleolus) and then go 3 cun (3 thumb widths) straight up just behind the tibia bone. This is an important point for tonifying and regulating the liver, spleen and kidney organ systems, as I often refer to it "the acupuncture hormonal point), promote Qi and Blood circulation, benefit overall skin condition.

- **SP 10:** The Chinese name, Xue Hai, means a sea of blood. If you think of your kneecap as a square, this point is two inches above the upper and inner corner. Working it promotes blood circulation, including to the facial area.

- **LIV 9:** This point on the liver channel, called Yin Wrapping, lays 4 cun (4 thumb widths) above the upper border of your kneecap, on the inners side of the thigh.

- **KI 3:** Between the medial malleolus (the inside ankle bone) and the Achilles tendon is a "great ravine" where lies the Tai Xi (or KI 3) energy point. The name, indeed, means "great ravine" or "canyon." It is called a "yuan" source point, meaning it contains vital kidney energy. It strongly nourishes the kidney organ system, tonifying dry wrinkled skin due to Yin deficiency.

- **LI 4:** This is the "Union Valley," a command point for your face that's located along the Large Intestine channel. On the back of your hand, find the web between your thumb and pointer finger. It's about an inch behind the front end of that web.

- **ST 9:** TCM considers the neck an extension of the face. This point, called Ren Yin ("men's welcome") is along the front side of each carotid artery at the level of the Adam's apple. It's a powerful energy point for facial complexion and blood flow to the face.

    Caution: *Since this point is on the course of the common carotid artery, the force of acupressure on this point should be extremely soft and gentle.*

    Now to the protocols. To master these massages, simply follow the steps in order, and refer to the accompanying illustrations showing you exactly where to massage or press. Enjoy!

The 5-Minute Anti-Wrinkle Facial Acupressure

This is a great, time-efficient protocol that's perfect for anybody who can't find the time for the more sophisticated routine to follow. You can do this one while you're watching television, just before bed, or whenever you have five minutes to spare.

You can apply a warm wet towel to your face for a few minutes followed by applying a natural herbal based facial cream or massage oil.

Then, to get started, sit down, make yourself comfortable, take three deep breaths, and let your face relax.

Step 1: To activate the channel system on the face, bring more Qi and blood flow, firmly press the following energy points with both index fingers for about 5 to 10 seconds, five times each: GB 20, Tai Yang, GB 14, LI 20, and ST 7, SI 18. *(See Fig. 6.3)*

Step 2: For the wrinkles on your forehead, use your index and middle finger of both hands to knead the skin in upward motions, starting at eyebrow level and following the solid lines on the face indicated in the drawing up to the hairline. The line in the center is the Du channel. Your kneading along that line starts at a point right between the eyebrows known as Ying Tang, or the third eye. The urinary bladder channel (UB) goes up from either eyebrow. The other line starts from Yu Yao on both sides of the eyebrow and go upward.   *(See Fig.6.4)*

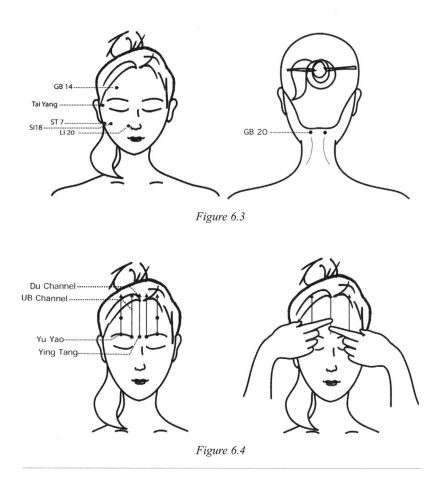

Figure 6.3

Figure 6.4

Step 3: For the wrinkles around your eyes, press the following points five times each: UB 2, Yu Yao, GB 1, Quo Huo. Also press one or two Ashi points, where your wrinkles are most noticeable. *(See Fig.6.5)*

Step 4: For crow's feet, use the thumb and pointer finger of one hand to "open" the wrinkles. With the pad of the index finger of the other hand, massage the opened area with a circular motion. Do this around both eyes. You can also use this method for wrinkles around the mouth and for smile lines. *(See Fig.6.6)*

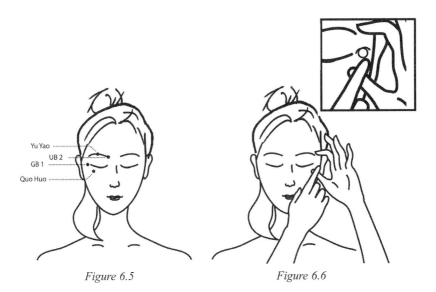

Yu Yao
UB 2
GB 1
Quo Huo

Figure 6.5   *Figure 6.6*

The 15-Minute Comprehensive Anti-Wrinkle Acupressure

This relaxing 15-minute acupressure session includes the steps in the first protocol, and much more. Make it a part of your everyday routine and you'll have a smoother face surprisingly quickly. It's best to do this in the early morning or at night.

Make sure your face is very clean and apply a nourishing skin cream or massage oil before you start. Put on some soothing music and sit in a position you find comfortable.

Step 1: Using either your entire hand or a 5-inch-long dry luffa, massage in a circular motion starting from just below the knee and moving slowly down the stomach channel to the ankle. Repeat five times on each leg. *(See Fig.6.7)*

Step 2: Massage ST 36 in a circular motion for about a minute, both sides simultaneously. *(See Fig. 6.8)*

Step 3: Now you'll massage along the liver, spleen and kidney chan-

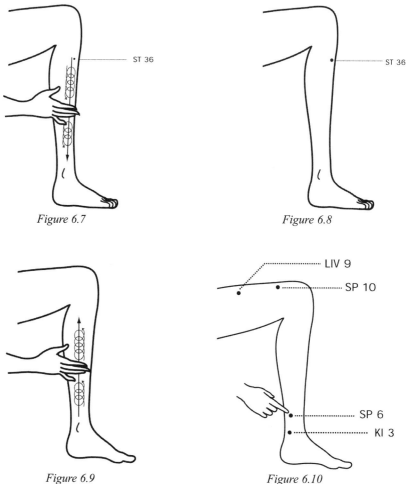

Figure 6.7

Figure 6.8

Figure 6.9

Figure 6.10

nels, simultaneously. Again moving your entire hand (or the luffa) in a circular motion, massage slowly upward along the inside of the leg, which covers these three channels together, from your ankle to your upper thigh. Repeat five times on each leg. *(See Fig.6.9)*

Step 4: Massage SP 6, SP 10, KI 3 and LIV 9 in a circular motion for 1 minute on both legs simultaneously. *(See Fig. 6.10)*

Step 5: Reaching behind you the best you can, massage (with your hand or a luffa) the Du channel from the back of your neck all the way down to the coccyx area at the bottom of your spine. Repeat five times. *(See Fig. 6.11)*

Step 6: Using both thumbs, use repeated digital press, working your way down two lines parallel to your spine and about one and a half inches to either side of it. This is the urinary bladder channel. Repeat the journey five times, working from as high up the back as you can reach down to the coccyx. *(See Fig.6.12)*

Step 7: Perform the entire first acupressure protocol described above.

Step 8: Locate ST9 on each side of your neck and very gently massage the point in circular motion for 3 times with your index fingers (remember just soft touch). Turn your head until you can feel the neck muscle. Massage for about a minute along that muscle from behind the ear to the collarbone with gentle strokes. Then turn your head the other way and massage the other side with gentle strokes. *(See Fig.6.13)*

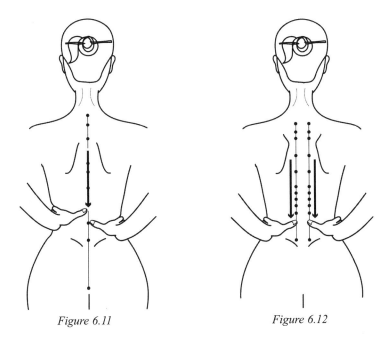

Figure 6.11   *Figure 6.12*

Figure 6.13

Ear Acupressure for Facial Wrinkles

Here we take advantage of the ear's own "total body system," mimicking the whole body in miniature. Stimulating certain points on the ear activate the organs that correspond to wrinkling. There are also "facial points" in the ear itself. Points are simply named for the organ they activate.

The easiest way to follow these steps, refer to the illustrations with each instruction.

Step 1: Lift the ear apex upward, pull the ear helix outward, then the ear lobe downward. Do each motion three times, working both ears simultaneously. *(See Fig.6.14)*

Step 2: Using your thumbs and index fingers, take each ear at the apex and then massage down slowly in a circular motion to the ear lobes. Repeat three times.*(See Fig.6.15)*

Step 3: Using your thumb and index finger press (squeeze) the following points three times each: Brain cortex, kidney, lung (2 areas), heart and face. *(See Fig.6.16)*

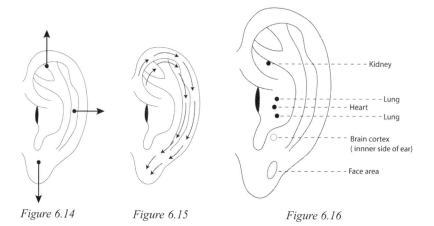

Figure 6.14   *Figure 6.15*   *Figure 6.16*

Tips From Ping

You can also try the "jade stick facial massage." The famous Chinese empress Chi Xi used this method. Her secret was using a stick of jade to "iron" her face. She'd put on the stick a mixture of pearl powder and egg yolk. You can use it with or without the mixture, rolling it along the wrinkled area the same way you'd apply a facial cream. Jade sticks aren't easy to find. See http://www.nefeli.com for more information. I often suggest my patients to use jade stick to massage their face once a day with nourishing facial cream, which brings great results.

CHAPTER 7

Smoothing Away Wrinkles With Qi Gong

As we've learned, Qi Gong exercises help the three treasures — Qi (energy), essence and spirit. It helps fill the internal organ system with essence, which has an immediately beneficial effect on many organs, including facial skin.

The Qi Gong methods I'll describe for you are not difficult by any means. They will definitely help your pursuit of a wrinkle-free complexion. What's important to keep in mind about these exercises is that they harmonize both your external and internal beauty. They are purifying exercises that improve your character and personal life as well as your actual skin. Remember, it's that combined external-internal healing that makes TCM utterly different — and much more effective — than any other beauty method.

You can practice these exercises every day as part of your wrinkle-smoothing strategy, eventually tapering down to a twice-a-week "maintenance" schedule.

The Energy Ball

This is a wonderful 15-minute, four-step Qi Gong exercise that energizes your face to rid itself of wrinkles. It's based on using the power of your imagination to create healing energy in the form of an "energy ball." Although it starts in the mind, the energy ball is quite real and full of body essence and Qi that will help beautify your face and take care of its wrinkles.

In this exercise, you'll focus your attention on an area about two inches below your naval called Dan Tian *(See Fig.7.1)*, which will be your energy ball's home. You'll be "sending" the energy ball on a route that will take it along the Ren meridian (channel) which is the conception channel that runs in front of the body right up the center of your torso to the upper lip. It will also follow the Du meridian (or governing channel) *(See Fig.7.1)* that runs from under the coccyx to the spine, straight up to the top of the head down to the upper lip.

Start by sitting in a chair, your eyes lightly closed and your mood relaxed. Focus on your breathing, keeping it slow, even, and natural for about a minute. Then follow these four steps:

Step 1: Concentrate on the Dan Tian area for half a minute, holding both hands on Dan Tian area, palms facing it. Then begin to imagine

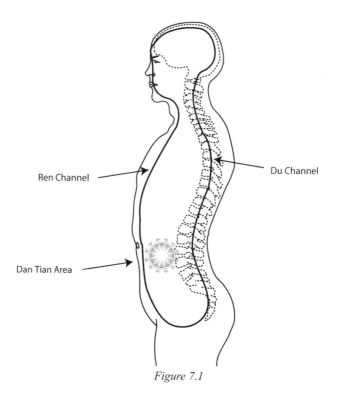

Figure 7.1

a small energy ball, about the size of a ping-pong ball, coming togeth-er there. Visualize its form and energy. Use your imagination to "exer-cise" the ball by making it become smaller and bigger by turns in your Dan Tian area. *(See Fig.7.2)*

Step 2: Now let your imagination send this energy ball via the Ren meridian (conception channel) up the front middle line of your trunk to the top of your head, then down the governing channel along the middle line of your back. Let it end up back in the Dan Tian. You can let this ener-gy ball circle around the Ren and Du meridians for five cycles before having it come to rest in the Dan Tian. *(See Fig.7.3)*

Step 3: The energy ball that you now control has acquired healing power. Use the power of your imagination to take in with your breath the essence of the clear sky and fertile land (that is, from heaven and earth), imagining these vital nature essences entering through the opened skin pores, nourishing and replenishing the skin. Bring the breath all the way down to the Dan Tian. Then imagine the pores opening wide as you breathe out the accumulated toxicity in your face. Repeat this breathing technique 5 to 10 times until you feel a slight heat sensation or dampness in your face. Concentrate your attention in your Dan Tian area as you finish.

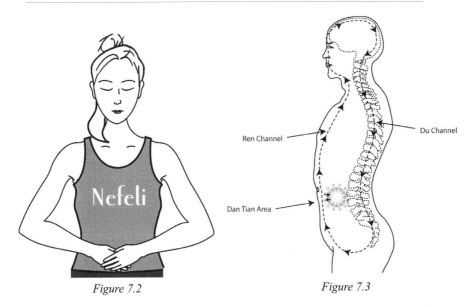

Figure 7.2

Figure 7.3

Ren Channel

Du Channel

Dan Tian Area

Tips From Ping
Remember that the goal of Qi Gong exercises is to use your body's energy to rejuvenate your face. The skin has to actually feel the energy of your breath through its pores.

Step 4: Use your hands to draw out the energy ball from the Dan Tian, imagine it exiting in the form of a light-stream.

Step 5: Now move the energy ball with your hands up to your face, separating the ball into two half-balls, one in each hand.

Step 6: Massage the forehead area with these half-balls of energy, one on each hand, with palms (about 1 inch away from the face) facing the area of the forehead that needs work on, use 10 circular motions. *(See Fig.7.4)*

Figure 7.4

Step 7: Using the same motion, massage each side of the face simultaneously (one half ball on either side), imagining the wrinkles being ironed flat as you complete 10 circular motions. Do this without actually touching your face, keep your hands about an inch away.

Step 8: Massage with the energy half-balls the wrinkled areas around the eyes, giving each side 10 slow circular massage motions. Imagine your eyes brightening and the wrinkles smoothing out. Focus on the area where your wrinkle concern is.

Step 9: Bring the energy half-balls back down to the Dan Tian area, uniting them into a full energy ball again. Exercise the energy-ball with your palm facing together, make it smaller and smaller in front of your Dan Tian area.

Step 10: Slowly reinsert the energy ball into the Dan Tian, again in the form of a stream of light. Take three deep breaths to finish the session.

Golden Fluid, Jade Liquid

This Qi Gong exercise is an ancient Chinese beauty method that takes advantage of the healing power from our own essence — clear, nourishing and lubricating liquid in the form of saliva. Strange as that may sound, TCM has long seen our clear saliva (called the "golden fluid" or "jade liquid") as our body's own spring water and a basic essence that nourishes and replenishes the body.

In TCM literature, our own clear saliva is considered an herb formed by heart Qi and kidney fluids. It is spoken of in almost reverential terms, with various Chinese names meaning wonder liquid, magic water, the body's spring water and even "premium fine wine." To the Taoists, saliva was a precious body fluid that irrigates the internal zang organs and the fu organs, beautifying skin in the process. There are even two acupuncture points in the saliva-forming area under the tongue, one called Jin Jing and the other Yu Yie.

Modern science recognizes that healthy saliva contains hormones, mucin, and a glycoprotein that lubricates food. It also has an antibacterial agent called lysozyme, and an important enzyme called salivary amylase, which breaks down starch into maltose.

Other traditional Chinese medical texts abound with praise for saliva's beautifying properties. One reads, "The saliva generated at the tip of the tongue and frequently swallowed into lower Dan Tian, where it enters smoothly, can in one hundred days make the face beautiful." Another notes, "Taking jade liquid each morning makes a person strong, and makes the face glow."

Here are two ways for you to use your own saliva to smooth or prevent wrinkles. Do both of them one right after another, every other day.

First way: Swallow the Golden Fluid and Jade Liquid

Step 1: In the morning time when you get up, brush your teeth well, and drink a glass of warm water slowly while you relax your mind. Then sit on a comfortable cushion with your legs crossed in the lotus position. (If you prefer, you can simply sit on a chair with both legs relaxed.) Regulate your breathing to a slow, even rhythm.

Step 2: Focus on taking your breath in and down all the way to the Dan Tian area, about two inches below your naval. Breathe in through the nose and out through the mouth. Each time breathing in and hold for a second in Dan Tian area before breathing out. Continue doing this for about 1 to 2 minutes till you feel a slight warming sensation in Dan Tian area. Then move to the next step, but continue relaxed breathing down to the Dan Tian instead of just the chest.

Step 3: Lightly clench your teeth against each other rhythmically 36 times.

Step 4: Keeping the mouth closed, move the tongue (the "red dragon") inside your mouth in a circular motion. Make sure the tongue touches all over the inner side of the mouth wall so the inner wall of your mouth will be massaged by the tongue. After 10 to 15 circles, plenty of clear fluid should be generated in your mouth. Swallow all that liquid little by little, imagining it reaching the Dan Tian. Then move on to the second way.

Second Way: Warm Golden Facial Massage

Step 1: Make more fluid in your mouth just as you did in the first version of this saliva exercise. At the same time, rub both hands 36 times together until they feel hot.

Step 2: Using the palm of your hands massage your face from the chin area, one hand on each side of the face, taking deep, slow breaths. As you breathe in, massage from the center of your face upward. As you breathe out, massage lightly down the sides of your face. Repeat 9 times. *(See Fig.7.5)*

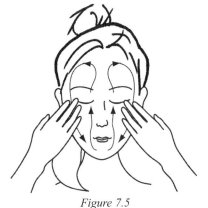

Figure 7.5

Step 3: Re-warm up your hand by rub 36 times and repeat the massage strokes as step 2. Then repeat Steps 1 and 2 for a third time (but no more). During any or all of these three facial massages, you may do a little extra massaging of wrinkled areas using your middle and index fingers. Imagine your face being nourished by essence and filled with energy during the massage session.

Step 4: Finally, concentrating your breath in the Dan Tian area, imagine for a relaxing period your face being nourished by the precious fluids from inside of your body. See and feel it glowing, smooth and beautiful.

Tips From Ping

Please remember the caution I mentioned in Chapter 3. Don't do these exercises if you're pregnant or sick. If you experience a strong reaction while performing any Qi Gong routine — such as too much warmth, discomfort, and shortness of breath or palpitations — stop and relax. Discontinue Qi-Gong for several days before you try again.

CHAPTER 8

Food To Fight Wrinkles

Your friendly family practitioner down at the HMO clinic will tell you the same thing any Traditional Chinese Medicine healer will tell you. Namely, eat a healthy, balanced diet with plenty of fruits and vegetables. But TCM theory goes beyond "good nutrition" and makes use of food as a therapeutic agent. So one way you'll be using Chinese medicine to smooth your face is by adding some anti-wrinkle foods to your diet. In this chapter, I will show you how.

Food therapy, as we learned in Chapter 3, is based on precisely the same theories that lie at the heart of all TCM healing. Like herbs, some foods have properties that can help eliminate the imbalances that cause specific symptoms — in this case, wrinkles. Certain foods "enter" certain energy channels, regulate certain organ systems, and help balance Yin and Yang.

Over the centuries, the Chinese identified foods with components that delay aging, improve the elasticity of facial tissue, and reduce wrinkling by (among other things) replenishing the needed body essence, like collagen, for example.

We're going to spend the rest of this chapter exploring some of these excellent anti-wrinkle foods. Many are also available as herbal supplements, but the idea is to complement your herbal treatments (and your Qi Gong and acupressure treatments) with food you actually eat at meals. Some of the food choices may surprise you (pig's skin), but they've worked for the Chinese for millennia. They'll work for you too.

Rule # 1: Keep that Acid-Alkaline Balance Steady

Before we get into specific foods, it's important that you bear in mind an essential general nutrition rule for a smooth and vibrant face. PH balance — that is, the right combination of acidic and alkaline foods in your diet — is essential for beautiful and healthy skin.

Common acidic foods are meat and other animal products, pasteurized milk (but not organic raw milk), processed wheat flour, egg yolk, shrimp, crab, duck meat, fish, rice and some other grains, white sugar, citrus fruits (such as oranges. lemons and cranberries) and beer.

Common alkaline foods include fruits such as watermelon, cherries, peach, papaya, mangos, green vegetables and sea vegetables (like seaweed), all beans and lentils, potatoes, sweat potatoes and yams, lotus root, onion, mushrooms, green tea, sesame seeds, garlic, organic and unpasteurized milk, and egg whites.

Most people tend to overload on the acidic side, with predictable results. Too much acidic food means acidic blood and an acidic over-all internal environment. That leads to rough, lusterless skin that tends to loosen and wrinkle, as well as dark spots and other unwant-ed skin conditions. You'll also notice that you get tired easily, lack concentration, and are often irritable.

The solution is simple — and nothing you haven't heard before: Eat more fruits and vegetables. It's not that acidic foods are "bad" per se; in fact, many of the anti-wrinkle foods I'm about to recommend are acidic. But balance is essential, and the best way to make sure you're not skimp-ing on alkaline foods is to eat plenty of fruits and vegetables.

Rule #2: Limit sweets and eliminate processed foods.

Processed foods are the bane of modern nutrition. The best gift you can give your face is to get out of the habit of eating packaged foods that have been processed, refined, and contaminated with preservatives and other chemical additives. Replace them with "real" food straight from nature — fruits, vegetables (especially dark green and red), whole grains, beans, nuts, organic fish, organic meat and dairy products.

Rule #3: Learn the Art of Drinking Water

Drinking enough high quality water helps provide your skin cells a clean and healthy living environment to replenish themselves. Not drinking enough water can sabotage all the other good efforts you're making to beautify your skin.

How much is enough? Drink at least eight glasses of clean water a day. That's about 64 ounces. TCM considers water consumption to be an art, and offers a number of suggestions for optimizing the ben-efits of good old H20:

- **Choose good, clean water.** Fortunately, that's easier to do these days, with lots of quality-bottled drinking water available.

- **Drink water warm or at room temperature.** Ideally, you should boil your water for less than five minutes, and then drink it as it reaches room temperature in the cooling down process. According to nutritionist point of view, boiled water when cooling down to warm or room temperature takes on a molecular structure more compatible with the water in our cells. If you have a cold, drink the water at a warmer temperature, inducing sweating to push out toxins.

- **Drink a glass upon awakening**. Your first glass of water should be on an empty stomach.

- **Drink evenly throughout the day.**

- **Choose hydrating herbs.** Certain Yin tonic herbs help keep you hydrated. They include American Ginseng, Tian Men Dong (Chinese asparagus), Tremella (a mushroom you'll be reading more about shortly), He Shou Wu (fleeceflower root), and Da Zhao (Chinese dates).

- *There's one caution with water. Under normal conditions, drinking lots of water will detoxify your body. But those with certain health condition might suffer from water retention if they change their drinking habits. Check with your doctor first.*

The Top 10 Anti-Wrinkle Foods in Traditional Chinese Medicine

Chances are you've never even heard of some of the foods on the following list, let alone tasted them. But they've all been found by TCM practitioners to have a profound effect on the prevention of wrinkles. If you want to keep your face as smooth as you can, these foods should be part of your regular diet.

1. Bird's Nest

This Chinese delicacy and health food is exactly what it sounds like — the edible abode of birds called swiftlets who fashion their nests from the male's saliva. Available as a food or supplement in Chinese grocery stores or by mail order, bird's nest is considered one of the most precious nutritional aides for beauty and rejuvenation.

Its specific wrinkle-smoothing properties come from its action on the skin and lungs, and its ability to moisturize and help to support body's healthy immunity. Modern research has found that bird's nest contains epidermal growth factor, a water-soluble glycoprotein, as well as vitamins and minerals.

2. Chinese Dates (Jujube Fruit)

This is a fruit (not a candy) that's often called Chinese dates. Its medicinal value has been recognized in China for 4,000 years, and there's even an old saying that "three dates a day keeps old age away." Its special function is to nourish the digestive system, but its ability to generate energy and blood nourishes the skin, promoting a healthy glow and smoothing wrinkles. Rich in antioxidant vitamins and minerals, it's the ideal fruit (fresh or dried) to moisten dry skin and lips. Make sure to take pits out of dates before preparing them. Just use a scissor or a small knife to cut it open and take the pits out.

3. Black Sesame Seeds

Those little black seeds you may know best from the outside of bagels are anti-aging wonders that in TCM terms nourish the internal organs, the blood, and body fluids in general. As such, long-term, regular consumption of black sesame seeds is especially good for wrinkles resulting form dry skin conditions. From a Western point of view, they're rich in plant protein, vitamin E and lonilenic acid, all essential for healthy, wrinkle-less skin.

4. Peanuts

There's a reason peanuts are a staple in Chinese cooking. TCM literature refers to peanuts as "ever-live fruits" -- meaning they have an anti-aging effect when eaten regularly. Peanuts fight wrinkles by nourishing the lungs and strengthening the stomach and spleen. Western nutritionists have recognized the value of peanuts, which are rich in readily absorbable amino acids, with a protein concentration (about 30%) nearly equal to chicken, eggs and red meat. Though they contain fat, peanuts actually help lower cholesterol levels. One caution: Make sure any peanuts you eat are fresh, because old or spoiled peanuts can contain carcinogenic toxins. Choose high-quality, organically grown peanuts.

5. Black Soy Beans

There is a traditional Chinese text called the "Yian Nian Mi Lu" that focuses on anti-aging secrets — and it raves about how soybeans benefit the facial complexion. Black soybeans especially promote tissue growth, replenish bone marrow, tonify deficient organs, and moisturize the body according to TCM. As is well known in the West, soy is one of the best plant sources of protein, rich in natural estrogens known as isoflavones, essential fatty acids including omega-3, vitamin E, and several important minerals. For best results, choose the black beans, or soy products made from the black beans.

6. Pig's Skin

It may not be most Westerners' idea of a healthy food, but the Chinese discovered long ago that pig's skin is an "herb" that nourishes Yin, relieves irritability and is used effectively for dry and wrinkled skin based on the concept of ancient Chinese medical theory that "like heals like."

According to modern science, pig's skin (fresh or dried) contains basic nutrients that our skin needs in order to delay wrinkle formation. It has abundant protein, mainly gelatinous protein and fibrous protein (collagen fiber, elastic fiber). It's also rich in minerals, and the vitamins B1 and B2. And the fat content of the pig's skin is only half that of pork meat itself.

Moreover, pigskin has a cell structure similar to our own skin, with a very compatible kind of protein (large cell protein). All of these qualities make pig skin an important food for delaying the skin aging process, for softening and beautifying skin, and for reducing and preventing wrinkle. You probably don't need to find a Chinese market to get pig's skin or pig's feet. They're usually available from any local butcher.

7. Walnuts

Walnuts are another time-honored Chinese "treasure" for nourishing the complexion and smoothing facial wrinkles. They're actually an ingredient in many ancient Chinese herbal formulas for beauty. Walnuts are also recognized in the West as a beneficial food. They're rich in cholesterol-lowering unsaturated fats and omega-3 fatty acids, linolenic and oleic acids, the antioxidant carotene, vitamins B1 and B2, and a number of other natural anti-aging substances.

You'll do well to eat a handful of walnuts every day, perhaps by using this ancient Chinese way of getting started with walnuts as a beautifying food: Eat one piece each night, before going to bed, for five days. On the sixth day, eat two and continue adding one every five days until you reach 20.

8. Cherries

Cherries are energizing food that beautify the skin by nourishing the spleen and stomach (the middle Jiao). Because of their high iron content, they're a wonderful skin-smoothing fruit that also improve skin color as they enrich the blood. They're so effective that besides eating them, you can simply crush cherries and apply the juice directly to your face.

9. Honey

If your daily sweet treat uses honey, you will find over time that your will power is heightened, your body is "enlightened," your aging process has slowed down and your face is less wrinkled. Honey tonifies energy and calms the five internal organs. It's a superb skin-nourisher, and its unique antibacterial and anti-viral function helps protect the skin.

Honey is rich in vitamins, amino acids, organic acids, complex carbohydrates, hormones, proteins, fructose and glucose. Many of these nutrients are easily absorbed by the skin, making honey an excellent food for nourishing the skin, as well as improving skin function and regeneration.

TCM considers honey an herb as well as a food, and you can enjoy its anti-wrinkle benefits in supplement form if you don't care to include it as part of your meals. One way is to simply swallow a teaspoon of honey each morning on an empty stomach, like (very sweet) medicine. Or mix a teaspoon of honey and a teaspoon of vinegar in 6 ounces of water and drink half of that mixture at a time. Be sure to use only pure, organic honey.

Honey can also be used as a great facial mask. Combine 1/4 teaspoon of honey, 3 drops of olive oil, and 1/2 teaspoon of pearl powder. Mix it well in the palm of your hand with some water and apply it to your face once every other day. Wash it off with warm water after 20 minutes. You'll see amazing results the very first time you use it.

If sugar intake is a concern for you, try substituting royal jelly for honey. It's not sweet and it's less sticky. This is an especially beneficial food for women with low sex drive and wrinkled skin. Use it as you would use honey but with a low dosage. 1/4 teaspoon daily.

Caution: *Some people are allergic to bee products. If you know or suspect that you have such an allergy, don't use honey or royal jelly, or any other bee product. If you get a surprise allergic reaction from either (such as rashes or wheezing), stop using it and see a physician.*

10. Tremella

This is a mushroom that has long been used in China for general skin beauty, either as a food or as a supplement. Its fluid-generating properties make it an excellent food choice for dry, wrinkled skin. But it's a do-all food that nourishes lung Yin, increases energy, and benefits the blood, the brain, the heart and the body's healthy immune system. And its Yin-nourishing function makes it especially beneficial for those with dry, wrinkled skin who also suffer bouts of irritability or who are going through menopause. It's rich in vitamin B and minerals, including iron, sulfur, phosphate, magnesium, calcium and potassium.

You'll see tremella in already prepared form with sugar added form at health food stores or Chinese supermarket. Better to buy the actual mushrooms (they'll be cultivated, not wild) at a Chinese market.

One convenient way to prepare them is as follows: Soak 2 ounces of tremella mushrooms overnight. Then section them by hand into small pieces, throwing away the yellowish part at the bottom. Simmer slowly in 75 ounces of water (about eight full coffee mugs) for two and a half hours. Or use a pressure cooker, adding 5 measuring cups of water, keeping a mid-boil going for about 30 minutes.

When it's cooked, add two teaspoons of honey and let cool. Keep the cooked tremella in a glass jar in a refrigerator, eating about 1/2 a measuring cup worth each morning until it's finished.

More Great Anti-Wrinkle Foods

There are more than 10 ways to utilize dietary therapy to combat wrinkles. Get in the habit of including the following foods in your regular diet. They all have natural healing properties that include wrinkle prevention and facial smoothing. Most are readily available; a few you'll need to find in Chinese markets.

Pine nuts

Sea cucumber *(sometimes called "Ginseng from the sea" because of its high nutritional value)*

Lotus root

Pork or chicken cartilage *(boil it as a soup)*

Pork bone *(boil as a soup)*

Fish *(all kinds)*

Squid *(or calamari)*

Lingon berries

Wild yam *(also an herbal supplement)*

Chinese cabbage

Luffa *(the fresh form of the same plant that serves as a scrubber or massager)*

Tomato *(it's also a detoxifier)*

Cucumber

Seabuckthorn

Black mushrooms

Reishi mushrooms

Olive oil

Coix seed

Bee Pollen

Euryale Seed

> **Tips From Ping**
> Luffa is a very good vegetable for overall body health. It beautifies the skin taken internally as a food as well as externally as a massager. For long-term use, try planting it in your backyard. It's a vine that grows easily as long as you give it a trellis or something similar to climb on. Try cutting the fruit when it's ripe and letting the liquid drain into a container from the stem where you cut. You can use it to apply directly to your face.

Foods That Detoxify

Traditional Chinese Medicine's strong belief that our body is able to detoxify itself when given the chance is directly relevant to your wrinkle-smoothing quest. The accumulation of toxins in your body upsets your internal balance, contributing to wrinkling. The following foods energize your body's natural detoxification systems, helping to rid your bloodstream and organs of toxins and beautifying your skin. Make them a part of your regular diet.

- **Green Tea:** It's well known in Chinese medicine as a super detoxifier, and in Western medicine as a super antioxidant — two ways of saying the same thing. Green tea is loaded with antioxidants in the form of polyphenols, flavonols, vitamin E, vitamin C, carotene, and much more. That antioxidant effect helps protect your skin from the damage caused by the sun's ultraviolet rays, toxic food additives, secondhand tobacco smoke, and stress. A good way to take advantage of green tea's detox power is to combine it as an infusion with one of the anti-wrinkle herbs given earlier. Remember, though, that it contains caffeine, so limit your intake and try to drink it only in the morning if you tend to get hyper with caffeine. If a physician has instructed you not to take caffeine, don't drink green tea without consulting your doctor.

- **Bitter Melon:** Fresh bitter melon can be found at Chinese or other Asian grocery stores (you'll also find it as a juice or a supplement in liquid extract form). It's nutrient-rich, and is thought to stabilize blood sugar levels. More important, bitter melon contains properties that, in TCM terms, clear away heat, relieve lethargy, sharpen the eyes and nourish the skin. If you buy the whole fruit, wash it and remove the seeds and boil it in soups or cook as dish.

- **Niu Bong:** Also known as burdock root, this is a vegetable used to detoxify the body, especially the blood. It contains trace minerals, foliate, vitamins C and B, and amino acids. Buy it fresh in Asian markets. Wash one long stick and cut off some to add to you soup or decoct by boiling to make a tea.

- **Coix Seeds:** They're from a kind of barley. Coix seeds benefit the skin by strengthening the digestive system, leaching out dampness, and detoxifying the body. You'll find them at most herb stores or Chinese markets. Mix them with rice or in a soup.

- **Pomegranate:** This fruit benefits and detoxifies the digestive system.

- **Black Fungus:** Used throughout the centuries as a body cleanser and detoxifier, this wonderful food/herb has such powerful cleansing properties that Chinese workers often use it to offset occupational contamination hazards. We will address it again in chapters dealing with age spots. Because it is rich in vitamins, minerals (especially iron), and proteins, and is such a powerful cleanser of the digestive system, it will help clear your wrinkles as well. Buy it at an herb store or Chinese market, soak it in hot water until it spreads and softens, boil, and include in soups, salads, or just about any main dish.

- **Lotus Root:** It's a delicious food/herb and available at Chinese markets. Wash the root, dice it or cut it into small pieces, and use it raw in salads or include it in soups. The lotus root clears heat, moistens the lungs, cools the blood, benefits the digestive system, enlightens the body, beautifies the skin, and helps delay the aging process .

- **Celery**

- **Garlic**

- **Seaweed**

Chinese Herbal/Food Porridges for Beauty

Chinese medicine has known for centuries that mixing boiled rice with a decoction of an herb delivers that herb's healing properties to your system in an easily absorbable form. Rice itself is considered an herb that nourishes the digestive system, preparing the stomach to digest the herb it's partnered with.

Rice — whether its white, semi-processed, or sticky sweet rice — is also the perfect vehicle for delivering anti-wrinkle foods. This combination of boiled rice with a healing food is often called herbal porridge. Following are a number of easy-to-prepare porridges that you can use to include many of the anti-wrinkle foods in your diet.

I use traditional cooking methods in the following recipes. To save time, you can use a pressure cooker. Make sure you follow the safety instructions and don't exceed the recommended volume so no pressure overloads will develop. If you need to adjust the ingredients proportionally to stay within the recommended pot volume, then you can.

The measurements I'll be giving you are generally suitable for a 4-quart pressure-cooking pot.

- **Pig's Skin and Soybean Porridge**
  Especially recommended for skin that's dry as well as wrinkled.

  1/4 pound of fresh pig's skin.
  1/4 measuring cup of black soybeans.
  1/4 measuring cup of euryale seed.
  a quarter teaspoon of pearl powder.
  1/8 cup of rice.
  Wash the soybeans and euryale seed and soak in hot water overnight.

Clean and cut the fresh pig's skin (it's easier if you use scissors). Make sure you removed any fat clinging to the skin.

Cook all the ingredients together in 80 ounces of water for about two hours at a low to medium boil.

If you use a pressure cooker, use 45 ounces of water to the above ingredients, boil for 25 minutes.

Add 3 teaspoons of honey (or whatever flavoring you like) after boiling but while it's still hot. Eat about one measuring cup daily until it's gone.

■ Tremella and Soybean Porridge

This is essentially a vegetarian version of the pig's skin and soybean porridge, with the same anti-wrinkle results.

Simply follow the same cooking instructions, substituting 1 ounce of soaked tremella for the pig's skin.

Also, add

1/4 measuring cup of black beans.

1/4 measuring cup of euryale seeds.

1/8 cup of walnuts.

Soak the seeds and tremella overnight. Section the soaked tremella into small pieces. The rest is the same as the above recipe.

You can make it a dessert by adding two pieces of unrefined "rocky" sugar, each piece about the size of an egg yolk. Three teaspoons of wild honey will also work.

■ Reishi Mushroom and Pig's Skin Porridge

This is an anti-aging recipe that helps support the body's healthy immune system and smoothes wrinkled skin by replenishing collagen in the body. Reishi mushrooms are bitter and astringent in nature, this dish is on the bitter side. If you can tolerate the taste, the benefits are definitely worth it. But if the bitter taste is too much for you, choose another recipe. You'll need:

1/4 pound of fresh pig's skin.

9 grams of reishi mushrooms (available at any good natural foods store or Asian market).

1/8 of a measuring cup of shelled peanuts.

1/8 cup of rice.

3 teaspoon of honey.

Wash the reishi mushrooms. Wash and cut the pig's skin into small pieces.

Cook all the ingredients together in 65 ounces of water at a low to medium boil for 1.5 hours.

Add 3 teaspoons of honey toward the end of cooking.

Eat about a measuring cup a day until it's all gone.

If you choose to use a pressure cooker, use 45 ounces of water, bring to a boil and then mid-boil for 25 minutes.

■ Bird's Nest Porridge

Consider bird's nest porridge a gift for your skin. The Chinese hold the firm belief that this precious food offers a tremendous beautifying effect. This dish does not contain rice. You'll need:

3 grams of bird's nest.

1 teaspoon of honey or one piece of rocky sugar about the size of an egg yolk.

Soak 3 grams of bird's nest in warm water until it's soft.

Clean the soaked bird's nest by removing any small feathers or other deposits that don't belong there.

Use your hands to section it into small pieces.

Low boil it in 12 ounces of water for 30 minutes.

Add honey or rocky sugar.

Eat half and finish the rest the next day.

Tips From Ping

Bird's nest was considered a super skin and body food in ancient times, and it still is today. But pay attention to the possibility of having an allergic reaction to it. Some people do. If you experience any discomfort after eating it, change to tremella soup.

■ Chinese Date Porridge

This is a sweet porridge that's great for wrinkles with dark spots and blemishes. You'll need:

20 pieces of Chinese dates (jujube) with the pits removed.

1/4 measuring cup of lotus seed, without the green part in the middle. (Either take it out yourself after soaking or buy them "opened" at a Chinese grocery store, with the green part already removed.)

1/4 measuring cup of coix seed.

1/8 measuring cup of shelled walnuts.

1/2 teaspoon pearl powder.

1/8 measuring cup of sweet rice.

1 teaspoon of honey or one piece of rocky sugar about the size of an egg yolk.

Soak the coix and lotus seed in hot water, and dates in cold water, all overnight.

Cook all the ingredients together in 72 ounces (9 measuring cups) of water over a low flame until everything is soft (about 2 hours).

Add one piece of rocky sugar (each the size of an egg yolk) or 2 teaspoons of honey as it's cooking. Make sure to stir the mixture often during cooking so it won't stick to the pot.

It's good to take one cup a day of this porridge until it's all gone.

If you're using a pressure cooker, use 40 ounces of water with all the ingredients, bring to a boil, then mid-boil for 25 minutes.

- **Ginseng and Tremella Porridge**

If you have wrinkles and low energy, this one's for you. It has no rice in it. You need:

9 grams of ginseng root, preferably Choung Bai Mountain Ginseng, it's neither too hot nor cold in nature. If you have high blood pressure, however, use American ginseng.
1/4 measuring cup of euryale seed.
1/8 measuring cup of shelled peanuts, and
1 ounce of tremella.

Soak the tremella and euryale seed in a separate bowl overnight.

Clean and section the soaked tremella into small pieces.

Add all the ingredients to 72 ounces of water and cook over a low flame for 2 hours, making sure to stir the mixture frequently to avoid sticking.

Add 3 teaspoons of honey or one egg-yolk-sized piece of rocky sugar during the cooking.

Take the ginseng root out before serving and take a cup a day until it's finished.

If using a pressure cooker, use 40 ounces of water with all the ingredients, bring to a boil, then mid-boil for 25 minutes.

More Face-Saving Recipes For a Youthful You

While porridges are usually used to parcel out modest quantities of therapeutic food on a daily basis, there are also plenty of more substantial dishes and beverages you can prepare to take advantage of anti-wrinkle foods. Here are some of my favorites:

- **Homemade Soy Milk**

It's easy to make soymilk at home from soybeans. It will help fight wrinkles, and is a great source of protein and calcium for vegetarians. Start by soaking a half pound of soybeans (black is best but yellow soybeans are fine), and 1/4 measuring cup each of the coix and euryale seeds together overnight.

Rinse the soybeans/seeds mix and put it in the blender with 20 ounces (2 1/2 measuring cups) of clean water. (You may have to blend half the mix at a time in 10 ounces of water each time if your blender isn't big enough to take the whole load at once). Blend for about 1 minute or until all the beans are totally crushed.

Use a clean cheese cloth, squeeze the liquid into a large pot, leaving the pulp behind.

Now add two and a half cups more fresh water and bring the liquid to a boil. Lower the heat and scrape the foam away. Then return to a full boil for a half minute. Turn the fire off and let it cool, making sure it doesn't stick to the side of the pot.

This fresh soymilk can be kept cold in the refrigerator for three days. Make sure the container is clean and oil-free.

You might add a teaspoon of honey to a glass when your drink it. Another option: Blend in almonds and/or pine nuts with each glass you drink.

■ **Seed and Nut Blend with Soy Milk**
Blend equal amounts of black sesame seed, peanuts and walnuts together in a food processor or blender for about a minute, until they mix together well almost in a powder. (Tip: Lightly roast the seeds and nuts first for better taste).
Keep this potent anti-wrinkle mix in a glass jar in dry place.

To serve, stir 2 teaspoonfuls of the mix in a cup of your homemade soymilk. Add some honey if you like.

■ **Anti-Wrinkle Fruit-and-Vegetable Juice**
The surest way to get lots of anti-wrinkle foods into your system is to throw them together in a juice. The key to a successful anti-wrinkle juice is to follow the five-element theory from Chapter 2. Remember, five different colors go to five different organ systems, so you want to try to get one of each in your smoothie. A potent combination I recommend is to put the following together in the juicer:
1/2 tomato
3 strawberries
1/4 measuring cup of blackberries
1/4 measuring cup of blueberries

1/4 measuring cup of cucumber

1/4 measuring cup of green apple

1 kiwi

1/4 pound of kale

1/4 measuring cup of pear

1/4 measuring cup of papaya

1/4 measuring cup of mulberry

10 grapes

Put them all in a juicer and drink the juice each morning.

You can use pretty much any combination of fruits and vegetables to achieve color variety in your juice -making, choosing at least a few from the anti-wrinkle food list. For example, you can include cherries, watermelon, lime or lemon, blueberries, grapes, Chinese cabbage, and/or mulberries.

■ **Bone Soup**

As you've surely noticed by now, Chinese medicine doesn't fear pig meat. Pork bone and the meat touching it (without the fat) are very rich in nutrients. Moreover, pork bone also contains bone collagen, so eating it fairly regularly can help the healthy body to fight wrinkle formation. The ancient Chinese herbal texts also emphasize pork's detoxifying effects, and its ability to strengthen your own bones. Here's a soup recipe that makes it easy to get the benefits of pork bone:

Place a 1.5 pound pork bone in a pot with 80 ounces of water (10 measuring cups). You can leave some attached meat on the bone, make sure there's no visible fat attached.

Add 3 scallions, cut into 2 inch long strips, 5 pieces of fresh ginger, 2 teaspoonfuls of cooking wine, 1/4 teaspoon of salt, and any herbal seasoning that you prefer, it won't affect the healing power. Bring to a boil, then low-boil for 1 1/2 hours, occasionally clearing the foam away.

Enjoy a small bowl twice a day until it's gone.

This pork bone soup also makes a fine base for a hearty vegetable soup.

If using a pressure cooker, you need to boil the bone in water for 10 minutes in a regular pot, throw away the resulting soup so that no foam is left, then put it in pressure cooker and add 45 ounces of water, bring to a boil, and mid-boil for 20 minutes.

■ **Tasty Cold Pig's Feet**

You'll find pig's feet at any Chinese market with a meat department, or more than likely at any supermarket or butcher. Have the butcher cut one pig's feet into small pieces for you. Wash them thoroughly when you get them home. Then follow these steps for a very potent anti-wrinkle treat:

Drop about 1 pound of pig's feet pieces into a pot with 80 ounces of water, 4 slices of ginger, 1 teaspoonful of cooking wine, and 1/8 teaspoon of salt.

Bring to a boil, then cook over a low flame for about 2 hours, until it is fully cooked.

Remove the ginger.

Separate the meat from the bones, using a fork (it should be easy to do). Remove the bones.

Use the fork to squish the meat into smaller pieces. Add it back to the boiled soup.

Add 1 teaspoonful of fresh cut spinach leaves and 1 teaspoonful of fresh cut cilantro and simmer for about 1 minute.

Turn the flame off and let the pot cool down.

Once cooled, put the pot (covered) into the refrigerator. It will take on a gelatin texture by the next day. Scrape the surface fat off.

Serve the gelatin-like mixture cold, keeping what's left over in the refrigerator for up to three or four days

If using a pressure cooker, use 40 ounces of water with 1 pound of pig's feet. Bring to a boil, then mid-boil for 25 minutes without the spinach and cilantro added. (You can put them in afterward while it is still hot).

■ **Cucumber and Luffa Juice**
Use 1/2 of a cucumber and the same amount of fresh luffa vegetable, available at Chinese markets. Simply juice them together with 1/2 tea-spooon of organic honey. Drink this juice every day to nourish the skin, beautify the face and smooth wrinkles. You can also use this juice topically on your face as a mask for 15 minutes and wash off.

■ **Treasure from the Sea**
If you like seafood, you'll love this ultra-delicious and nutritious anti-wrinkle seafood soup that's especially good for dry skin.
Wash and then low boil 1/2 pound of sea cucumber (you'll find them at Chinese markets) in 32 ounces of water for 40 minutes, take it out, wait until it cools down, and cut it into small pieces.

Combine the sea cucumber with 1/4 pound of fresh scallops, 1/4 pound of shelled shrimp, 1/4 pound of fish (any kind), all cut into small pieces.

Sautee the mixture in 2 teaspoon of olive oil for about 1 minute.

Put the sautéed mixture in a pot with 24 ounces of water.

Bring to a boil and then add 1/2 teaspoon of salt, and a 4" cube of soft, silky tofu that's been diced.

As it reaches a boil again, add 2 tablespoons of thick starch in liquid form, and several drops of sesame oil.

After it boils again, slowly dip in one beaten egg white.

Continue boiling for 1/2 minute and add one handful of whole spinach leaf and 1 tablespoon of fresh copped cilantro. Immediately turn off the heat.

Serve. There's plenty for your friends and family with this recipe.

Anti-Wrinkle Masks Made from Food

Sometimes getting food on your face can do you a world of good. The following anti-wrinkle masks are made from food. They're easy, fun and they work.

If you tend to have dry skin, you can add several drops of olive oil to any of the following masks. Or to increase their potency, you can also add 1/2 teaspoon of pearl powder and several drops of lemon juice.

Caution: It's possible to be allergic to any of the following natural masks. Before you use one, test it on a small part of your inner wrist by applying a dab there and wait a day. If an irritation occurs, don't use the mask and consult a health care professional about your possible allergy. If nothing happens, go ahead and use the mask.

- **Banana and Strawberry Mask**
  Blend 1/4 banana and 3 strawberries, and apply the mixture to your face for 15 minutes. Wash clean.

- **Egg, Honey and Milk Mask**
  Mix one egg, one teaspoon of honey and one teaspoon of milk together and mix well. Apply the mixture to the face and wash it out after 15 minutes.

- **Luffa and Cucumber Mask**
  Use 1/4 of a cucumber and a cut of fresh luffa that's about the same size. Blend them together with an egg white and a 2" by 2" piece of tofu. Apply the mixture to your face once every two days for 15 minutes.

■ **Kiwi and Milk Mask**

Blend one kiwi with 1/8 cup of whole milk and apply half the mixture to your face, massaging it in. Leave on for 15 minutes and wash.

■ **Pig's Foot Mask**

Cut about a pound of pig's foot into small pieces. Boil the pig's foot in 64 ounces (8 measuring cups) of water for about 2 hours or until only about a cup of liquid remains. Take out the meat and put just the soup in the refrigerator, where it will form a gelatin. Use it as a regular mask by applying some to your face at night, washing it away the next morning.

If you use a pressure cooker, use 45 ounces of water with a pound of cut-up pig's foot. Bring to a boil, then mid-boil for 25 minutes. Follow the rest of the instructions as normal.

■ **Chestnut and Honey Mask**

Collect about a gram of the inner skin of the chestnut shell. Crush it and mix it with 2 teaspoonfuls of organic honey. Apply it to your clean face at night and wash away in the morning.

■ **As You Like It Mask**

You can always go to your local market to pick up something natural and seasonal to make your own mask, such as banana, pumpkin, apple, aloe, carrots or eggplant. Blend your choice with and egg and some milk to make a mask.

Your Alternatives

As an alternative, you may consider to just use Nefeli **"Facial Rejuvenating Mask"** and **"Intensive Wrinkle Care Mask"** from Nefeli Anti-Wrinkle/Aged Skin Care Collection when you cannot make the food masks mentioned in this chapter.

PART THREE

BRIGHT, BEAUTIFUL EYES;
THE CHINESE SECRET

CHAPTER 9

Beyond Your Eye Beauty Concerns

I've never had a patient yet who felt okay about puffy bags or dark circles in the eye area. It's true that those problems are almost never painful. And it's also true that neither Traditional Chinese Medicine nor modern Western medicine considers eye bags or dark circles a "disease" per se. But if you look in the mirror and see puffiness or discoloration around your eyes, you naturally want to do something about it. And you have good reason to want to correct the problem.

First and most obvious, eye bags and dark circles are unsightly. They make you look tired and spiritless, as well as older than your years. When they get really bad — as they often do — even make-up won't cover the problem. If you suffer from these conditions, you don't need me to tell you any of this.

But there's another reason to be concerned about puffy eye bags under and around your eyes. They reflect an internal imbalance, an underlying health problem that may stem from purely internal conditions, from aging, or from external factors such as an unhealthy lifestyle, inadequate sleep or a poor diet.

Whatever the origin of this internal imbalance, it can be addressed with traditional Chinese remedies. Applying these remedies at home regularly will make those dark circles or eye bags disappear before your very eyes. In their place you'll find healthy eye areas that make your entire face look young and full of life.

Before I present to you in the next four chapters the specific Chinese herbs, food, acupressure routines and Qi Gong exercises that will clear up your eye area, let's take a brief look at the kind of internal imbalances that are causing the puffiness and discoloration in the first place. That way you'll understand why and how your home remedies are working.

Your Eyes and Your Internal Organs

In Traditional Chinese Medicine, eyes are literally windows of the soul. They serve as a sort of messenger from your inner emotional and spiritual world to the outside world at large. Since emotion and spirit are inseparable from physical considerations as determinants of your health, bright clear eyes surrounded by healthy, radiant skin reflect inner spiritual and physical balance. Eyes marred by puffiness or dark circles reflect an imbalance.

The outer condition of your eyes — including the lower and upper eyelids and the flesh around them — is so significant in Traditional Chinese Medicine that many vast tomes have been written about it. The "Yellow Emperor's Inner Classic," for example, gives tremendous importance to the close relationship between the eyes and the Three Treasures of Jing, Qi and Shen (essence, life energy and spirit).

The eyes are also integrally connected to the main five organ systems, which is why they are such notable indicators of the health of the organs. It's through the channel (meridian) systems, of course, that the eyes are connected to and nourished by the organs. Take a look at any of the meridian maps and you'll see that many meridians either start or end near the eye area.

The eye-organ connection is often thought of as "Five Wheels" because Chinese medicine actually divides the eye area into five "wheels" or parts. Each wheel has a direct correspondence with one of the five internal organs. Here they are, one by one:

- **The wheel of flesh and the spleen.** This refers to the flesh that is found around the eyes, mainly the upper and lower eyelids. The corresponding organ is the spleen, so not surprisingly spleen function is most important in dealing with eye bags. Remember, the spleen rules the flesh, therefore it rules the muscles responsible for the opening and closing of the eyelids. Many of the herbs you'll be taking enter the spleen channel, and many acupressure points you'll be pressing are along the spleen channel.

- **The wheel of blood and the heart.** You'll recall that in TCM, the heart rules the spirit. You'll also recall that the eyes are outer orifices that directly reflect the condition of the spirit. The wheel of blood is the eye part that corresponds to the heart and spirit. It's located in the inner and outer canthus, where the eyelids meet.

- **The wheel of wind and the liver.** Blood from the liver plays a big role in the eyes' capacity to actually see. It also irrigates the eyes, keeping them able to open and shine. The eye part that corresponds to the liver and is called wheel of the wind is the iris.

- **The wheel of water and the kidneys.** The Yang energy in the kidneys is what keeps fluids moving through the body. In Traditional Chinese Medicine, the dampness accumulation that results from fluids not moving easily through the body is a cause of puffiness in the eye area. Hence the importance of the "wheel of water," the kidneys and the corresponding eye part, the pupil.

- **The wheel of Qi and the lungs.** The lung system does play a role in fighting eye bags and dark circles, but not as important as other organs. The corresponding eye part is the sclera, the membrane covering the eyeball.

What Really Causes Those Eye Bags and Dark Circles?

To get rid of your eye bags or dark circles, you will use Chinese herbs and other treatments that deal with the root causes. Those root causes are not in the eyes themselves but in the internal organs, mostly the spleen and kidneys. The main problem: phlegm and/or dampness (fluid accumulation) obstructing the channels leading from the organs to the eye area. This can come about in several ways:

- **Spleen Qi deficiency.** Weak spleen energy impairs the transportation of body fluids, which leads to phlegm accumulation and fatty deposits in the eye area — that is, eye bags. TCM, by the way, considers fat deposits to be the same thing as phlegm accumulation. If you have a weak spleen, you're likely to suffer not only from puffiness around the eyes but also cellulite, water retention and excess weight. Also, as we've seen, too little energy (Qi) rising from the spleen inhibits the spleen's flesh-nourishing function, resulting in drooping eyelids.

- **Kidney Yang deficiency.** In our bodies, kidney Yang works like fire in a boiler. If the fire is weak, things don't move easily in the body and dampness accumulates. That fluid retention causes eye bags. In fact, women often swelling around the eyes during their periods, in a large part due to temporary kidney Yang deficiency at that time.

- **Liver Qi stagnation.** In TCM, the liver regulates the flow of emotions and coordinates the functions of other organ systems. If liver energy stagnates, one consequence is the smooth flow of Qi and nutrient-rich blood to the eye area will be interrupted, causing facial swelling, puffy eyes, and dark eye circles. Again, women will often report these symptoms during menstruation, when liver Qi tends to be more stagnated. As the result of qi stagnation, blood flow will be impeded which can eventually cause dark circles.

The obvious question is: What's making the liver Qi stagnated and spleen energy and the kidney Yang weak in the first place? There are many possibilities, and they often coincide with modern Western explanations for eye bags and dark eye circles. One, of course, is simple aging. You can't stop aging, of course, but you can use the Chinese remedies I'll be giving you to slow its effects and undo its damage.

Lifestyle factors can also damage the energy and Yang of key organs. Over-exertion, too-little sleep, and constant irritability, for example, create liver Qi stagnation. So before moving on to the herbs and other remedies, do your eyes a favor by making sure you do the following:

- **Get enough sleep.** That usually means seven hours a night for most people.

- **Don't over-exert yourself.** That goes for work or play.

- **Control your emotions**. Don't over constrain, nor over-express.

- **Moderate your alcohol consumption and no smoking.** Too much alcohol intake or smoking causes irregular blood flow to the eye area, produces more body toxins, which can cause eye puffiness and dark circles.

- **Limit your sun exposure.** As we all know now, too much sun exposure causes skin aging including the eye area.

- *See your doctor. Your need to rule out any serious underlying medical conditions that may be causing your eye bags or dark eye circles before you consider using any of the modalities suggested here in the book.*

Fortunately, TCM has developed over the centuries many of the natural, safe and effective remedies to clear your eyes of puffiness and dark circles. In the next four chapters, you will learn which herbs to take and foods to eat for healthy eyes, as well as some excellent but simple acupressure and Qi Gong routines.

I strongly recommend that you choose one or more remedies from each category. By creating for yourself a well rounded and multi-faceted eye health program from those four categories, you're on your way to getting back those youthful, lively eyes.

CHAPTER 10

Herbal Eye Care

Traditional Chinese Medicine is rich in herbal resources for eye beauty. Not surprisingly, after thousands of years of practice and research, Chinese healers have identified and used many very effective herbs that are aimed at eye care.

Specifically, there are herbs that address the problems you care about the most — in this case, puffy eye bags, unattractive dark eye circles, and dull, tired-looking eyes. In this chapter I'll be describing to you many of the best herbs for these conditions, herbs you can buy and take on your own to return your eyes to the bright and beautiful state you want.

It's important to emphasize (yet again!) that it would be misleading to say that these Chinese herbs work directly on your eyes. They are not simply superficial "eye treatments." If they were, they wouldn't be nearly as effective.

Instead, the herbs I recommend in this chapter correct the underlying health conditions that show up as unattractive problems in the eye area. In other words, these herbs address the root problems of your eye woes. They help create a healthier body and spirit, which is reflected in healthier, younger-looking eyes. That is the Chinese way.

The herbs work in a variety of manners, but the main action of most of them is to replenish kidney essence, clear the liver channel to facilitate blood flow, and improve spleen function to get rid of accumulated dampness. These actions help clear away the blood and energy (Qi) stagnation in the eye area that causes the puffiness and discoloration. (You can always refer back to the first part of this book to refresh your memory about TCM terms such as essence, Qi, and channel.)

So let's get to the herbs you'll be taking advantage of to beautify your eyes. As always, keep the following points in mind:

- All of the herbs described here are of the "superior class" unless I specify otherwise. Superior class means (among other things) that they are non-toxic and generally safe for long-term use.

- Don't take more of any single herb than the recommended doses I give. This is for effectiveness as well as safety. More is not better. Everything, according to the Chinese healing philosophy, is best in the right amount — even gold.

- Use these herbs as part of your complete eye-beautifying routine, which includes food therapy, acupressure, and Qi Gong exercises. Herbs alone, although helpful, are not enough to get the results you want.

- Obviously, you won't want to take all the herbs described below. Start out with at least the first two (Fu Ling and Bai Zhu) and add others based on the information given, their availability, and your own preferences.

The Two Best Single Herbs for Puffy Eyes and Eye Bags

There are many Chinese herbs you can use to help get rid of those eye bags or dark eye circles. Some of them you've already been introduced to, because they are also very effective in smoothing away and preventing wrinkles. The two herbs I'm recommending here are especially for puffy eyes and eye bags, and have shown remarkable results with my patients.

If eye bags and general puffiness in the eye area are concerns for you, I recommend you try both these herbs for at least several months. I'll introduce (or re-introduce) many more eye-rejuvenating herbs in this chapter, of course, but these can form the core of your program.

Fu Ling *(Poria)*

Fu Ling is one of the most highly regarded "vital" herbs in the Chinese tradition. A fungus, it's a powerful healer of the body and spirit that, from the Chinese point of view, concentrates the evergreen energy of a variety of conifers upon whose roots it grows.

You'll be taking Fu Ling as an herb in capsule form, but for centuries the Chinese have been using it as both a medicinal herb and a health-imparting food. Chi Xi, the "Last Empress" of China counted Fu Ling as a favorite. You can find Fu Ling even today in Beijing food stores, and traditional Fu Ling pie is still popular as a dessert in China.

When you take Fu Ling, you're prolonging a tradition that goes back to the ancient Taoists, who considered the herb a special gift from nature. The earliest Chinese medical literature recognizes Fu Ling as a superior anti-aging herb that improves sleep quality, calms hunger, relaxes the mind, replenishes the spirit, and prolongs life. Accordingly, it's a powerful herbal remedy for insomnia and other sleep disorders, as well as tension, nervousness and stomach problems.

All those qualities help prevent puffiness around the eyes as well. The beautifying capacity of Fu Ling was recognized in the Taoist holy book by Bao Po Zhi, which says, "Taking this herb once per day can make the face glow and shine like jade, looking as young as a child's."

- **How Fu Ling beautifies your eyes.** Its calming effect is not the main reason Fu Ling is such a wonderful herb for eye beauty. Credit goes to its action of leeching out accumulated dampness in your body, which is the primary underlying cause of eye bags and puffiness. That water retention is the result of spleen Qi deficiency. As a bland, neutral herb, Fu Ling enters the spleen channel and facilitates its energy transport system. The smoother flow of spleen Qi releases stagnant accumulated fluid.

  Fu Ling's actions of tonifying the spleen and strengthening its energy rejuvenate the eye area in another way as well. The re-energized spleen system helps prevent the sagging of facial flesh, an unwanted result of low spleen Qi. Also, Fu Ling regulates the Qi of the entire "Fu" internal organ system — that is, the spleen, stomach, small intestine, urinary bladder and gallbladder. Your digestive functioning thus improves, and shows in your eyes.

  Fu Ling is probably the first Chinese herb anyone should try who wants to get rid of eye bags or any kind of puffiness around the eyes. But because of its special properties, which include its outstanding ability to unblock accumulated dampness and to promote urination, Fu Ling is especially recommended if your stool is loose, if you often feel bloated or heavy, or if you have problems with your digestion.

- **Finding and taking Fu Ling.** You should be able to buy Fu Ling in capsule form at most health food stores, Chinese markets or off the Internet. It's sometimes referred to as Poria. If in doubt, check the botanical name on the bottle. If it says Poria cocos, you've got the right herb. Take 3 grams a day.

- ***Cautions concerning Fu Ling.*** *Fu Ling is a very safe herb that you can take for a long period of time.*

Bai Zhu *(Atractylodes Root)*

Bai Zhu offers the same benefits as Fu Ling. But Bai Zhu is not a fungus. It's a root that you'll be taking in powdered form. It's classified as a warm, sweet herb. Like Fu Ling, it enters into the spleen channel, and acts as a Qi tonic. Bai Zhu is especially suitable for treating your puffy eyes if you also suffer from weak digestion and low energy.

- **How Bai Zhu beautifies your eyes.** As a Qi tonic that activates energy in the spleen channel, Bau Zhu expels phlegm and water from skin layers as it regulates the digestive system. This unblocking of the free flow of blood and energy to the face returns luster to the skin around your eyes.

Western medicine — both herbal and conventional — also recognizes Bai Zhu's ability to reduce water retention. It's main ingredients, including atractylol, give it diuretic properties and promote the excretion of electrolytes.

- **Finding and taking Bai Zhu.** Get Bai Zhu in powder form and take 1 gram per day. The botanical name is Atractylodes macrocephala.

- *Cautions concerning Bai Zhu. Bai Zhu is a safe herb, but it is not traditionally used as food. So, you can take 10 days in a row, rest for a week, and restart again. Repeat this for 1 month.*

Three Facial Beauty Herbs for Dark Circles and Eye Bags

Many of the Chinese herbs that I recommend for smoothing facial wrinkles are also excellent treatments for dark circles and other eye concerns. Here are three of the best. For more information on each, refer back to Chapter 5.

Dang Gui *(Chinese Angelica Root)*

This very popular root is an excellent all-around facial beautifying herb because it promotes blood circulation, bringing much needed nourishment to the facial skin and clearing away "garbage" that accumulates in the skin layer.

It's also valuable for improving PMS symptoms, constipation, and a number of conditions that result from blood deficiency, including feelings of weakness and a pale complexion.

Dang Gui is specially recommended if your periods are painful, with dark clotting and mood swings. These are all signs of Qi and blood stagnation, for which Dang Gui is very effective.

- **How Dang Gui beautifies your eyes.** Dang Gui's capacity to promote blood movement helps clear away discoloration around the eyes. At the same time, the increased blood flow brings needed nourishment to the eye area, helping reduce puffiness.

- **Finding and taking Dang Gui.** Look for it as Chinese angelica root (Angelica sinensis). Low-boil 3 grams of the crushed fresh root in 16 ounces of water for 15-20 minutes and drink half of the resulting decoction one day and the other half the next. In powdered form, take 1 gram a day. If you prefer to take capsules, 1 gram a day is a good dose.

- ***Cautions concerning Dang Gui.*** *Dang Gui is a blood-moving herb, so you need to consult your physician before taking it. This is especially true if you are on blood-thinning medication. Dang Gui should not be taken during pregnancy or if you have diarrhea. This herb is recommended to take periodically. Take for one week in a row, stop for a week, and then restart. One month is considered a course.*

Huang Qi *(Astragalus)*

Huang Qi is the top herb in the energy tonic category, and one of the best Chinese herbs there is for all-around beauty. It is a rich source of antioxidant plant chemicals, especially flavonoids. This herb, usually called astragalus in the West, is especially recommended if in addition to puffy eyes, eye bags, or dark eye circles, you suffer from low energy, frequent colds, poor digestion or low appetite.

- **How Huang Qi beautifies your eyes.** Astragalus raises the Yang Qi of the spleen and stomach systems. Deficient spleen and stomach energy can lead to prolapse, or sagging of the face. If that occurs in the eye area, it contributes to the creation of eye bags. Huang Qi helps correct that underlying problem.

  It also strengthens the Qi of the middle Jiao, which improves both your digestive system and the energy transportation function of the spleen. You're familiar by now with how those two improvements help clear up the area around your eyes.

- **Finding and taking Huang Qi.** This herb has become popular in the West and easy to find. Low boil 6 grams of the root in 16 ounces of water for 25 minutes. Drink half of it one day, the other half the next. If you buy capsules, look for the words Astragalus membranaceus somewhere on the label. Take 1 gram a day.

- ***Cautions concerning Huang Qi.*** *Huang Qi is a very safe herb, unless you have any kind of respiratory infection and high blood pressure then avoid taking it.*

Di Huang *(Rehmannia)*

The "prepared" and dried forms of this superb all-around anti-aging tonic are not only effective against wrinkles but also help clear away your eye bags or dark eye circles. The dried Di Huang root is called Sheng Di Huang. If the root is prepared by steaming, it's called Shu Di Huang, or "cooked" Di Huang. The third "fresh" form, neither cooked nor dried, is not what you want for your eyes.

According to Traditional Chinese Medicine, Sheng Di Huang moves and cools stagnated blood, replenishes bone marrow, promotes healing of the flesh, tonifies kidney essence and replenishes essence and blood.

- **How Di Huang beautifies your eyes.** TCM's five element theory, where the liver rules the colors of green and blue, and the kidney rules the color black (see Chapter 2). When your liver and kidney Qi is depleted, the weak energy flow shows up around your eyes in the form of the liver and kidney colors. Hence, dark eye circles. Di Huang tonifies the liver and kidney, boosting their QI and nourishing the eyes.

  That makes Di Huang a good choice for your dark eye circles if you overindulge in physical activity or show signs of liver and kidney energy deficiency. Those signs can be chronic weakness or dizziness, a pale complexion or low back soreness.

- **Finding and taking Di Huang.** Combine 1/2 gram of Shu Di Huang with 1/2 gram of Sheng Di Huang and take it for 10 days. Rest for a few days and start again.

- *Cautions concerning Di Huang. Use with caution if your digestion is weak..*

Five Excellent Herbs for Brightening Your Eyes

We've been focusing on the well-defined eye-area problems we are most familiar with — eye bags, eye-surrounding puffiness and dark eye circles. For overall eye beauty and health, you're probably as much concerned about the eyes themselves as the skin around them. And for good reason: Sparkling, clear, alert eyes also reflect your inner health.

Dull, red or withered-looking eyes are what you want to avoid. They reflect unhealthy internal conditions, and make you look sickly and low-spirited. TCM uses hundreds of different herbs to deal with these conditions and brighten up your eyes. So even if you're lucky enough (and healthy enough) not to need the herbs we've already discussed for eye bags and dark circles, your eyes will benefit from one or more of the eye-brightening herbs described below.

Tu Si Zi *(Chinese Dodder Seed)*

Tu Si Zi is classified as sweet and neutral. It enters through the liver and kidney channels to tonify those organs as well as to stabilize and replenish essence. The ancient Taoists lauded Tu Si Zi as a longevity herb that tonifies both the Yin and the Yang at the same time.

This marvelous seed has a myriad of medical uses. TCM practitioners prescribe it for such conditions as diarrhea, pregnancy problems, urinary tract disorders, and pain in the back or knees.

- **How Tu Si Zi brightens your eyes.** In TCM and other forms of herbal medicine, Tu Si Zi is used to improve blurred vision due to liver and kidney deficiency. Brighter eyes are a welcome consequence of its healing powers.

- **Finding and taking Tu Si Zi.** You may be more likely to find Tu Si Zi labeled with its Western common names, usually Chinese dodder seed or cuscuta. You know you have the right herb if the botanical name Cuscuta chinensis appears on the label. For the best possible eye-brightening results, combine 1 gram of Tu Si Zi powder with 1 gram of Gou Qi Zi (the next herb on this list). Take this combo once daily and within several weeks you'll see some great results.

- *Cautions concerning Tu Si Zi. Tu Si Zi is a very safe herb. You can take it periodically for long time. However, avoid it if you have heat signs like constipation or dark, scanty urine.*

Gou Qi Zi *(Chinese Wolfberry)*

Like Tu Si Zi, this is a neutral sweet herb that enters the kidney and liver channels. But Gou Qi Zi is a fruit, not a seed. You've already met Chinese wolfberry as a wrinkle-reducing herb, but for centuries Chinese healers have considered it a treasure for eye health and brightness.

- **How Gou Qi Zi brightens your eyes.** Modern studies confirm what TCM has known for years — wolfberry enhances liver function. Since TCM theory maintains that the liver rules the eyes, it's logical that this herb has been shown to help alleviate blurred vision and contribute to eye brightness.

  Gou Qi Zi does more than enhance liver function. It replenishes Qi, generates nourishing blood, replenishes vital essence, and expels internal "wind" and dampness. All of these benefits contribute to brighter eyes as well as a healthier body.

- **Finding and taking Gou Qi Zi.** Combine 1 gram of powdered Gou Qi Zi with 1 gram of Tu Si Zi, dissolve into 2 oz. of warm water and take daily.

- *Cautions concerning Gou Qi Zi. Gou Qi Zi is a safe herb that can be taken daily for years. Avoid it, though, if you have the flu or a loose stool. Unlike many other eye-benefiting herbs, wolfberry does not leach out dampness. Don't take it if you are suffering from water retention.*

Ju Hua *(Chrysanthemum)*

Chrysanthemums make for a cold, sweet and bitter herb that enters the liver and lung channels. Usually the white blooms are used as food or herbs, while the less sweet yellow flowers work better as herbs — that is, taken in concentrated doses rather than eaten with meals. I've already mentioned Ju Hua as a wrinkle-reducing food. Its function of clearing deficiency heat from the liver and kidneys makes it a valuable herb for brightening the eyes.

Ju Hua has long been a much-revered herb in the Chinese culture. Taoists have considered it a source of extended longevity. A well-known ancient poem pays homage to this "superior flower" that "eliminates a hundred diseases." There's even a special day for harvesting Ju Hua, whichin the Chinese calendar is the equivalent of September 9. And it'sbelieved that making a pillow of pure chrysanthemum petals will brighten your eyes and clear them of superficial obstructions.

- **How Ju Hua brightens your eyes.** Like many other eye-care herbs, Ju Hua mainly enters the liver channel, which opens to the eyes. By improving energy flow through that channel, it clears the eyes. As a flower herb, Ju Hua is naturally "light," which helps its effectiveness in raising energy from the liver to the eyes. (That, of course, is a striking example of the difference in the kind of thinking that marks Western and Chinese medical philosophy.)

  More specifically, Ju Hua treats the "wind" and "heat" conditions in the liver channel that contribute to red, painful and or dry eyes. TCM practitioners also use it to treat blurry vision and "floaters" in the vision caused by liver deficiency.

- **Finding and taking Ju Hua.** It's become quite common in herb stores, the herbal sections of health food stores, and Chinese markets. If you buy the loose, dried flowers, you'll probably prefer the sweeter variety. Simmer 3 grams of it in 16 ounces of water. Strain and drink it all throughout the day. Also available are chrysanthemum tea bags. Use one or two per day.

- *Cautions concerning Ju Hua. As with all Chinese herbs that are cold in nature, use with caution if you have weak digestion, diarrhea, or low energy.*

Ju Ming Zi *(Cassia)*

How good an eye herb is this bitter, sweet, and cool seed that enters the liver, kidney and large intestine channels? Well, Chinese lore holds that if you take Ju Ming Zi daily for 100 days, you'll be able to see in the dark. Useful as that ability would be, perhaps it's best not to take that claim too literally and instead be content with this potent herb's very beneficial effects on the beauty of your eyes. And keep in mind that the name Ju Ming Zi translates as "eye-brightening seed."

- **How Ju Ming Zi brightens your eyes.** This cool herb is another effective option for treating wind-heat conditions that results from external influences such as constant exposure to heat, dryness, etc. That makes it effective for eliminating redness, pain and itchiness in and around the eyes.

■ **Finding and taking Ju Ming Zi.** Its botanical name is Semen cassiae, which may help you confirm you're getting the right stuff if ordering off the Internet. Low-boil 9 grams of the seed in 2 cups (16 ounces) of water for 20 minutes. Drink the liquid a little at a time throughout the day.

■ *Cautions concerning Ju Ming Zi. It is a safe herb. However, I suggest you take it only periodically when for brightening the eyes. Since it's a moistening herb that loosens stool to unblock the bowels, use with caution if you have diarrhea. Avoid Ju Ming Zi if you have low blood pressure.*

Zhen Zhu *(Pearl/Margarita)*

You've already met this herb as an ingredient in topical facial treatments for wrinkle reduction (see Chapter 5). It may be strange to think of pearl powder as an herb, but as I've said, the Chinese make no distinction between animal, mineral and vegetable "herbs." This one, of course, is calcium-rich and has been considered a precious beauty herb for thousands of years in China. It is also an excellent eye-brightener.

■ **How pearl powder brightens your eyes.** Sweet, salty and cold in nature, pearl enters the heart and liver channels. Its eye benefits are mostly due to its ability to clear the liver channel, allowing energy and blood to flow to the eyes.

■ **Finding and taking pearl powder.** You may see the Chinese name Zhen Zhu Mo (Margarita is its pharmaceutical name) at health food stores or at Internet sites. Take 0.3 grams a day, stirred into water.

Your Alternatives

Herbs introduced in this chapter should be relatively easy for you to find. They are safe, natural and are the first choice of Traditional Chinese herbal medicine that will work for your eyes. However, if you still find it trouble some to find and prepare them as internal taking herbal tea, here are your alternative:

■ You may consider using Nefeli herbal supplement **"Eye Refresh"** as your internal herbal/food supplements. It is carefully blended with all natural Chinese eye healing herbs – many of them have been discussed here as individual eye healing herbs

Eye-Beautifying Herbs to Apply Topically

Many eye-brightening herbs work wonderfully when applied directly to the eye area. You need to take a selection of single herbs internally, of course, but herbal wraps, washes and masks provide a worthwhile complement to your eye-beauty program. And they feel great.

Herbal wraps especially promote relaxation and deep-tissue cleansing around the eyes. Simply dip a small towel in the hot water in which your herbs have been soaked and hold the warm towel to your eyes. The best times for warm applications of herbs are in the morning upon rising and in the evening before retiring.

Some of the recommended topical herbs below are better applied as a mask — that is, by rubbing or patting thick, sticky mixtures onto the skin. Or you can simply wash the area with the herbal liquid, being careful not to splash it into your eyes.

Please note, since the eye area tends to be very sensitive, you should test any eye wash or mask in your inner wrist for 24 hours to make sure you are not allergic.

- **Chrysanthemum Flower Wash**

  This is an exceptionally pleasant treatment for eye bags. Boil about 3 grams of loose, dried chrysanthemum flowers (Ju Hua) in 6 oz of water for 10 minutes. When the water cools down enough, use the liquid to wash the eye areas thoroughly.

  Or try this variation: Boil 3 grams of dried chrysanthemums along with one green tea bag in 6 oz of water for 10 minutes. When the water cools down, take out the tea bag and place it right on your puffy eye bag without squeezing it out. Leave it there for 10 to 15 minutes. Do this on each eye.

- **Rose Petals**

  As a blood-moving herb in TCM, rose petals are great for dark eye circles. Rose flowers move blood and detoxify the body, relieving swelling around the eyes. Buy or pick fresh roses and wash the flower petals thoroughly after you separate them. Then make a paste by crushing the petals with water and flour (oat, whole wheat or soybean). Apply the mask for 15 minutes and wash off. Peach blossoms also work fine.

- **Mint**

  As an external wind-relieving herb in TCM, the volatile oils in fresh peppermint or other garden mints are very effective for reducing dark circles and eye bags, especially if they result from emotional constraint. Dampen and press the leaves directly to your problem areas.

- **Rosemary Wash**

  Rosemary is well known as a fine tonic for the scalp, which is why it's an ingredient in many commercial shampoos. It helps keeps the skin free from wrinkles, and also will rejuvenate the area around your eyes. Simply boil a handful of fresh rosemary leaves and flowers and use the cooled-down (but not cold) liquid as a face wash, concentrating on the area around your eyes.

■ **"Moving" Dark Circle Mask**

This simple blend lets you take advantage of pearl's skin purifying function and Dan Gui's ability to promote blood flow around the eyes. Make the mask by mixing one gram each of pearl powder and Dan Gui powder (Chinese angelica root) with 8 drops of fresh carrot juice or vitamin E oil. Apply the blend under each eye, making sure you avoid contact with the eye itself. Leave on for 15 minutes, and then gently wash it out. Follow up with a light application of olive oil.

Herbal Formulas for Eye Beauty

Professionally, Chinese herbal medicine is often administered as formulas that combine several herbs for optimum results. That holds true for herbal eye care. Again, however, I do not recommend that you try to blend and take these formulas on your own at home. They are complex and have to be geared toward your individual body conditions. And have to be precise in ratios.

Still, it's helpful for you to know some of the formulas available so you can talk to a Chinese herbalist or Traditional Chinese Medicine practitioner about what you need to beautify your eyes. Here are some of the most effective herbal formulas for your eyes you might want to ask about:

■ **Bu Zhong Yi Qi Tang**

This formula is particularly good for swelling eye bags due to spleen Qi deficiency with phlegm accumulation. It benefits the digestive system and overall Qi.

■ **Xiao Yao Wan**

An emotion-harmonizing formula used for treating eye bags and dark eye circles that result from emotional constraint.

■ **Eight Treasures**

A famous formula that addresses eye bags and dark circles by tonifying Qi and blood at the same time. It consists four blood-tonifying herbs and four Qi-tonifying herbs.

■ **Kai Yu Xing Xie Tang**

This one is a Qi-moving and blood-moving formula which consists of nine different herbs. It is especially effective for dark eye circles caused by stagnant blood flow.

■ **Shi Hu Ye Guong Wan**

This one is often used for blurred vision and other eyesight problems. But it also brightens up eyes that have taken on a dull look due to liver and kidney deficiency

Your Alternatives

Herbs introduced in this chapter should be relatively easy for you to find. They are safe, natural and are the first choice of Traditional Chinese herbal medicine that will work for your eyes. However, if you still find it trouble some to find and prepare them as external masks, here are your alternatives:

You may consider using Nefeli Herbal-based Eye Care Collection. It includes:

- Nefeli **"Essential Eye Care Cream"**. This is an All-in-One herbal-based cream consisting of Safflower, Ginseng, Ivy, Persimmon leaf, White Peony, Reishi Mushroom that takes care of all eye beauty related concerns, including dry skin around eyes, fine lines around eyes, sagging of eye lid, dark eye circles, eye bags and eye puffiness.Use mornings and evenings. Ideal base for make-up.
- Nefeli **"Eye Rejuvenating Mask"**. This herbal infused serum mask works as an immediate rescue remedy for eye concerns including eye sagging, fine lines around eyes, dark eye circles, eye bags and eye puffiness. Use as needed or 2 times per week for skin repair and rejuvenation around the eyes.   .

> **Tips From Ping**
> All the herbs introduced in this chapter should only be used if you are not suffering from any disease, not taking any medication, and not pregnant or nursing. Consult your doctor before taking any of the suggested herbs.

CHAPTER 11

Acupressure for Healthy, Beautiful Eyes

While others spend fortunes on synthetic creams and ointments in a futile effort to "rub away" those unsightly eye bags or dark eye circles, you'll be taking advantage of one of Chinese medicine's most powerful methods for activating your body's natural healing power — acupressure. By applying pressure to certain body points that I will show you, you will stimulate energy flow to improve the function of the organ systems most vital for clear, health, youthful-looking eyes.

Acupressure (unlike acupuncture) is a true do-it-yourself healing technique. You need absolutely nothing but a comfortable place to sit, your fingers, and my instructions. Essentially, acupressure turns on your body's natural delivery system, sending needed blood, energy and nutrients to the eye area. If you combine the simple techniques that follow with a healthy lifestyle, and also use the herbs, food therapy and Qi Gong techniques described in the other chapters in this section, you will be pleased at the reduction in puffiness and discoloration around your eyes.

Getting to The Points

What's most significant about the dozens of points you'll be "pressing" is that not all of them are near the eyes. Local stimulation is important for eye healing, but your main objective is "root treatment," that is, to stimulate the liver, kidney and spleen systems that are so vital for clear, healthy eyes. Key body points related to those organs are in various positions along those organs' meridians. So get your fingers ready for body-wide travel.

Let's start with a brief tour of the points you'll be concentrating on for your eye-rejuvenating acupressure routines. We'll look first at the points around the eyes, and then at the rest. Some of the points have already been described in Chapter 6, but they're described again here to save you the trouble of going back.

Here are the acupressure points near your eyes that are involved in the upcoming routines. You can also pinpoint the location of these points by finding them in the accompanying illustrations. *(See Fig.11.1)*

UB 1: This is the "bright eye" point along the urinary bladder meridian, known to the Chinese as the Jing Ming. It is in the corner of the inner canthus.

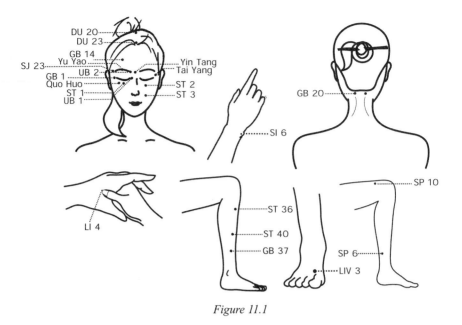

Figure 11.1

GB 1:   On the gall bladder meridian, called the Tong Zi Liao. You'll find it in the bone hole near the corner of outer canthus.

UB 2:   This point on the urinary bladder meridian is found right where each eyebrow begins above the nose. The Chinese name, Zhan Zhu, means "an assembly of bamboo," which is a pretty good way of describing the first hairs of your eyebrows. Like all facial points above the nose, this one clears away wind (an external evil), smoothing frown lines and forehead wrinkles.

ST 1:   Located just below the eye, it's the ideal spot to "receive tears," which is the translation of its Chinese name, "Cheng Qi" or "tear container." As your eyes look straight forward, it's directly below either pupil on the inward side of the lower ridge.

ST 2:   It is call "Si Bai" in Chinese, meaning "Four Whites". It is just below ST-1 where the depression is.

SP 6:   This is a key point on the inside of the leg between the knee and ankle where the liver, spleen and kidney channels meet. Its name is San Yin Jiao, which literally means the crossroads of the three Yin meridians. Feel for the big bone protruding from the inside of your ankle (the medial malleolus) and then go 3 cun (3 thumb widths) straight up just behind the tibia bone. Important point for tonifying and regulating the liver, spleen and kidney organ systems, as I often refer to it "the acupuncture hormonal point", promotes Qi and blood circulation, benefits overall skin condition.

SJ 23: The Chinese name of this point along the San Jiao or "Triple Burner" channel means silky bamboo hole. It's in the depression at the outer end of the eyebrow.

Yu Yao: This means the "waistline of a fish" and you'll find it at the very center of each eyebrow. It's an "extra point," meaning it doesn't belong to any meridian. This is good for forehead line and wrinkles around the eyes.

Quo Huo: You'll find it along the ridge bone under your eyes two thirds of the way to the inner corner. Massage it gently bringing blood flow to the eye area and help local drainage.

Tai Yang: This refers in this case to a point at either temple, not the urinary bladder channel. It's a special point, not belonging to any meridian. It is a powerful point for pulling the Yang energy together. Gently massage on it helps smooth wrinkles around out side of the eyes.

Now here are the "root treatment points" from around the body that you'll be working on. *(See Fig.11.1)*

ST 36: Called Zu San Li, this is a point along the stomach meridian just below each knee. Activating these symmetrical points gives you the strength to go for three miles, which is what the Chinese name means. Find it by locating the mushy point just below your kneecap and then moving 3 cun (3 thumb widths) down along the shinbone, then one thumb-width toward the outer side. This is one of the most important points that tonifies Qi and blood, helps support body's healthy immune system, and improves your overall skin condition.

ST 40: This is a key point for dealing with eye bags and puffiness. It is a "master point" for treating phlegm. It's called the "bountiful bulge." From the protruding knob on the outside of your ankle, trace up eight Chinese cun (about eight inches) almost to the middle of the lower legs. Then move in toward your shinbone, stopping just an inch from it. That's ST 40.

GB 37: It means "bright light." Trace up the outer side of you leg just as you did for ST 40, but stop five inches up from the protruding ankle knob. Then move your finger slightly toward the shinbone to find the spot.

GB 20:   Known as Feng Chi and occupying the pool-like depression under the occipital bone at either side of the base of your skull. You can find it by bending your head forward and run your fingers up the muscled part of the back of your neck to the points just before hitting the skull bone.

SI 6:   This spot, which the Chinese call "Nourishing the Aged," also nourishes the eyes. Hold your hand in front of you, palm down and then turn your hand with thumb up and you will see a bony knob at the outside where your wrist starts, the point is in the center of the bony knob.

LIV 3:   This is a "source point" for the liver system, meaning any activation of the point directly affects the liver itself. It's located an inch behind the forward edge of the web between your big toe and second toe.

DU 20:   This is the "Bai Hui" point on the Du meridian. It's on the vertex of your head. If you fold in both ears, you'll distinguish a "high point" at the top of each. If you trace an imaginary line from high point to high point, going over the top of your head, DU 20 is where that imaginary line crosses the middle of your skull.

GB 14:   Called Yang Bai, it's another facial point along the gallbladder channel. Activating it benefits the whole eye area and helps smooth forehead wrinkles.

SP 10:   The Chinese name, Xue Hai, means a sea of blood. If you think of your kneecap as a square, this point is two inches above the upper and inner corner. Working it promotes blood circulation, including to the facial area.

LI 4:   This is the "Union Valley," a command point for your face that's located along the Large Intestine channel. On the back of your hand, find the web between your thumb and pointer finger. It's about an inch behind the front end of that web.

DU 23:   This is "Shang Xing" or "Upper Star," located at the very center of your skull one inch behind where your hairline starts (or used to start).

Acupressure Routines for Your Eyes

Now let's get to your acupressure protocols, or routines. There are two of them for your eyes. Start with the first one, practicing it daily. Then move on to the second, which is actually an extended version of the first. Do it daily. Both are excellent routines for getting rid of eye bags and dark eye circles, as well as for overall eye rejuvenation.

You can think of these routines as massages; they certainly offer similar relaxation benefits. But acupressure goes well beyond typical massages. These routines are a form of self-healing. They stimulate blood and energy flow through the channels. They promote lymph drainage and improve cell activity and regeneration. These benefits, in turn, improve the function of the kidney, liver and spleen organ systems. The result: Bright, beautiful eyes surrounded by smooth, supple, youthful skin.

At the start of each routine, apply slight pressure to your eyes with a warm towel for one or two minutes, then press a cool towel to both eyes for one minute.

5-Minute "Inner Circle" Acupressure For Your Eyes

Step 1: Open up the two body points LI 4 and Liv 3 by pressing each nine times. You can locate these 2 points from *(See Fig.11.1)*

> **Tips From Ping**
> In Chinese Medicine we often use nine repetitions of any movement because that's the number associated with the maximum therapeutic benefit. That's why I'll often be asking you to repeat things nine times, or 36 (4 times 9) times.

Step 2: Using both middle fingers, gently tap the inside of each upper eye ridge at the UB-1 point. Keep tapping as you work your way around the edge of the eye socket toward the outside. Then do the same thing along the lower ridge, going from inside out. Repeat the cycle three times. *(See Fig.11.2)*

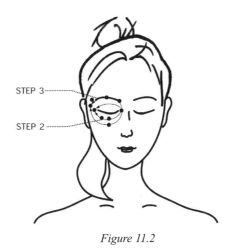

STEP 3

STEP 2

Figure 11.2

Step 3: Now you'll work the bigger outer circle of your eyes, starting with the upper half circle. Using your middle fingers, one for each eye, press the following points one after another, lightly sliding your finger from one point to the next. Start by pressing UB 1, and then move to UB 2, to Yu Yao, to SJ 23, and finally GB 1. Now do the lower half circle by going back to UB 1, and from there moving to ST 1, to Qu Hou, and finally GB 1. Repeat the whole cycle three times. *(See Fig. 11.2)*

15-Minute "Inner and Outer Circle" Acupressure For Your Eyes

Step1: Start by performing Step 3 of the previous 5-minute exercise, following the exact same instructions.

Step 2: Now you'll move to the outer circle of your eyes. Using the same digital pressing technique (pressing with one middle finger for each eye, lightly sliding from one point to the next), press the following points in the order given: Starting by pressing Yin Tong, move to GB 14 and then to Tai Yang. Then start again, this time at UB 1, moving to ST 2, and then to Tai Yang. Repeat the entire process three times. *(See Fig.11.3)*

Step 3: Press GB 20, the master point, nine times to activate all the opening orifices on the face, such as the eyes and nose. *(See Fig.11.4)*

Step 4: This final stage focuses on the body points. Use both thumbs (or your index and middle fingers) to massage the following body points with about 50 presses each: GB 20, LI 4, SI 6, ST 36, GB 37 and SP 6. If your main problem is dark eye circles, also massage SP 10. If your main problem is eye bags, add ST 40. *(See Fig.11.4)*

Figure 11.3

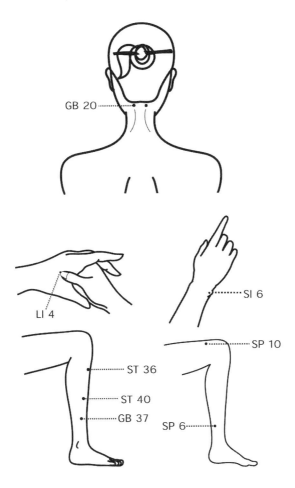

Figure 11.4

Tips From Ping

Here's a simple eye relaxation technique you can do in the morning and evening just after you wash your face: Rub your hands together 36 times to get them hot. Then put your palms over your eyes and lightly press for 30 seconds.

CHAPTER 12

Qi Gong Eye-Brightening Exercises

Just like herbal treatments, acupressure and food therapy, the mind/body exercises known as Qi Gong improve the appearance and health of your eyes by balancing your body's internal environment. One of Traditional Chinese Medicine's core beliefs is that your eyes reflect the overall health of your body, mind and spirit. Perhaps no other kind of remedy embodies that holistic approach as Qi Gong.

In fact, when it comes to your eyes, Qi Gong is considered to be at the highest level of healing power. More than any other technique, Qi Gong uses only the natural ability to heal that you already possess. You are adding no ingredients, no outside material, not even physical pressure (as in acupressure). With Qi Gong, the cure is in you.

As you do the exercises I'm about to describe, keep in mind that Qi Gong is much more than just breathing exercises or relaxation techniques (though it is those things too). Rather, it's a high level of "spirit adjustment," a way to coordinate your mind with your body, and improve the energy that runs through both. These Qi Gong exercises improve the health and appearance of your eyes by directing energy through the appropriate channel and organ systems to achieve a healthier balance that will be reflected in and around your eyes.

Three Simple and Powerful Exercises for Beautiful Eyes

Now it's time for you to take some action to brighten your eyes by learning and performing mind/body techniques passed down through the ages by Chinese sages. By doing so, you will find yourself in a very special category of health-conscious individuals. Most people do absolutely nothing for those special treasures we call eyes. Congratulations!

I learned these routines many years ago from my TCM masters in China, and brought them with me to New York to help American men and women who are concerned about dull eyes, eye bags and dark circles in the eye area.

When I teach these Qi Gong exercises at professional seminars and in my private practice, my students and patients always express amazement that such simple routines can rejuvenate eyes so quickly. They can sense the tension relief from the eye area, see their eyes brighten,and feel the skin around their eyes free from puffiness and discoloration. You can too.

Even though the routines are simple, they'll take a little time to master. After all, most people aren't used to creating energy balls with their minds or breathing in through their eyes! Relax, take your time, and enjoy the tranquil feeling you'll get right from the beginning. Be sure that you perform at least one of these three Qi Gong exercises every day, working your way up to all three.

Eye Irritation Qi Gong Exercise

This simple technique uses your internal energy to exercise the muscles around the eyes, promoting blood and energy flow for healthier eyes.

Step 1: Sit or lie down in a position you find comfortable. Gently close your eyes and put both your palms on the Dan Tian area, about two inches below your navel. Your fingers may overlap slightly. Take 3 deep but soft breaths.

Step 2: Focusing your mind on your eyes, imagine that as you inhale through the nose that you are inhaling energy through both eyes. You'll feel a gentle inner pressure in the eye area as you do. As you exhale through the nose, push out the energy from the eyes. Repeat 9 times.

Step 3: Here you'll use your mental power to put healing energy into your eye bags and puffy eyelids. As you breathe in deeply, imagine pulling energy into your puffy eye bags and eyelids. While you breathe out, let the vibrating energy circulate around your eyes, like making wider and wider concentric circles from throwing a pebble into a pond. Repeat 3 times. *(See Fig.12.1)*

Step 4: Rub your palms together 36 times to warm them. Press one palm to each eye for 30 seconds. Repeat 3 times.

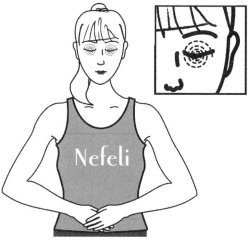

Figure 12.1

Energy Ball For the Eyes

This is essentially the same "energy ball" exercise introduced for wrinkles in Chapter 7, but adapted to bring vital energy to the eye area, specifically to brighten and refresh your eyes. I've found it to be wonderfully effective for relaxing the eyes and increasing the Qi and blood circulation around the eyes, which is very beneficial for relieving puffiness and dark circles.

Step 1: Hold your palms close together, fingers overlapping, facing the Dan Tian area about two inches below your navel. Breathe in slowly through your nose (if you find that difficult, it's okay to breathe in through your mouth) all the way down to the Dan Tian. As you continue this breathing, imagine the clear air you're taking in to be forming a ball of energy inside the Dan Tian. After a few minutes, you'll feel warmth in the Dan Tian, meaning the energy ball is getting stronger.

Step 2: When you sense the energy ball inside you is strong, use both hands to draw it out of the Dan Tian and hold it in your cupped palms. Then separate your hands to divide the energy ball in half, one half-sphere in each palm.

Step 3: Bring the two halves up to the eyes, each palm facing on eye but not touching it. Massage each eye socket with the half-ball in a circular motion, with your eyes closed and relaxed. As you massage, use your mind to instruct the energy half-balls to flatten the eye bags, or to smooth away the black circles around your eyes. Continue your massage until the entire eye area feels warm and relaxed. *(See Fig.12.2)*

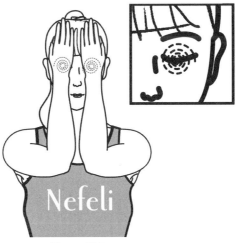

Figure 12.2

Step 4: Then bring both hands back down, bring them together to re-unite the energy ball, Slowly reinsert the energy ball into the Dan Tian, again in the form of a stream of light.

Step 5: Rub your palms together 36 times to warm them, and then press one palm gently to each eye. Hold them there for about 1 minute. Repeat two to three times to finish.

Organ Tonification for Overall Eye Health

In addition to doing one or both of the Qi Gong exercises above, you can also do the following Qi Gong to fortify liver and kidney energy for overall eye health. This routine is especially helpful if you have dark eye circles accompanied by liver and kidney deficiency signs such as tired eyes, low back soreness, weakness, irritability, or insomnia.

A key energy point you need to know for this Qi Gong exercise is called DU 20 *(see the previous chapter, Fig.11.1)*.

Step 1: Sit comfortably on a chair. Relax all the muscles and joints in your body. Place the palm of one hand over the back of the other, and hold them in front of your Dan Tian area. Slowly, deeply, breathe into the Dan Tian area three times. Imagine that your eyes are like fish in a calm sea — relaxed, comfortable and weightless.

Step 2: Now very slowly lift both arms parallel to your sides, cupped palms facing upward. As you lift, imagine your palms gathering the pure energy of the natural world. *(See Fig.12.3)*

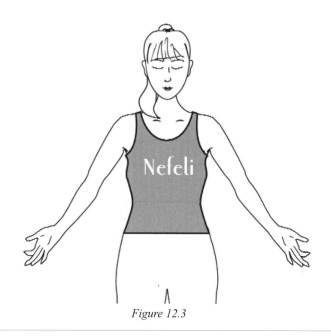

Figure 12.3

Step 3: As your palms reach shoulder continue raising them to create a circle, bending your elbows slightly so the palms end up almost touching the top of your head. The center of each palm (the Lao Gong point) should face directly toward DU 20. Continue to breathe deeply and slowly, in through the nose and out through the mouth. *(See Fig.12.4)*

Figure 12.4

Step 4: Now, with each inward breath, "send" that clear energy you gathered in your palms into the DU 20 area, where it will combine with the internal energy of your body. As the clear energy enters, expel your body's unclear energy out through the mouth. Imagine the clear energy forcing out the unclear energy. Also imagine the unclear, toxic energy moving down your channels to exit from the bottom of your feet, disappearing into the ground below you. Continue this energy cleansing for one minute. Then move on to one of the following two specific-organ exercises.

Step 5A: The liver and kidney systems are linked in TCM, so they go together here. Pull the liver and kidney energy to your eyes by imagining breathing in clear energy down to the Dian Tan. Then, imagine this clear energy spreading through your body, it will naturally cover the liver and kidney area, activating those organ systems. As you breathe out, imagine the liver energy as green and the kidney energy blue, forming a blue and green stream of energy that flows to your eyes. Repeat 3 times then move to 9 times as you get more comfortable with the exercise.

Step 5B: To pull spleen energy to your eyes, imagine breathing in clear energy to the stomach area between your rib cage and naval. As you breathe out, imagine the energy now inside you to form a yellow stream to your eyes. Repeat 3 to 9 times.

CHAPTER 13

Feasts for the Eyes

Food therapy does for your eyes exactly what herbs do — that is, they balance the internal organ systems to achieve an inner health that's reflected in clear youthful eyes. The foods I'll be recommending to you in this chapter will be important weapons in defeating eye bags and dark-circles because they are especially effective in strengthening the liver, spleen and kidney functions. As you know by now, these are the organ systems that need to be addressed to you in order to get rid of puffy eye bags and dark circles.

From a modern Western point of view, these eye-rejuvenating foods are considered healthy because they're all rich in vitamins, minerals, and antioxidant phytonutrients ("phyto" means plant) such as beta-carotene. But you could say the same thing about supplements. In Traditional Chinese Medicine, what counts is the totality of all the food's properties, including its taste, its color, the channels it enters, and its function inside the body.

Some of the foods that I recommend for your eyes will be familiar to you. Others will strike you as exotic. But the Chinese people in their daily diet actually quite commonly eat all of them. Most have made the journey from East to West and are generally available throughout North America. You shouldn't have any trouble finding these foods in good health food stores or Chinese markets.

Keep a few things in mind as you incorporate these foods into your meal plans:

- These foods will help your eyes tremendously, but only in conjunction with the herbs, acupressure routines and Qi Gong exercises described in the previous three chapters. Chinese beauty is all about combining all four techniques.

- Work these foods into your diet gradually. I think they're all delicious, but some of the tastes take a little getting used to. Don't stop with just one or two. There's room in your diet for just about all the foods you'll be learning about, so you'll eventually want to include several every day. You'll feel great knowing that every bite you take is helping to beautify your eyes and face.

- I've organized the recommended foods based on which are best for dark eye circles and which for puffy eye bags. I've also included a special list of foods for general eye health and brightness. You'll naturally want to focus first on the category that fits your condition. But don't be too strict about it. All the foods in this chapter are excellent for all-around eye health and beauty.

The Three Best Foods for Eliminating Dark Eye Circles

If dark eye circles are your main problem, look for the following foods at a good health food store or a Chinese grocery. They directly address the stagnation and kidney Yin deficiency that are often the inner cause of those unsightly discolorations.

Try to include as many of these foods as possible in your meal plan, and as often as possible. Later in this chapter I'll give you some ideas for using many of these foods in delicious recipes, based on Chinese tradition.

■ **Hei Mu Er** *(Black Fungus)*

This is a common food among the Chinese people, a staple in just about every vegetarian dish. You should have no trouble finding Hei Mu Er at any Asian market, good health food store or herb market. Make sure you're buying true Chinese black fungus, however, and not just any dark mushroom.

Used throughout the centuries as a detoxifier, this wonderful food/herb has such powerful cleansing properties that Chinese workers often use it to offset occupational contamination hazards. In TCM, it's considered a "sweet," neutral herb (though it doesn't taste sweet) that enters the stomach and large intestine channels to tonify body energy and promote blood flow. Because its rich in vitamins, minerals (especially iron), and proteins, and is such an effective cleanser of the digestive system, it's also one of the best foods you can eat to clear the area around your eyes of dark circles, as well as wrinkles

Hei Mu Er is simple to prepare. Simply soak the fungus pieces in hot water until it spreads and softens. Rinse clean and boil. You can include them sliced in soup or salads, or add them to any hot dish.

■ **Chi Xiao Dou** *(Azuki Bean)*

Here's one of the best and easiest things you can do to help get rid of dark eye circles. Simply substitute this reddish, oval bean for whatever kind of bean you usually prepare as a side dish. It's an ancient Chinese bean that's been popular in the Orient for thousands of years and it's readily available in North America. You may find it under some variation of its Western name (such as adsuki, adzuki or aduki. It's botanical name is *Paseolus angularis.*

As common as this bean is, few foods are better for rejuvenating your eye area. Chi Xiao Dou has ideal properties for healthier eyes. It

enters through the heart and small intestine channels to clear dampness out of the body as it eliminates toxicities, strengthens the digestive system, moves blood stagnation and relieves swelling. That
makes it an ideal food for eliminating dark eye circles (and puffy eye
bags, as well).

Prepare Chi Xiao Dou as you would any dry bean. Soak overnight
in clean water, drain, rinse and simmer until soft, using about 4 cups of
water for every cup of beans. If you forget to soak them overnight,
unsoaked beans will cook in about 15-20 minutes in a pressure cooker.

■ **Dao Zao** *(Chinese Dates)*

You met this magical fruit earlier as an all-around beautifier that
helps smooth wrinkles. I'm including it here because Dao Zao is also
wonderfully effective for clearing up discoloration in the eye area. I
especially recommend the Chinese Date Porridge (see Chapter 8) to
anybody having trouble with dark eye circles.

Dao Zao rejuvenates your eye area by strengthening your digestive
system, which in turn generates abundant Qi via the post-natal sea of
energy. It also improves blood flow. The overall effect of eating
Chinese dates regularly is increased nourishment in the eye area and
a reduction in swelling around the eyes. Remember to take out the
pits inside the dates.

The Three Best Foods for Eliminating Eye Bags and Puffiness

Here are three foods you'll want to include in your diet if puffy eye
bags are making your eyes look tired and old. Each addresses the
organ imbalances most often related to eye puffiness. Specifically,
each helps correct the dampness accumulation caused by spleen Qi
deficiency. And they help remove the "fatty ball" type of eye bag —
what Western medicine might call a fat deposit but what TCM considers to be phlegm obstruction.

■ **Kun Bu** *(Kelp Thallus)*

A big difference between Oriental and Western diets is the liberal use
of sea vegetables that Chinese, Japanese and other Asians eat. The most
valuable sea vegetable for reducing eye puffiness is a kind of kelp called
Kun Bu. If you eat it regularly, it will clear out phlegm congestion,
reduce dampness accumulation and the swelling that goes with it.

Kun Bu (*Laminaria japonica algae*) is popular as a supplement in
pill form, but you can also find it as a food. (If you can't, any other
dark "seaweed" will be an acceptable substitute.) If you buy it dried,
usually in thin strips, soak it in hot water for several hours and then
simmer it to make a broth. Or boil it for just 10 minutes and use the
cooled and chopped kelp as a condiment or garnish. Dry or fresh,

Kun Bu is something you can eat almost daily, sprinkling it on your salads or adding some to any main dish without altering the main flavor too radically.

■ **Carp Fish**

From the TCM point of view, fish vary not just in taste and texture but in the healing properties they impart. For eye rejuvenation, carp is king of the sea. As it clears away heat and detoxifies the body, carp addresses the causes of eye puffiness by strengthening the digestive system and reducing swelling from dampness accumulation. For your eyes' sake, try to eat carp at least once a week, preferably more often.

■ **Yi Yi Ren** *(Coix Seed)*

You were introduced briefly to these barley seeds in a number of wrinkle-reducing recipes. This all-purpose skin beautifier is even more valuable as an eye-rejuvenator. The main reason for Yi Yi Ren's effectiveness is that it helps clear dampness from the body, thus reducing swelling. But coix seeds are also excellent for the digestive system. And they're easy to add to just about any dish.

Healthy Foods to Brighten and Energize Your Eyes

Even without eye bags or dark circles, your eyes may tend to look tired and spiritless. Your vision may blur on occasion, or your eyes tear up. These symptoms, especially if they tend to occur after you overstrain yourself physically or emotionally, usually mean your liver blood is deficient and your kidney essence is depleted. Since the liver meridian opens to your eyes and kidney essence nourishes and replenishes the eyes, weakness in those organs spells trouble for your eyes.

Fortunately, there are plenty of foods that help improve the situation. Following are some of the most powerful. Work some of them into your meal plan each day and you'll make noticeable progress toward regaining your healthy eyes. And you'll notice that many of them are also recommended for dark circles and puffiness.

Yam	Almonds
Carrots	Soybeans
Fish	Seaweed
Walnuts	Lotus root
Chrysanthemum flower	Apricots
Liver (beef)	Sesame seeds
Mulberry fruit	Sunflower seeds
Millet	

Nutritious Dishes for Bright, Beautiful Eyes

Now it's time to put these eye-saving foods into tasty dishes. Here are five of my favorite simple recipes that use many of the foods that work to rejuvenate your eyes. Of course, you won't want to limit your use of the line-up of eye-rejuvenating foods to just these simple soups and teas. Once you get used to including these foods in your meals, you'll be able to come up with any number of variations on your own.

■ **Fish Soup**

Here's a soup for your beautiful eyes that makes good use of carp (the super eye-saving fish) and of Hei Mu Er, the dark circle-removing Chinese fungus.
You'll need:

1 lb of carp fish, marinated with cooking wine and 1 tsp of cornstarch.

One handful of Hei Mu Er (dried black fungus). It should be soaked in hot water until it's soft, washed, and then cut into bite-sized chunks (if the pieces aren't that small already)

3 thin, 1-inch slices of fresh ginger
Some cilantro, cut it into small pieces

1/4 tsp of sesame oil.

2 tablespoons of olive oil.

Lightly fry the fish, the fresh ginger and black fungus for 1 minute with two tablespoons of olive oil. Add 32 ounces of water and bring to a boil. Then low boil for 30 minutes. Add the cilantro, sesame oil and a dash of powdered white/black pepper and salt. Serve hot.

■ **Liver and Spinach Soup**

This may sound like a child's culinary nightmare, but if you have tired and blurry eyes with dark circles around them, this is an excellent (and tasty!) soup to prepare often. You'll need:

1/4 lb of liver (beef), sliced into small pieces, and marinated in cooking wine with a 1/4 teaspoon of sesame oil.

A large bunch of fresh spinach (best if you include the root), washed and cut into big pieces.

2 egg whites, beaten.

3 slices of fresh ginger.

Two tablespoons of olive oil

Salt to taste

Dash of powdered white pepper

Heat the olive oil in a large saucepan and add the marinated liver, the fresh ginger, and salt. Stir fry for about a minute and then add 34 ounces of already boiling water. Add some more salt to the liquid and let it boil for no more than 5 minutes, or until the liver is done. Be careful not to overcook the liver. Turn off the heat and stir in the egg white slowly. Only now do you add the spinach (it doesn't need to cook much), along with a few drops of sesame oil and a dash of white pepper. Serve hot.

■ **Black and White Soup**

Here's an ideal combination of black fungus, white fungus (tremella), Chinese wolfberries and Chinese dates (jujube), without internal pits. A great choice for fighting eye bags as well as dark circles, and for general eye brightening. You'll need:

1 handful of black fungus, soaked in hot water until soft and cut into small pieces.

1 handful of white fungus (Soak it in hot water for over night, then cut out the root and cut the rest into small pieces)

15 pieces of Chinese dates without pits, washed.

9 grams of Chinese wolfberries

15 grams of sea weed, clean and cut into small pieces.

Simply add all the above ingredients to 4 cups of water (or bone soup base), bring to a boil and simmer for about 1 hour. Serve warm or cold twice a day.

■ **Chrysanthemum Flower and Wolfberry Fruit Tea**

This is a decoction — boiled instead of steeped. Boil 4 cups (32oz) of water with 3 grams of chrysanthemum flower and 6 grams of wolfberry fruit. Drink daily for beautiful bright eyes. For even better results, add a third of a gram of pearl powder to the tea.

■ **Fruit and Nut Soup**

Here's a wonderful soup for overall eye beauty, combining jujube (Chinese dates), winter melon, lotus root, walnuts, mulberries (if available) and water chestnuts. You'll need:

10 pieces of Chinese dates, washed and remove the pits.

10 pieces of fresh water chestnuts, diced.

1/4 pound of winter melon, cut into inch-sized cubes.

1/4/ pound of lotus root, cut into pieces.

10 pieces of walnuts.

1/2 cup of fresh mulberries.

2 carrots. Cleaned and sliced.

1/2 cup of red beans, pre-soaked for 30 minutes first.

Add the above ingredients to 5 cups of chicken broth or bone soup (or plain water, if you prefer). Bring to boil and then lower the heat for soup to low-boil for 45 minutes.

Five-Element Fruit Blends

Remember that in TCM, the healing value of food goes well beyond Western medicine's emphasis on chemical ingredients. At its most advanced levels, Chinese food therapy is a complex scheme of relationships in which flavor and color are important determinants of which organ systems will be affected and which "elements' come into play.

For example, "sour" flavors enter the liver (the wood element), which is associated with green. "Salty," blue or black foods enter the kidney (water element). And "bland," yellow foods enter the spleen (earth element). Since the liver, kidneys and spleen are the key organ systems for eye beauty, fruits and vegetables of those descriptions will blend well into eye-healing juices or smoothies.

Thankfully, generations of TCM healers have done the complicated work for you. All you have to do is mix together whatever combinations of the following fruits and vegetables suit your fancy. Add a little honey and you'll have yourself a daily dose of eye-beautifying refreshment.

Carrots	Ginger root (with peel)
Oranges	Mulberry fruit
Lotus root	Green apple
Blueberries	Banana
Blackberries	Bitter melon

Food Masks and Washes
for Bright and Beautiful Eyes

Certain foods can provide their healing benefits when applied directly to the area around your eyes. Try some of the following easy-to-make masks or washes, using them at least every other day. Note that the skin of most fruits or vegetables, because of its astringency, is especially effective in reducing swelling around the eyes. Note: Do not forget to do a test in the inner side of your wrist for 24 hours to see if you are allergic to these fresh made masks and washes.

■ **Chrysanthemum Flower Wash**

This one is especially good for dark eye circles and eye bags. Pour 6 ounces of boiling water into a cup with 6 grams of chrysanthemum flowers. Let it steep for 10 minutes. When it cools down soak a hand towel in the warm "tea" and press the towel over both your eyes for 1 minute. Then re-soak the towel and repeat. Do this five times. Option: Include 1 gram of pearl powder in the tea.

■ **Sesame Seed Oil Mask**

Especially for eye bags. Simply apply sesame seed oil around your eyes before you go to sleep and wash it off in the morning. You can also apply a thin layer of sesame oil around the eyes and massage the eye area with a warm hard-boiled egg (with shell on).

■ **Persimmon Peel Mask**

Peel the skin off a fresh, ripe persimmon and press the skin to your eye bags, avoiding touching the inside of the eye . The skin should be moist enough to stick on by itself. Leave it there for 20 minutes. Do this once a day.

■ **Potato or Apple Skin Mask**

Pare off two pieces of skin from a raw potato or apple and press them onto each eye bag. Wait for 10 minutes and wash.

Your Alternatives

Food mentioned here and in the next section as masks for different eye concerns are mostly ready to be found in the local super-maket. To prepare them correctly follow the recipes, they will benefit your eyes greatly. However, if you still find difficultly in preparing them, you may consider using Nefeli's **"Eye Refresh"** as an alternative food supplement and Nefeli's **"Eye Rejuvenating Mask"** to substitute the hand made masks. They will work great too.

PART FOUR

THE COMPLEXION YOU WANT, NATURALLY

CHAPTER 14

Understanding Your Complexion Problems

In all my years of treating patients and teaching students, I've met very few people — male or female — who are completely satisfied with their facial skin. That includes lots of women and men who are either young enough or healthy enough not to have wrinkles. Sure, wrinkles get the most attention, and deservedly so. But even a wrinkle-free face can suffer from complexion problems that detract from your true beauty and rob your face of its youthful look and natural glow.

I've found that these more generalized, non-wrinkle-related complaints usually consist of one or more of the following: A dull or withered-looking complexion. Discoloration of the facial skin. Dark spots or splotches on the face.

Over the centuries, Chinese healers have developed countless ways to take care of those general "complexion" problems. In the next four chapters, I'll tell you how to take advantage of many of these Chinese treatments — safely, inexpensively, and in the comfort of your own home. These time-honored treatments will return your complexion to its natural clear and radiant state.

Since ancient times, the Chinese have placed tremendous importance on achieving and maintaining a clear, radiant complexion. In fact, the Chinese have traditionally cared more about the general complexion of the face than any other beauty concern. A famous Chinese saying holds that, "One fair, spotless skin can cover up three ugly bodies."

Of course, like anybody else, Chinese people want to look good. But that's not the only reason for this strong emphasis on a clear complexion. It's also because they recognize that a bright, clear, unspotted complexion reflects inner health. So complexion problems are more than just a superficial beauty concern - they are an outward manifestation of internal imbalances that need to be corrected to restore your health.

TCM's remedies, including those I'll be describing to you for home use, treat the root causes of your complexion problems rather than merely the symptoms you see on your face. By working from the inside out, these TCM remedies will not only help get rid of the dullness, discoloration or spotting, but will improve your internal health so the symptoms won't come back.

What's Really Causing Your Complexion Problems?

If you recall the role that the spleen, liver and kidney systems play in TCM treatments for wrinkles and eye puffiness, it probably comes as no surprise that those same organ systems are involved with complexion treatment as well. What may surprise you, though, are some of the original causes of the imbalances that lead to discoloration, dullness or spotting. Three stand out:

Emotional stress. Western and Chinese medicine agree that constrained emotions or ongoing emotional stress can lead to health problems. As far as TCM is concerned, a spotted or discolored complexion is one of those emotionally induced health problems.

Here's why: In a healthy state, each of your internal organ systems works in coordination with the others. That balance ensures a smoothly functioning body with Yin and Yang in balance, and Qi and blood flowing freely. Since the TCM system holds that each of the seven emotions affects a particular organ system, an emotional imbalance can disturb the harmony of the organ systems. Just as an auto accident can tie up traffic in many different directions,

One organ system in imbalance can inhibit the energy and blood circulation controlled by another organ system. Emotional constraint or excess can have that effect, decreasing the Qi and blood flow to your face. That decrease, in turn, can create local blockages of energy and blood in the face. Result: dark spots, dullness, or discoloration.

An irregular lifestyle. Again like Western medicine, TCM recognizes the unhealthy consequences of what might be called bad habits — poor eating, overwork, obsessive thoughts, excessive worrying, and so on. Chinese healers see these lifestyle irregularities as negatively affecting spleen function. Since TCM considers the spleen to be responsible for the transformation and transportation of body fluids, a weakened spleen system causes dampness accumulation that blocks the channel systems leading to the face. With insufficient Qi, blood and essence making it to the face, dark spots and facial discoloration can result.

One of the irregular lifestyle choices singled out by the Chinese as causing facial discolorations (including dark eye circles) is overindulgence in sexual activity. This is not to say that an active and fulfilling sex life is unhealthy, but it does mean that sexual obsessiveness or simply overdoing it can consume too much kidney Yin and kidney essence. Yin and essence are key factors in the nourishment of your facial skin, so if there's not enough available, discoloration, especially around eyes, can occur.

According to TCM, in a healthy body, Yin (associated with water) and Yang (associated with fire) intermingle in perfect balance. Sex is a Yin-consuming activity. When to much Yin (water) is consumed, the fire of the Yang can burn out of control, since there's not enough water of the Yin available. This is known as "empty fire." As it rises, the resulting dryness creates local energy stagnation in the face, resulting in facial discolorations.

Exposure to the elements. External factors such as heat, dryness and wind can create internal conditions that lead to spotting, discoloration and dullness. When wind, for example, invades the body surface, it disturbs the harmony of Qi and blood at the skin level. Once again, the flow stagnates and complexion problems can result over time.

Overexposure to sunlight is a major cause of spotting, on your face and elsewhere. Here again, Western and Chinese medicine are in complete agreement in terms of the cause, (though not of the treatment). That's why the Chinese people have traditionally placed much emphasis on avoiding skin damage from too much sun exposure. The umbrella was first invented by the Chinese — not to keep rain off their heads but to protect them from the sun. The emperor's carriage was always outfitted with a parasol.

The Safe, Natural Way to Clear Your Complexion from The Inside Out

Based on the external causes just mentioned, the first steps you should take to rejuvenate your complexion are exactly what a Western doctor might recommend. Bring your emotions under control, neither bottling them up nor letting them get out of hand. Eat a balanced, healthy diet and practice moderation in all things. And limit your exposure to extreme environmental conditions, especially sunlight.

These simple preventive measures will not only decrease the likelihood of future complexion problems, they'll also help you get rid of the ones you have.

Just how to get rid of them is where the TCM techniques I'm about to give you part ways from Western medicine. Typical modern treatments for dark spots include a "peel," in which trichloroacetic acid is applied to remove the top layer of skin. Bleaching is another method, using such chemicals as hydroquinone to fade out the spots. A number of other synthetic topical products will supposedly address complexion problems. So will laser embrasions, and other modern interventions. These Western techniques tend to treat the symptoms rather than the root causes.

The TCM techniques and treatments you'll learn in the next four chapters are not only safer and much less expensive methods for clearing and brightening your complexion, they also work noticeably better in the long run because they fix the internal imbalances that create the problems in the first place.

Thousands of years have gone into perfecting these herbal remedies, food therapies, Qi Gong exercises and acupressure routines that directly address the root causes of dull, withered complexions, facial discoloring and dark spots. If you practice daily a selection of treatments from each of these four categories, you'll enjoy the same complexion benefits that the Chinese have known for thousands of years.

CHAPTER 15

Your Face's Herbal Allies

Chinese herbs work wonders for your complexion for many of the same reasons they smooth wrinkles and brighten your eyes. Working mostly through the liver and kidney channels, they act to correct the internal imbalances that lead to facial spotting, discoloration and dullness.

The herbs I'm recommending to you in this chapter have been proven effective in improving the complexion through literally thousands of years of experimentation and practical use. In many cases, however, modern Western medicine acknowledges some of the health benefits that can be found in certain ingredients of the herbs you'll be using. But as you've learned, the Chinese medical philosophy is less concerned with individual ingredients than the properties of the whole herb and how they act on the energy channels and organ systems in the body.

These herbs' beauty uses are only part of their effectiveness. Many are used to treat conditions that have little to do with facial beauty. When you remember that the key to beautifying your face is to resolve inner health problems, then the herbs' versatility makes sense.

Herbs in this chapter are safe, non-toxic, "superior" herbs. Many can be found at Western-style health food stores and herb centers. The rest are available at Chinese markets, Chinese herb stores or via the Internet.

Remember that herbs by themselves are only part of your complexion-brightening program. You also need to take advantage of the acupressure routines, Qi Gong exercises and medicinal foods outlined in the next three chapters.

Top Ten Herbs For A Cleaner, Brighter Complexion

Here are five amazing herbs that you haven't met yet. Each has been used traditionally in TCM to reduce facial discoloration and eliminate dark spots.

Yu Zhu (Solomon's Seal Rhyzome)

The Chinese name for this healing root means "jade bamboo." It's a member of the same genus as Huang Jing, the "yellow essence" herb that I recommend for treating wrinkles. Both are often called Solomon's seal, and both are superior Yin tonics. But their actions differ slightly, and Yu Zhu is best for complexion problems other than wrinkles.

Like Huang Jing, Yu Zhu is one of those "superstar" herbs that have been highly lauded since ancient Taoist times. It is considered an "enlightener" of the body and prolonger of life. But it also has the reputation as a facial beauty herb, bringing nourishment to the complexion to free it of spots and blotches, restoring youthful radiance.

■ **How Yu Zhu beautifies your complexion.** Sweet and slightly cold in nature, Yu Zhu enters and nourishes the stomach and lung channels. For wrinkles and eye puffiness, we talked mostly about the spleen, kidney and liver functions. But the lungs rule the skin, and the abundant lung Yin that Yu Zhu helps create is essential for a radiant and clear complexion.

Another Yu Zhu's action is tonification of the "middle burner" — that is, the digestive system. Recall that the middle burner is the source of the body's post-natal sea of energy, a generator of the Qi and blood that nourishes facial skin.

■ **Buying and taking Yu Zhu.** In Chinese markets or TCM-oriented Internet sites, you'll be able to find it under its Chinese name and easily differentiate it from Huang Jing. But if you're buying Solomon's seal at a Western-style herb or health food store, look for the Latin botanical name Polygonatum odoratum to be sure it's Yu Zhu.

You might find the fresh, whole root, which the Chinese often eat as a beautifying food. Wash about 6 grams of it and use it as an ingredient in a soup. You don't need to eat the actual root; just drink the soup. If you prefer the loose, powdered root, stir 1 gram of it into some warm water (or any juice) and drink it daily.

■ *Cautions concerning Yu Zhu. All cold herbs, including Yu Zhu, should be avoided if you have diarrhea or phlegm in the stomach.*

Bai Jiang Can *(Silkworm)*

This is dried silkworm, a common and multifaceted Chinese natural medicine with a marked ability to clear away internal heat and wind. Chinese herbal texts have recommended its use for such diverse ailments as headache and Bell's palsy.

■ **How Bai Jiang Can beautifies your complexion.** As an herb, silkworm is salty and acrid and enters through the liver and lung channels. According to TCM, it reduces dark discoloration and scarring by eliminating wind locked in the facial skin layer.

■ **Buying and taking Bai Jiang Can.** You can buy it in dried, powdered form. Take .5 gram a day, stirred into water.

Dong Gua Ren *(Winter Melon Seed)*

You already know about winter melon, a popular Asian vegetable that the Chinese eat in soups. According to Traditional Chinese medicine, the seeds are a powerful medicinal herb that works like magic to reduce facial dark spots and discoloration. The saponins and fatty acids found in winter melon seeds are beneficial to the skin.

- **How Dong Gua Ren beautifies your complexion.** Winter melon seed is sweet and cold in nature. It enters the lung, stomach, large intestine and small intestine channels. Its complexion- beautifying actions include moisturizing, as well as relieving wind from the facial skin.

- **Buying and taking Dong Gua Ren.** You'll find winter melons in Chinese grocery stores. If you like, you can take about 6 grams of raw, shelled winter melon seeds and boil them in water. Drink the liquid and eat the cooked seeds. Make sure you only eat the inside seeds, not the shell. To buy winter melon seeds ready to use as an herb, you'll probably need to find a store that specializes in Asian herbs, or consult the Internet. The seeds come as a dried powder. Take .5 grams per day stirred into warm water.

Rou Gui *(Cinnamon Bark)*

Cinnamon is more than a pleasant seasoning, in both the Chinese and Western herbal tradition. As an herb, cinnamon is acrid, sweet and hot, excellent for expelling cold from the body. TCM texts emphasize Rou Gui's ability to enlighten the body, which promotes longevity. It's also very effective for improving the complexion, according to TCM texts, bringing radiance and beauty, "like that of a child's face."

- **How Rou Gui beautifies your complexion.** Cinnamon tonifies the body's Yang to expel cold from the body. That promotes blood flow through the channels to the face, nourishing the facial skin. .

- **Buying and taking Rou Gui.** Cinnamon is especially recommended for your complexion if you often feel cold, or suffer from digestion problems. Buy the bark sticks anywhere, including supermarkets, and grate it liberally into drinks, desserts, and even main dishes. For the full herbal benefits, stir at least a half-gram a day, up to one gram, into a glass of juice or warm water and drink it down. Cinnamon tea is another option.

- ***Cautions concerning Rou Gui.** If you have a lot of heat signs in your body, you should not use this hot herb. Heat signs include constipation, acne, thirst, and yellow urine. If you are pregnant, use Rou Gui with caution. Consult your doctor.*

Tao Hua *(Peach Flower)*

The blossom of the peach tree is a bitter tasting, neutral herb that enters into the kidney and liver channels. It is considered a different herb that the kernel of the peach fruit (Tao Ren). Both promote blood flow, but the blossoms are better for reducing facial discoloration and spotting.

- **How Tao Hua beautifies your complexion.** Peach flowers, like silkworms, expel wind from the skin, which improves local circulation to bring more nourishment to the face.

- **Buying and taking Tao Hua.** In season, help yourself to cut peach blossoms from the tree. TCM lore holds that flowers on the south- and east-facing sides of the tree are best for beauty results. Otherwise, buy dried peach flowers at a Chinese herb store. Pour 8 ounces of boiling water in a cup with 2 dried peach flowers and let it steep for 20 minutes. Enjoy the tea.

  Another option is to soak 9 grams of Tao Hua in a bottle of grain alcohol for a month. Take 10 milliliters of this tincture measured in a dropper daily.

- *Cautions concerning Tao Hua. If you are pregnant, have heavy menses, or are taking a blood thinning medication, don't use Tao Hua.*

Many herbs recommended for smoothing away wrinkles or beautifying your eyes can also do wonders for your complexion. Here are five of the best.

Zhen Zhu *(Pearl)*

This salty-tasting, cold herb brightens your complexion by calming the liver Yang and clearing away liver heat. According to Traditional Chinese Medicine, it detoxifies the skin and help to regenerate the flesh. It's especially recommended if your dark spots or facial discoloration are accompanied by irritability, disturbing dreams, or swelling around the eyes. Take 0.3 grams of the powder each day, dissolved in warm water.

Fu Ling *(Poria)*

Fu Ling is as great for your complexion as it is for your eyes. Its spleen-strengthening action expels phlegm and dampness that inhibit the flow of blood and energy up to the face, dulling and discoloring your complexion.

It's a good herb for you if you also suffer from weak digestion and a heavy, swollen feeling in your body. Boil about 6 grams of Fu Ling in fresh water, add to a soup or drink it alone. Or buy it in powdered form and drink 1 gram dissolved in water per day.

Bai Zhu *(Atractylodes Root)*

Another eye herb that also clears the complexion. It's a Qi tonic that enters the spleen and stomach channels to promote digestion. By strengthening the spleen system it clears channels of dampness, improving the flow of blood and Qi to the face. It's a particularly good choice if your facial discoloration looks dull gray or dull yellow (but not jaundiced), if your overall complexion is withered-looking, or if you suffer from loose stool, water retention, low energy or poor appetite. Low-boil 3 grams of the raw root in 2 cups of water for 20 minutes and drink it daily as a tea. Or buy it in powdered form and dissolve 1 gram in warm water to drink once a day for 10 days.

Tu Si Zi *(Chinese Dodder Seed)*

You've met this herb, sometimes called dodder seed or Semen Cuscutae, when as a treatment for eye bags and dark eye circles, but it's also commonly used by TCM practitioners to eliminate dark spots on the face and brighten dull complexions. It's a Yang tonic, warm and sweet, that enters the liver, kidney and spleen channels. It's tonifying effect on kidney Yang (as well as Yin) helps nourish the facial skin. Try Tu Si Zi if your complexion is dull or spotted, and you exhibit such signs of kidney Yang deficiency as frequent urination, blurred vision, or ringing in the ears. Buy the raw seeds, low boil 6 grams in water for 20 minutes, strain and drink.

Tian Men Dong *(Chinese Asparagus)*

This is a Yin tonic long praised by Taoists as the ultimate facial beauty herb, smoothing wrinkles as well as brightening and evening out the complexion. It helps your complexion by tonifying kidney Yin, thus eliminating the fluid-consuming heat that leads to dark spots and discoloration. Try Tian Men Dong if your complexion problems include dry skin, or if you show such signs of kidney and lung Yin deficiency as dry mouth, irritability, insomnia or constipation. Low-boil 6 grams in 2 cups of water for 20 minutes strain and drink one cup per day. Continue for 10 days and then rest for five days before starting again.

Caution: *Since it is cold in nature, do not take Tian Men Dong if you have diarrhea or a cold. Do not take this herb with tremella (Bai Mu Er), Ku Shen (Radix Sophorae Flavescentis), or Kuan Dong Hua (Flos Tussilaginis Farfarae).*

Homemade Herbal Masks for a Spotless and Radiant Complexion

Some herbs work wonders for your complexion when they're applied directly to your face, as a mask or a wash. Here I'll give you some of the most common topical herbs that have been very successful for my patients with complexion problems.

Remember to do your allergy test first. Put a little of the mask or wash on a small area of your wrist. Wait for 24 hours to see if you have an allergic reaction. If not, try some or all of the following.

Pearl Powder Mask

To repeat, pearl is an excellent herb both internally and externally for a radiant and even complexion. Applied topically, it will gradually eliminate dark spots. Put 2 grams of pearl powder into a bowl with 1/4 teaspoon of honey and 1/4 teaspoon of olive oil, and blend together to make a mask. Then apply the mask to your face and leave it on for 15 minutes. Wash thoroughly.

Dong Gua Ren Mask

Winter melon seed can be taking internally and applied externally .to brighten your face and even out your complexion. To prepare a mask, simply mix 2 grams of the powdered seed with 1/2 teaspoon of honey. Put it on your face for 15 minutes and wash out.

Bai Zhu Wash

Take a piece of the dried root about the size of two quarters stacked, soak it in 1 ounce of vinegar for seven days, and then dilute the liquid by adding 4 ounces of water. Wash your face with this wonderful solution each morning and followed by clear water rinse.

Yu Li Ren *(Semen Pruni)* Mask

This herb is called Bush cherry pit in the West. It's traditionally used by the Chinese people as an external mask for treating facial discoloration and age spots. It's rich in lipids and vitamins beneficial to your skin.

You can buy the actual pits and then roast them (if they're not already roasted) yourself in the oven, like chestnuts. After they cool, rub off the skins. Take a good large double handful of them and blend them into a fine powder. Keep the powder in a tightly lidded glass jar, stored in a cool place.

Each night, take a teaspoon of the powder and mix it with an egg white to create your mask. Leave it on your face over night. Do this every day for seven days, rest for a few days and renew your regimen.

Feng Wang Jiang *(Royal Jelly)* **Mask**

If you are not allergic to bee products, Royal Jelly will be your great choice for your complexion. Royal Jelly is a great source of complete protein, with all the essential amino acids. It's also rich in unsaturated fats, natural sugars, minerals, and vitamins, especially the B Vitamins. The Chinese use it as a food, but they've also found that applying Royal Jelly (called Feng Wang Jiang) directly to the face works wonders for the complexion. It's already in a liquid form, so just buy it, apply it to your clean face, leave it on for 20 minutes and wash it off.

Tao Hua *(Peach Flower)* **Mask**

Pick fresh peach flowers from a tree if you can, rinse them clean, and soak them in water for a few minutes. Place soaked flowers some water into the blender, add some pearl powder, and blend into a pasty liquid. Pat the blend onto your face and wait 20 minutes before rinsing.

Tips From Ping

Sometimes the body can easily get an allergic reaction to something applied externally for skin care. You should test your homemade food/herbal washes and masks by applying it to a small area on your inner wrist. Leave on for 24 hours. If any allergic reaction occurs (such as a rash, redness, swelling or itchy), do not use that herb or food formulas. If there is no reaction feel free to use it.

Traditional Herbal Formulas for Your Complexion

Over thousands of years, Chinese medicine has documented countless formulas for treating dark spots, blemishes and dullness of the face. These combinations of herbs, blended in precise proportions and taken internally, represent some for the most advanced and successful herbal treatments of complexion problems. Though some Chinese herbal formulas are available over the counter, for reasons of safety they are best administered by a trained TCM practitioner. I seldom recommend them for do-it-yourself home treatment.

Here, however, I'll introduce some of the better-known formulas for treating the complexion. If you're interested in exploring any of these further, talk to your Traditional Chinese Medicine professional.

Shui Dynasty "King and Queen" Face-Brightening Powder

This ancient formula is traditionally used to nourish and brighten the face by relieving dampness, ridding the channels of phlegm, promoting blood flow. It consists of citrus peel, winter melon seed and peach flower in powdered form. It's usually taken 1 gram per day after each meal for ten days.

Six Rhumennia Formula

This is a classic TCM Yin tonic formula that's often used to treat facial discolorations and dark spots due to kidney Yin deficiency.

Your Alternatives

Needless to say, the above mentioned herbs, including internal taking and for external applications are the best choices to use for facial discolorations and age spots. However, you may use Nefeli products as your alternative if you find it troublesome to find and prepare. Fortunately, Nefeli's line of Skin Brighting Collection includes internal taking herbal formulas, and external skin care application. This includes:

1. Nefeli **"Bright Complexion"** herbal Supplement. It is made by 100% pure Chinese herbs/foods that nourish the body from inside out to help correct the imbalances that cause facial discoloration and dark/age spots.

2. Nefeli pure herbal-based Skin Brightening Collections.

This line of pure herbal-based creams and washes are designed to help protect the skin from environmental factors, promote energy and blood circulation in the skin so it helps to tap the root of the cause for facial discoloration and dark/age spots. This collection includes:

■ Nefeli **"Skin Brightening Facial Wash"** which is made with Ginkgo Biloba and Papaya removes make up and cleans the skin at the same time initiating the skin healing process from the start. Use mornings and evenings.

■ Nefeli **"Intensive Day-Time Skin Brightening Cream"**. Formulated with Rhodiola, Coix Seed, Safflower, Seaweed, Trichosanthes, Phellodendron Bark, Winter Melon, transforms a dull complexion into a bright luminous one. It helps diminish the appearance of facial discolorations and dark/aging spots.

■ Nefeli **"Intensive Night-Time Skin Brightening Cream"**. With the combination of herbs leading by Pearls – a legendary herb considered by Chinese healers as "the Queen of all minerals" for facial beauty, Chinese Asparagus, Poria, Licrice, Winter Melon and Tremella, this formula is designed for either dull and/or discolored, spotted complexion. It does this by deeply promoting the energy and blood circulation to the skin area, so the skin's own healing power is strenghtened, thus, a healthy flawless, even toned complexion with a true glow and radiance is created on your face naturally.

CHAPTER 16

Facial Discolorations, Dark Spots and Acupressure

In this chapter you'll master some do-it-yourself acupressure techniques that will help rejuvenate your face by fading away dark spots and discoloration. Though quite simple, these acupressure routines work because they activate important body points along certain meridians that promote energy and essence flow to your face.

Some of the points you'll be stimulating are "local," that is, on the face itself. Activating them promotes Qi and blood flow in the immediate area, and helps detoxify your face via improved lymphatic drainage

But in accordance with TCM theory, most of the acupressure benefits come from activating non-facial points that smooth Qi and blood flow throughout the body. As I've repeated countless times, your face is the mirror that reflects your internal health. That health depends on proper functioning of the internal organ system, the smooth flow of Qi and blood, and a balanced emotional state.

These routines have long helped Chinese men and women achieve brighter and clearer complexions, free of spots and inappropriate coloration. But they are not quick "cures." They are part of a health-inducing TCM facial beauty program that includes herbs, Qi Gong and diet therapy.

Practice the acupressure routines daily. Be patient. Soon, your consistency will pay off, and you'll notice the long-term benefits that activating certain points and channels can give you.

The Exercises

A special feature of one of these acupressure routines is that you'll be stimulating not individual points but entire channels (meridians) — the kidney channel (KI), the liver channel (LIV), the spleen channel (SP), and to a lesser extent the stomach channel (ST).

The other exercises will concentrate on energy points, so let's get familiar with those points before we move onto the actual routines. Some points you've been introduced to before, but I'll describe them again here.

Be sure to check for all points on the accompanying figure to help you pinpoint their locations. The body points you'll be working are: *(See Fig.16.1)*

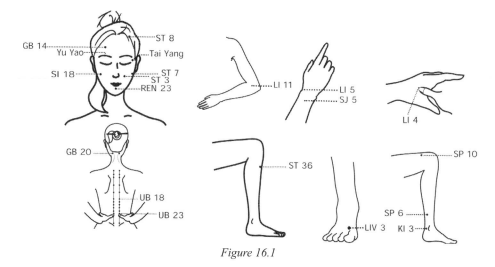

Figure 16.1

LI 11: To find this point on the large intestine channel, called the Qu Chi, bend your arm at the elbow and you should be able to clearly see the ending of the crease on the underside of your elbow. The point is in the depression right at the ending of that crease.

SP 6: This is a key point on the inside of the leg between the knee and ankle where the liver, spleen and kidney channels meet. It's name is San Yin Jiao, which literally means the crossroads of the three Yin meridians. Feel for the big bone protruding from the inside of your ankle (the medial malleolus) and then locate this point 3 cun (3 thumb widths) straight up just behind tibia bone. Important point for tonifying and regulating the liver, spleen and kidney organ systems, promote Qi and blood circulation, benefit overall skin condition.

SP 10: The Chinese name, Xue Hai, means a sea of blood. If you think of your kneecap as a square, this point is 2 cun (2 thumb widths) above the upper and inner corner. Working it promotes blood circulation, including to the facial area.

LIV 3: This is a "source point" for the liver system, meaning any activation of the point directly affects the liver itself. It's located an inch behind the forward edge of the web between your big toe and second toe.

ST 36: Called Zu San Li, this is a point along the stomach meridian just below each knee. Activating these symmetrical points gives you the strength to go for three miles, which is what the Chinese name means. Locate the mushy point just below your kneecap and then moving 3 cun (3 thumb widths) down along the shinbone, then one thumb-width toward the outer side.

This is one of the most important points that tonifies Qi and blood, helps support body's healthy immune system, and improves your overall skin condition.

UB 18: This one, although it's on the Urinary Bladder channel, is known as the Gan Shu, with "gan" meaning liver and "shu" meaning the point on the back where the Qi of corresponding organs is gathered. It's the point where liver Qi is infused into the back. Reach behind you and touch the lower tip of your wing bone (scapula). Move your finger down 1 cun (1 thumb width) and over 1 cun and a half toward your spine. The point is about one and a half cun away form your vertebra on either side.

UB 23: Another very important point on the Bladder channel where kidney Qi is infused into the back. Put each pointer finger on your outer hip bone and move them up about two inches. Now move them toward the center behind you, stopping about 1 cun (1 thumb width) and a half before the spine. The point is there, on either side.

LI 4: This is the He Gu, or "Union Valley" energy point that's a commander point for the face. Spread index finger and the thumb, use the other thumb and press on the web between the index finger and the thumb, where the tip of your thumb touches it, there's your He Gu.

LI 5: This is the "Yang Ravine." Put your hand in front of you, palm down, and open it up by spreading the fingers. The point is in the depression of your wrist on the thumb side, between the two tendons.

SJ 5: A very important "gate" point on the Triple Burner channel. Bend your spread hand back toward you without moving your forearm and you'll see a line right where the wrist and hand meet (the wrist line). The point is two inches up from that line, right in the center of the forearm.

KI 3: Between the medial malleolus (the inside ankle bone) and the Achilles tendon is a "great ravine" where lies the Tai Xi (or KI 3) energy point. The name, indeed, means "great ravine" or "canyon." It is called a "yuan" source point, meaning it contains vital kidney energy. It strongly nourishes the kidney organ system, tonifying dry wrinkled skin due to Yin deficiency.

The facial points you'll be working are: *(See Fig16.1)*

SI 18: Look carefully at the accompanying illustration to find this point on the small intestine channel. Trace straight down from the outer corner of each eye until you come to your cheekbone. Go down a little further to the lower part of that bone and you'll feel a depression start. At the border of the lower cheek bone and the depression is SI 18.

GB 14: Called Yang Bai, it's another facial point along the gallbladder channel. Activating it benefits the whole eye area and helps smooth forehead wrinkles.

GB 20: Known as Feng Chi and occupying the pool-like depression under the occipital bone at either side of the base of your skull located by bending your head forward and run your fingers up the muscled part of the back of your neck to the points just before hitting the skull bone.

ST 3: Trace your fingers down from the very middle of the lower eye socket and stop at a point just in level with the lower border of your nostrils.

ST 7: Or Xia Guan. It's a motor point along the stomach channel just below the zygomatic bone. It is a powerful motor point. Massage on ST 7 can activating abundant Qi and blood flow in the facial area since it belongs to the stomach or Yang Ming channel which is full of Qi and blood. It's also an excellent point for lifting chin wrinkles that have resulted from muscle "prolapsed" or "falling down."

ST 8: A point at the corner of the hairline, about a half cun (thumb width) into the hair.

Tai Yang: This refers to a point at either temple, not the urinary bladder channel. It's a special point, not belonging to any meridian. It is a powerful point for pulling the Yang energy together. Gently massage on it helps smooth wrinkles around out side of the eyes.

Yu Yao: This means the "waistline of a fish" and you'll find it at the very center of each eyebrow. It's an "extra point," meaning it doesn't belong to any meridian. This is good for forehead line and wrinkles around the eyes.

REN 24: It's right below your chin, in the center.

20-Minute Face Workout For Blemishes and Blotches

Do this acupressure massage once or twice a day, every day.

Step1: Wash your face, apply a thin layer of cream, especially if you have natural skin brightening cream, and sit in a comfortable chair. Let your body relax.

Activate facial points from the kidney, liver, stomach, large intestine and Du channels. Use both index fingers, massage in a circular motion each of the following points. In order, 25 times clockwise and 25 times counter-clockwise: UB18, UB 23, KI 3, LIV 3, REN 24, SP 6, SP 10, LI 4, LI 5, SJ 5. *(See Fig.16.1)*

Step 2: Now you'll massage the facial points. Use both index fingers, massage the following points 50 times clockwise (except SI 18, ST 3 and GB 14, for which you'll make 100 clockwise circles each) and 50 times counter-clockwise (except S 18, ST 3 and GB 14, which will each get 100 counter-clockwise massage circles). Massage them in the following order, even though the number of circles varies: GB 14, SI 8, Tai Yang, GB 20, ST 8, ST 3, ST 7, LI 18, REN 24. *(See Fig.16.1)*

Step 3: Now for the Ashi points, which is simply the name of the spots where the discoloration is, use either your index finger or middle finger (or both) to massage each discolored or dark spot 50 times counter-clockwise

10-Minute Facial Bath Massage and Ear Acupressure

We call this a "facial bath" because you use your full palm to "bathe" the face with energy. Do this acupressure routine if you don't have enough time to do the facial massage exercise above. Both help clear up discoloration and give you a more radiant complexion.

Step 1: Wash your face and apply natural based skin brightening cream if you have. Sit comfortably on a chair and relax. Use the finger pads of your index or middle fingers, massage both sides of your nose from top to bottom, using 50 back-and-forth motions. *(See Fig.16.2)*

Step 2: Use both your palms, massage the cheek area, up and outward, for 50 strokes. *(See Fig.16.3)*

Step 3: Use the pads of four fingers on each hand, massage the forehead, rubbing from the middle toward the Tai Yang area. Rub 50 times. *(See Fig.16.4)*

Figure 16.2   Figure 16.3   Figure 16.4

Step 4: Use both thumbs to massage the UB 23 and UB 18 areas back and forth, 50 times each. *(See Fig.16.5)*

Step 5: Using the illustration as a guide, massage the following ear points, 30 time each with your index finger: Face, Liver, Kidney, Lung (2 places for both side of lungs), Endocrine, Ovary (for woman), Brain cortex, Adrenal Gland. *(See Fig.16.6)*

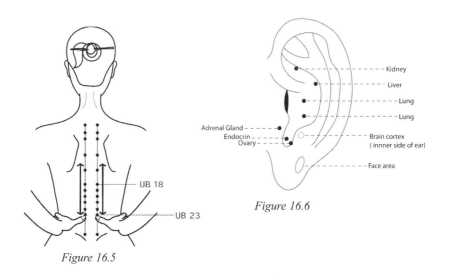

Figure 16.6

Figure 16.5

Channel Massage for a Radiant Complexion

Going through all the points in the two previous routines can be difficult. While mastering those techniques, take advantage of the following simple routine based on Yin/Yang paired channels, rather than points. Use the illustration to guide you. Start from as high as you can reach.

Step 1: The first pair of channels to massage is the kidney (KI) and urinary bladder (UB) channels, one at a time. Use dry luffa or both hands to massage the KI channels from the sole of each foot (which is the KI 1 point) along the channel all the way up to the groin area. Repeat 10 times. *(See Fig.16.7)*

Then do the same with the UB channels, going up and down from the UB-17 to the sacrum area 10 times. Massage the UB channel from the back of the thigh down to the end of the channel at the tip of the small toe 10 times. (Caution: pregnant women should avoid massaging lower back and the small toe.) *(See Fig.16.7)*

Step 2: Now you'll massage the lung (LU) and large intestine (LI) channels. They're both in the arms. Massage the LU channel

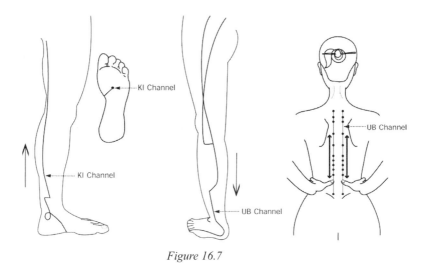

Figure 16.7

from the upper arm toward the fingers. Then massage the LI channel starting at the index finger and moving up to the arm. *(See Fig.16.8)*

Step 3: The third channel pair you'll massage is the liver (LIV) and gallbladder (GB) channels. Start with the LIV channel. From the big toe, work up to the inner thigh. Then move your fingers to the outside of the leg and from there, work the GB channel from the thigh down to your feet, stopping at the fourth toe. *(See Fig.16.9)*

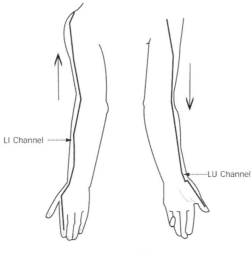

Figure 16.8

Step 4: One more extra channel to finish up: the SJ or Triple Burner. Go from the back of your upper arm to the end of your ring finger (go against the channel flow at this time), as shown. *(See Fig.16.10)*

Step 5: Now rub both hands together 36 times and give your face a warm massage, rubbing out and up (never down) from the chin.

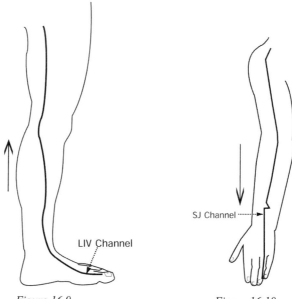

Figure 16.9   *Figure 16.10*

Tips From Ping

Gua Sha is a method in Chinese medicine to get rid of toxins and cleanse the entire body system. You can use it for facial discoloration. You use a device (called Gua Sha Board) to gently scrape the skin right where the dark spots are, or at points used in acupressure routines for discoloration.The force of the scraping should be slight but steady, enough to turn the skin surface just slightly red.

CHAPTER 17

Qi Gong For a Pure Complexion

As I've mentioned so many times, the root of all Chinese healing lies in the Three Treasures — energy, essence and spirit. Only when these Three Treasures are in balance can the body achieve a healthy state that is reflected in a smooth, youthful-looking face.

That concept is worth mentioning again as you begin to use Qi Gong exercises to help your face achieve its natural, clear and spotless complexion. Qi Gong is all about balancing energy, essence and spirit.

In Qi Gong, you use your mind, body and breathing to smooth the flow of life energy (Qi) and calm your spirit. This balance helps boost your body's ability to cleanse itself and dispel toxins. That not only promotes a clear facial complexion, but also greatly enhances your overall health, including your skin from head to toe.

This amazing healing ability of Qi Gong is not merely theory. It's a tried-and-true technique that helped countless people improve their facial coloration for thousands of years.

Keep in mind that as effective as it is, Qi Gong will not clarify your complexion and rid your face of dark spots on its own. It is one key element in an overall face-saving program that also includes herbal supplements, food therapy, acupressure, and a healthy life style.

Two Wonderful Face-Saving Qi Gong Exercises

I've selected two fairly simple Qi Gong routines to balance your internal organs, especially the kidney, liver and spleen systems. Traditional Chinese Medicine long ago discovered that those organs are strongly connected to the clarity of the complexion.

More specifically, the following exercises are designed to:

■ Promote Qi and blood flow to the facial area.
■ Tonify kidney and liver essence.
■ Balance the entire internal organ system.

You may find these exercises a little awkward at first. But practice every day and they'll soon feel natural.

Ancient Chinese Exhalation Exercise

This is an amazing Qi Gong routine that Chinese physicians have long practiced to strengthen the internal organs. It's primarily a breathing exercise, but as you'll see, there's a vocal component that adds an entirely new dimension.

The sounds you'll be coordinating with your breathing should be made softly, almost inaudibly. Even if there were somebody else in the area, only you would be able to hear them.

This exercise will nourish and purify your face by activating kidney essence, by moving liver and heart blood, and by building up spleen Qi and unblocking lung Qi.

Step1: Sit comfortably in a chair with your feet about shoulder-width apart on the floor, and your hands placed lightly on your knees. Relax your body. Relax your mind. Take three slow breaths, nice, natural and deep. Lightly clench your teeth 36 times. Then press your tongue against the roof of your mouth nine times. If you feel the need to swallow saliva as you do this, that's fine.

Step 2: Lower your face slightly toward the ground, keeping your hands loose as you breath in clean air through your nose. Then, as you breathe out, tighten both hands around your knees as you softly make the sound "Chuai" or "Choo-aye." According to TCM theory, this sound connects directly with the kidneys. Repeat six times.

Step 3: Now slightly (not tightly) close your eyes as you inhale through the nose and then exhale while making the sound "Shu." This is for your liver. Repeat six times.

Step 4: Take the breath in naturally and shape your mouth into a small circle as you breathe out with the (spleen) sound "Hu." Repeat six times.

Step 5: Breath in naturally through you nose, and make the lung sound of "Xi" or "Shee" as you breathe out. Repeat six times.

Step 6: This time as you exhale, slowly raise one hand out and up, palm up, to shoulder height while drawing out the sound "Ke." As you finish the sound, move your hand back down toward the Dan Tian, ending up with your palm facing the Dan Tian but not touching it. Repeat 6 times, alternating the hand you raise. The "Ke" sound is for the heart.

Step 7: Finally, still sitting in your relaxed position, concentrate on the Dan Tian area for a full minute. Breath naturally. Then imagine bringing the energy from the bottom of both feet along the inner sides of your legs, through the abdomen, chest and throat, all the way to the face. Feel the warmth in eyes, the nose, and the entire face. Repeat 3 times.

You don't need to go through the whole set each time when you do this exercise. You can rotate two or three organ systems and the sound that goes with them each time you perform this routine.

Zen Inner Visualization for Clear and Beautiful Skin

This ancient mind exercise comes from noted Tong Dynasty TCM physician Sun Shi Mao. Practice this routine daily to rejuvenate your entire body's skin, but with special emphasis on a bright, luminous complexion and lustrous hair.

Traditionally, this exercise has two steps. I added the 3rd step to emphasize facial complexion concerns. If on any particular day you find yourself short of time to finish the entire routine, simply start with the second step and make sure you include the third.

Do this exercise in the early morning, facing south.

Step 1: Sitting comfortably in a chair, let your hands relax as you place them on your knees. Slowly move all your body joints — wrists, neck, knees, and ankles — as you take easy, deep breaths. Imagine that you're breathing out unclean Qi and breathing in clear air from nature.

Now do the following 9 to 12 times each to get the body's Yang energy activated:

- Open up both arms, moving them up down, right and left.
- Open and close your eyes and your mouth.
- Alternately clench and unclench your teeth.
- "Comb" your hair back with all 10 fingers.
- Pull both ears in various directions.
- Pull your lower back forward and then push it back.
- Make soft coughs.

When you finish these movements, let your spirit calm back down. Sit still, relax, and move to the next step.

Step 2: Create in your mind a composite of the universe's harmonized Yin and Yang energy in the form of a purple cloud with the five color streams, namely, red, yellow, white, blue/black and green, representing the five elements, in a clean, after-it-rains sky. Imagine this beautiful cloud softly descending to your hair, then slowly entering through the vertex (crown) of your head, moving through the flesh and skull to your brain, and then penetrating to your abdomen and out to the extremities, like spring water seeping into fresh ground. Then feel your entire organ systems nourished by this energy cloud.

Notice the cloud's energy entering the Dan Tian area, and reaching a point at the bottom of each foot. This is the Kidney-1 point, called the Yong Quan or "Gushing Spring." *(See Fig.17.1)* Feel your body accept this energy as the Qi channels open up, nourishing all the organs.

Step 3: Now imagine all this energy circulating to your face, letting the face "breathe in" freely the nutrients being delivered by the energy and then "breathing" out the stagnation that creates the discoloration and dark spots. Keep focusing on this healthy energy exchange until you sense a warm, sweaty feeling in the facial area. It should take about one or two minutes.

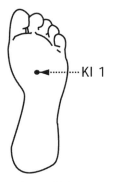

Figure 17.1

CHAPTER 18

Nourish Your Complexion With Healing Foods

There's beauty in your kitchen! A major part of your beautifying regimen is simply to include in your diet certain foods that have been shown for thousands of years to help brighten and even out your facial complexion. Beyond their nutritional value, the foods recommended in this chapter provide a therapeutic effect on your internal blood and Qi flow that will be reflected in your face.

Food therapy for your facial complexion adheres to the basic tenet of Chinese medical philosophy, which holds that external beauty is a mirror reflecting internal health. These foods help address the internal imbalances that result in a spotted or discolored complexion. Of course, their beneficial effect is gradual, and for best results your food therapy program must go hand in hand with the other complexion treatments — herbs, acupressure and Qi Gong.

10 Miracle Foods for a Spotless and Radiant Face

Some of the best foods that the Chinese associate with a good complexion are so common you'll be surprised at the benefits they hold. Others are more exotic, and might require a little searching around in Chinese or other Asian markets. There's no strict regimen to follow with these or any other skin-saving foods. Try to include as many of these foods as you can in your regular meals.

1. Dong Gua *(Winter Melon)*

You already know this gourd vegetable and its seeds as a healing herb, but it's also a very popular health food in China, especially as a soup. It benefits the heart, detoxifies the body and beautifies the skin. Whether eaten as a food or taken in herb form, Dong Gua improves your complexion by removing wind from the skin.

Winter melon is an especially worthwhile addition to your diet if you have complexion problems as well as eye bags or dark eye circles. Eating it regularly also helps you lose weight.

You should have no trouble finding winter melon most of the year in Asian markets or even in Western-style organic food stores. It's also called wax gourd or white gourd. Eat it as you would any melon, peeling off the outer skin. Remove the seeds and pulp, but save them for topical use for an even more radiant and spotless skin.

2. Si Gua   *(Luffa)*

You may only know this vine plant from the sponges made from the fibers inside the overripe fruit, but the young vegetable is a traditional food in China and one of my favorites for keeping my complexion young looking. It enters and clears the liver and stomach channels.

You can easily grow these zucchini-like vegetables yourself if you have the space. I do, and I enjoy their benefits all summer long. You also should be able to find them at Chinese markets. Prepare them as you would any squash. It also makes an excellent topical mask for dealing with wrinkles, dark spots and uneven facial discoloration.

3. Bai Luo Be *(White Turnip)*

This is a fairly common turnip, often called daikon, which offers plenty of medicinal benefits. In TCM terms, Bai Luo Be is acrid, sweet and cool in nature, entering the spleen and lung channels to detoxify the body and free up stagnating fluids in the channels. I've observed a definite beneficial effect on the complexion when Bai Luo Be is eaten regularly. The best way to use it for facial discoloration is to juice it every morning and drink about a half cup.

4. Shi Zi *(Persimmon)*

Most people know about this delicious fruit, but rarely eat them. If you want to reduce dark spots on your face, you should eat them often. Shi Zi has been known for centuries to clear heat from the body, nourish the lungs and moisten the skin — all actions that improve your complexion. They're also rich in vitamins C and A, potassium, calcium and iron. The leaves of the plant are also used as herbs.

You may find two different kinds of persimmons. The Chinese version is sometimes called kaki. Both the Chinese and the American persimmons are great for your complexion. You can eat them on their own, but make sure they're very ripe. Don't eat the skin. Dried persimmons are a special treat that you might be able to find in Chinese markets. Another way to use persimmon to brighten the complexion is by simply applying the fresh peel to the face.

5. Sang Shen Zi *(Mulberry Fruit)*

I've already recommended herbal extracts of mulberry as a wrinkle-reducing treatment. Now try eating the mulberry fruit itself, called Sang Shen Zi, to help clear and brighten your complexion. Mulberry trees have a long history in Chinese medicine. They're used to raise silkworms, which eat the leaves as their main source of nutrition. As we saw in Chapter 15, dried silkworm is an excellent complexion herb.

The fruit of the mulberry isn't a true berry, but it's berry-like in taste and appearance, and contains beneficial antioxidants also found in blueberries, raspberries and the like. One plant chemical (phytonutrient) found in mulberry fruit and berries, called cyanin, is responsible for the red or purplish color and is thought to have a strong therapeutic effect. From a TCM point of view, Sang Shen Zi is a blood tonic that benefits the Yin and kidneys, helps overcome weakness, and brightens a withered-looking complexion as well as clearing dark spots from the face.

Mulberry fruit is sweet tasting and a little tart, and can be eaten as you would any berry. If you can't find the raw fruit itself, try searching the net or your local health food stores for fresh raw mulberry juice.

6. Bai Gou *(Ginkgo Nut)*

The health benefits of ginkgo leaf extract have been widely discovered in the West. Much modern research indicates that the antioxidant plant chemicals in ginkgo benefit blood flow, and may even slow memory loss.

Not many are aware that in Chinese medicine, the nut of the ginkgo tree is more often used medicinally. Ginkgo nut extract is used herbally, but the whole nuts themselves, often roasted, are a traditional Chinese food that nourishes lung energy and calm wheezing. The best way to use ginkgo to clear the complexion is topically, crushing the fresh nuts into a paste and applying directly.

7. Yi Yi Ren *(Coix Seed)*

You've already met this wonderful barley-like grain as beneficial food for smoothing wrinkles and clearing the eye area. But it deserves special mention here for its ability to clear up discoloration of the facial complexion.

Yi Yi Ren is a very effective strengthener of the digestive system, and I constantly see it slowly but steadily clearing away yellowish facial discoloration in my patients. It also helps for age spots and other dark facial spotting.

Coix is a better protein source than most other grain seeds, and it's rich in vitamins. Coix oil is very good for your skin. It's easy to find at Chinese food stores, and you can eat it almost daily simply by cooking 12-15 grams of the raw seed in your soup. Another excellent way to include coix seed in your diet every day is to make and drink the Homemade Soy Milk recipe given in Chapter 8, which includes coix seeds.

8. Eggs

Chicken eggs are considered a superior herb/food in Traditional Chinese Medicine, with a surprising variety of beneficial effects. As a food, eggs anchor the heart and calm the five organ systems. The whites clear heat from the lungs, detoxify the body and nourish the skin. Those actions help brighten the face, smooth wrinkles and clear away dark spots. The yolks tonify the blood, helping to rejuvenate a withered, pale complexion, which is often the result of blood deficiency.

You can eat eggs every day if you have a healthy, balanced lifestyle. If you're not eating a lot of saturated fats in your diet, your body can handle the cholesterol in eggs without harm. If you do have a cholesterol problem, you can eat just the whites.

A good way to eat eggs is to put beaten eggs in soups, especially soups with luffa and tomatoes.

Another common use of eggs as a beauty product is topical. If you have discoloration in the face and dry skin, apply the raw beaten yolk and white together as a mask. If you have oily skin, use just the egg white as a mask.

9. Feng Mi *(Honey)*

The ancient Chinese Taoists lauded honey as a superior herb that calms the five organs and nourishes Qi. They thought of honey as the reliever of hundreds of diseases with the ability to harmonize the actions of hundreds of other herbs ingested into the body.

Having a little bit of honey every day in warm water or with your favorite tea will work just fine. Regular, long-term honey use strengthens will power and "enlightens" the body to prolong life. It also promotes a radiant, rosy complexion, making your face, according to one text, "as beautiful as a flower."

If you want to try something even more potent than honey, try Royal Jelly instead. Use it orally or topically. Use only 1/4 teaspoon in warm water if you're going to drink it down. Topically, apply Royal Jelly every night and wash it off the next morning.

Again, remember that if you are allergic to bee products, you should not use honey or Royal Jelly internally or topically. To know for sure, take just a tiny bit internally, or apply a dab to a small area on the inner side of your wrist. If there is any reaction, don't use it again.

10. Shan Yao *(Chinese Yam)*

Chinese yam is considered a main course in China, not a side dish. It's eaten as much for its medicinal properties as its taste. Shan Yao is sweet, warm and neutral. It tonifies heart energy, strengthens the stomach, spleen and lung systems, and nourishes kidney Qi. All those actions benefit the skin and hair, promoting a radiant facial complexion and helping to eliminate discoloration and dark spots.

Fresh Chinese yam is easy to find, and you should eat it often. For variety, buy dried yam at a Chinese market and include 12 grams in your soup. You can also grind the dried yam into a powder and add it whatever flour you're baking with.

Other Foods that are Great for Dark Spots and Facial Discoloration

- **Tomato:** Use it as a soup stock, or juice it and drink. It's also very effective as a facial application.
- **Eggplant:** Simply cut it into small pieces and rub it on the dark spot until the area is slightly reddened. Leave the area unwashed for an hour. Do this every day for 10 days.
- **Mung Bean:** Cook it as a bean soup or grind it into a powder to make a facial mask for dark spots and discoloration.
- **Black Bean:** Eat it often in soup, or cook it first and add it to salads or other dishes.
- **Peas:** Big green peas can be cooked any style you like. You can also mash them into paste and apply topically.
- **Cucumber:** It's great cooked, raw, in soups, or applied topically.
- **Chinese Cabbage:** Cook it any style, or juice it to include in a vegetable juice cocktail. It's also good applied topically.
- **Water Chestnuts:** Juice with other ingredients, or cook them any style you like.

Recipes For A Clear And Radiant Complexion

It's easy to incorporate complexion-improving foods into your diet. With most of them, it's simply a question of buying them and eating them. To give you an idea of how to get started, here are some extremely simple recipes. The ingredients include some foods or herbs introduced in previous chapters.

- **Vegetable Mix**
  Chop equal portions of tomato, cucumber, carrots, pumpkin (cooked), white turnip and Chinese cabbage and serve as a salad with a vinegar and olive oil dressing. On alternate days, you can throw this vegetable mix into the blender and drink it down as a juice.

- **Fruit and Yogurt Shake**
  Peel and core a tomato, persimmon (well rapped), pear and apple and put them in a blender. Add a handful of strawberries, 1/8 lemon (without the skin and seeds), 1/2 teaspoon of honey and a cup of plain yogurt. As a desert or simply a pleasure drink, this fruit combination cleans and purifies the skin.

■ **Face-Saver Soup**
Soak a handful of black fungus (Hei Mu Er) in hot water for 30 minutes and then cut it into small pieces. Put it into a pot with 6 cups boiling water and add 1/4 of a luffa (sliced), one chopped tomato, 1/4 of a lotus root (chopped), 1/2 pound of winter melon (sliced), 2 ounces of black beans, 10 seedless Chinese dates, and a pound of pork bone. Season to taste, bring to a fast boil and then simmer for about 1 hour. Add fresh cilantro at the end. Eat this soup daily to relieve toxicity, promote blood circulation and beautify your face.

Food on Your Face

As we've seen, many of the foods that benefit your complexion when eaten can also be applied to your face directly to enhance the results. Here are some of the food masks that I've found work best. Be sure to check for allergies first by applying a small amount on an area inside your wrist and waiting a day to see if there's a reaction.

For the following foods, you can assume that the mask treatments can be repeated daily for 10 days (unless instructed otherwise). Then rest for several days and re-start. Remember, you don't need to use these for your whole life. Use them periodically, along with other foods and other treatment modalities (herbs, acupressure, Qi Gong). Again, do not forget to do a skin test by applying a small amount of herbal mask or wash in the inner side of your wrist for 24 hours to make sure you are not allergic to them.

■ **Ginkgo Nut Mask**
Crush unshelled ginkgo nuts into a paste, adding a little water if necessary. Apply it directly to your face and rinse off. Do this every other day.

■ **Eggplant Rub**
Cut off a good-sized chunk of fresh raw eggplant and rub the fleshy part around your face until the skin gets a little red. Wait 20 minutes then rinse.

■ **Honey Mask**
Pour a little honey into a small bowl, dip your fingers in and rub the honey onto your face. Leave it for 10 minutes and wash out.
For an even better honey mask, mix a teaspoon of honey with a half teaspoon of Fu Ling (Poria) powder and half an egg to make a mask. Leave on for 10 minutes before washing off. Variation: Use Royal Jelly instead of honey.

■ **Honey and Fu Ling Mask**

Mix a teaspoon of honey with 1/2 teaspoon of Fu Ling (poria) powder. Don't use an egg with this combination. Apply it to your face and leave it on for 20 minutes before washing off.

■ **Winter Melon Mask**

Mash the fleshy part of a winter melon/or crash 1/2 cup of winter melon seeds and rub it right onto your face. Leave it there for 20 minutes, then rinse off.

■ **Egg in White Grain Alcohol**

Soak seven eggs in 500 grams of grain alcohol and store in a tightly sealed jar for seven days. Open and stir up one of the eggs each day and apply it to your face for a few minutes and wash off. Do this daily for one week.

■ **Luffa, Cucumber and Tomato Mask**

Mix together one fresh luffa, one cucumber and one tomato. Drink half of it and use the rest as a topical mask, rubbing some of it on your face and washing it off.

■ **Persimmon Leaf Mask**

Look for persimmons with leaves still attached or ask at a Chinese grocery for persimmon leaf. Dry the leaves and then crush them into a powder. Blend 50 grams of the dried persimmon leaf powder and mix with olive oil to form a sticky mask. Apply it to the spotted or discolored part of your face and leave it on overnight. Wash away in the morning. You should do this every night for at least two weeks, but not more than a month.

■ **Cilantro Wash**

Simply take several stalks of fresh cilantro, wash and boil in 6 oz of water for couple of minutes and then use the juice to wash the face daily.

PART FIVE

FINE TUNING YOUR BEAUTY STRATEGY

CHAPTER 19

30-Day Personal Holistic Program For Your Age Group

Unlike conventional Western medicine, Traditional Chinese Medicine is personal. We emphasize the individual.

As you've seen time and again throughout this book, TCM looks at the whole body, not just the area where the problem is (or seems to be).

We also base our diagnosis on all aspects of the individual — your mind, body, and spirit.

Chinese medicine doesn't look at disease in the abstract. Instead, it looks at the patterns of disease in you as an individual, your signs, symptoms, and overall mental and emotional condition.

One way you can apply TCM's personal emphasis to your at-home facial beauty program is to choose the remedies that suit your age. TCM divides life into distinct stages. Diagnosis and treatment varies according to the life stage.

The TCM age categories I use are "Young Adult" (18-25), "Prime Time" (25-50) and "Mature Prime Time" (50 and up). In this chapter I'm going to give you complete 30-day programs to follow based on your age category.

These programs stress the inside-out and natural approaches according to TCM that differentiate from standard Western medicine. The key points are:

- Beauty is health. These programs are designed to help you achieve the inner health that will be reflected in a bright, smooth, youthful-looking face.

- Inner health depends on balanced organ systems, with each system working well in and of itself, and in harmony with all the other systems.

- Facial beauty, as all health, depends on the Three Treasures — life energy, essence and spirit.

- Nature's way is the best way. The treatments you'll be using with these programs are the treatments we've dealt with throughout this book — all natural herbs, foods, acupressure techniques and Qi Gong exercises.

- A healthy lifestyle is an essential component of any beauty program.

Tips From Ping

Be sure to include your Qi Gong exercises and acupressure routines as you follow the lifestyle and food guidelines in these 30-day programs. All Traditional Chinese Medicine self-treatments work together to beautify your skin.

Young Adults (18 to 25)

If you're in this age group you're prone to excesses of all kinds, including Yang energy and unhealthy lifestyle choices. Skin problems are typically blemishes, oiliness and acne. Follow this 30-day program to clear up those problems, and delay the onset of wrinkles.

Young Adult Skin Care Program

Do these steps each day.

Step1: Exfoliate your face. Use 1 gram of pearl powder with a blend of 1/4 cup of crushed mung beans or brown rice. Use a blender or coffee grinder to crush the ingredients. Stir the powder into 2 ounces of water until it is dissolved. Use some of the resulting mixture to scrub your face. Save the rest of the powder mix for later use.

Step 2: Wash with chrysanthemum tea. Put five petals of wild chrysanthemum into two cups of water. Bring to a boil and then let it simmer for 15 minutes. Drink half of this as a tea. Use the other half as an external wash. Simply dip a face cloth into the tea (once it cools) and apply it to your face. Leave the liquid on for 20 minutes before rinsing.

Step 3: Use an herbal anti-acne powder. Make an herbal powder with equal amounts of the following ingredients (you can use 1 gram of each, and keep it for reuse until used up): gypsum powder, pearl powder, salvia, skullcap, rhubarb bark, safflower and cicada shell powder. Mix with water and apply to the problem area twice a day. Leave it on 20 minutes in the daytime, and overnight. If the acne spot is oozing, add 1 gram of Atractylodes lance powder.

Step 4: Use a good, natural facial moisturizer. It should be able to moisturize the face while working to close enlarged pores and regulate the secretion of oil glands.

Your skin is already aging at this early stage of your life, so now's a good time to take preventive steps. Keep your skin clean always, don't let it get dehydrated, and protect it from the sun. Do the anti-wrinkle massage described in Chapter 6 once a day.

Inner Body Adjustment For Young Adults

Young adults' skin problems, such as acne, result from inner body imbalances, especially hormonal imbalances. Pimples with pus are the accumulation of phlegm dampness intermingled with heat.

The solution calls for lifestyle adjustments, body cleansing, and the right diet.

To cleanse your body and balance your Yin and Yang, concentrate on the following for the next 30 days:

- *Regulate your sleep patterns.* Get to bed before 11:00. The period between 11 pm and 1 am is when your liver system is best rested and rejuvenated. Adequate sleep gives your skin a chance to self-repair.

- *Avoid fried foods, oily foods, spicy foods and sweets.* They cause fire and heat in the body. Instead, add more bitter greens to your diet, like spinach.

- *Avoid alcohol and smoking.* They cause fire and heat, aging the skin.

- *Control your emotions.* A balanced emotional state is essential for a balanced inner body. Out-of-control emotions are the biggest enemy of internal balance, and can cause many different kinds of skin problems, including rapid aging and acne. De-stress your self with meditation. And try to do a relaxing Qi Gong exercise every day.

- *Avoid constipation.* Get plenty of healthy fiber from vegetables and whole grains. This will also free your body of toxins. When the large intestine is blocked, the accumulated toxins flow to its paired organ, the lung system, which controls the health of your skin.

- *Avoid stimulating the acne.* Try to keep your hands away from the affected area.

Tips From Ping

It can sometimes be quite difficult for young people to calm down enough to perform the Qi Gong exercises. If that's the case with you, give yourself 10 minutes a day for relaxation, even if it's when you lie down to go to sleep. Tell yourself to empty your brain. Close your eyes and focus on the top of your head and repeat the word "relax" three times. Then focus on your face and repeat "relax" three more times. Keep this up as you move your focus down through the parts of your body, including the shoulders, chest, elbows, wrists, lower abdomen, knees, and the soles of your feet.

Practice this for couple of days. You'll begin to like it, you'll appreciate more the importance of taking care of your body, and you'll be able to do the Qi Gong exercises more easily.

Young Adults' Diet Cure

Now to your diet. The following is a food cure specifically for young adult complexion problems, including acne.

Breakfast: Make one of the following fruit-and-vegetable juices and drink 8 ounces of it each morning.

1. Blend together equal amounts of green grapes, cucumber, bitter melon, dandelion, lemon, and green apple. Add 0.5 grams of pearl powder. This juice is best for all kinds of acne conditions, and also acts as an internal body and skin cleanser.

2. Blend together equal amounts of watermelon (be sure to include the white part between the red and green parts), celery, fresh luffa, burdock root, dandelion, tomato, carrots, and pear. Add 0.5 grams of pearl powder. This is especially good for acute and cystic acne conditions.

Along with the juice, the main ingredients of your breakfasts should be yogurt (homemade if possible), whole grain bread, and boiled or poached eggs.

Lunch: Choose from the following lunches:

1. Mixed bitter green vegetables, boiled or fresh in salads. Lean meats (not fried), tofu, seaweed as a soup or salad.
2. A soup made with an equal amount of coix seed, black fungus, mung beans, seaweed, celery, tofu and lotus root, with a chicken or bone base.

With either meal, include a cup of tea made with chrysanthemum and honeysuckle flower. There are pre-made teabags in Chinese stores.

Dinner: Include the following:

1. Soup made with coix seeds, mung beans, bitter melon and seaweed with a chicken or bone base. Serve every night as part of dinner.
2. Make a salad from fresh vegetables and fruits like cucumber, tomatoes, lotus root, watermelon, turnips, carrots, or seaweed. Use a vinegar or lemon dressing (no cream).
3. A main course of your choosing, but be sure to avoid shellfish like shrimp or lobster, and fatty or fried meats. Avoid spicy foods and sweets.

Prime Time (25-50)

Aging signs, including wrinkles, begin to appear soon after reaching this age group. Both men and women experience more pressure in life during these years. Kidney function, the immune system, cell renewal and hormone release begin to slow down. Your metabolic rate starts to decrease.

This is also when the facial beauty concerns we've been dealing with in this book begin to appear. You may begin to notice eye bags, dark circles under the eyes, wrinkles, sagging, graying of hair, and hair loss. Women going through pregnancy are prone to facial discolorations and dark spots.

These are all related to a decreased function of the internal organ systems, as well as to the external environmental conditions we all live with.

For all these reasons, it's especially important for people in this age group to seek body rejuvenation and work to prevent disease. Wrinkles, dark spots, discoloration, eye bags and dark circles are signs of internal imbalance. The following 30-day programs are designed to restore the internal balance for prime-time adults.

Here are three different options for your 30-day program, depending on which facial problem most concerns you. One is for wrinkles and sagging, another is for age spots and discoloration, and the third is for eye bags and puffiness.

Prime-Time 30-Day Anti-Wrinkle Program

Start off by adopting the following lifestyle changes:

1. Cleanse your body by eating a lot of fresh bitter greens and drinking lots of water.
2. Avoid sugar and sugar products.
3. Don't smoke or drink alcohol.
4. Avoid excessive sun exposure. Use a good sun block with a high SPF to protect your face from UV ray damage.
5. Develop a regular schedule. It should include going to bed before 11:00 pm to benefit your liver energy,
6. Learn to let go of stress. It will show on your face.
7. Watch for your facial expressions. Frowning folds the skin and causes wrinkles.
8. Keep the skin in a good hydration condition.
9. Take the anti-wrinkle herbs you've chosen from Chapter 5. Remember to consult with your doctor before starting on any herbal programs.
10. Keep eating the anti-wrinkle foods you chose from Chapter 8. Incorporate them into the breakfast-lunch-dinner suggestions in this Prime Time 30-day program.
11. Follow the anti-wrinkle facial massage protocols from Chapter 6 every day this month.
12. Practice the anti-wrinkle Qi Gong exercises from Chapter 7 every day this month.

13. Use a self-made anti-wrinkle mask from Chapter 5 or 8 every other day this month.

14. Choose a natural based, non—irritating anti-wrinkle and hydrating cream.

Now, here are your meal suggestions for the Prime Time 30-day anti-wrinkle and   anti-sagging program.

Breakfast: For 30 days, this will be your morning breakfast:

1. One tablespoon of tremella with honey. Mix a month's supply and store it in the freezer in four bags of equal size. Take one bag out at a time to use for the week.

2. One cup of soymilk with black beans, apricot seed (sweet), sesame, and walnuts, with an optional teaspoon of honey. See Chapter 8 for preparation instructions.

3. 1 poached egg

4. A half cup of cherries, red grapes, blueberries, or strawberries mix with 1/4 of an avocado.

5. One cup of green tea mixed with 2 dried chrysanthemum flowers and 0.3 g of pearl powder.

Lunch: This is your lunch for the next 30 days:

1. A cup of porridge made with black beans, tremella, and 1/2 cup of pig's skin jelly. See the instructions in Chapter 8

2. Lean meat or fish with a salad made of a selection from the following fruits and vegetables (raw or steamed): tomatoes, snow peas, various seasonal dark greens, cucumber, kiwi, strawberries, celery, bean sprouts, broccoli, and carrots. Serve with fresh lemon juice, olive oil or sesame oil.

3. One piece of whole multigrain bread.

4. One cup of green tea with several pieces of orange peel.

Dinner: On most days, have a big bowl of an anti-wrinkle soup made from the following: Pig's skin jelly, fish, tofu, sea cucumber, Chinese dates, seaweed, black fungus, black mushrooms, squid, and quail eggs (boil first and then take out of the shell). You do not have to choose all these ingredients in the soup, but whatever you include will help because they all have anti-aging properties. You'll find preparation instructions in Chapter 8.

On other days, choose fresh steamed fish often. Other main courses can come from the recipes in Chapter 8. Accompany with a cup of brown rice made together with black beans and red beans.

Prime-Time 30-Day Anti-Discoloration Program

Follow the first seven-lifestyle recommendations in the Prime Time 30-day anti-wrinkle program above. Also do the following:

- Take the anti-discoloration and anti-spot herbs you have chosen from Chapter 13.

- Keep eating the anti-discoloration and anti-spot food from Chapter 16 and work them into the breakfast-lunch-dinner recommendations in this chapter.

- Follow the facial discoloration and age spots massage protocols in Chapter 14 every day this month.

- Make anti-discoloration and age spot masks at home by your self, and use one every day this month. See Chapter 13 and 16 for instructions.

- Practice the Qi Gong exercises from Chapter 15 every day this month.

Here are your eating guidelines for the 30-day program. You can basically follow the anti-wrinkle breakfast plan given above. But also use these guidelines:

Breakfast: Include the following:

1. A fruit and vegetable juice made of 1/2 cup of each of the following: winter melon, white turnip, Chinese cabbage, cucumber, celery, 1/2 orange, one kiwi, 1/2 tomato, and 1/4 cup of cilantro. Drink 8 ounces each morning.

2. Squeeze 1/4 lemon juice into a cup of green tea and mix in 1/2 teaspoon of honey. Add 0.3 gram of pearl powder and drink.

Lunch: Include the following:

1. A mixed salad (raw or steamed) with Chinese cabbage, broccoli, black sesame seeds, tomatoes, and dark green leafy vegetables. Use sesame oil or sunflower oil with lemon juice for dressing.

2. A bowl of soup made with 2 ounces of tender lean meat, 1/2 cup of tofu, 1/2 cup of black fungus, and 2 cups of fresh luffa, peeled and cut into thin slices. Simply boil them together and add seasonings and black sesame oil.

3. A cup of brown rice made with coix seed and black beans.

4. Eat a dried or fresh persimmon every day as a snack.

Dinner: Include the anti-aging soup given above on most days. Choose the rest from the dishes described in Chapter 16. You want to eat a balanced diet with lots of dark fresh seasonal vegetables, organic animal liver, beans, winter melons, Chinese cabbage, and white turnip.

Tips From Ping

You can make anti-discoloration cookies to snack on or eat in the morning. Mix 2 cups of almond powder, a half cup of poria powder (Chinese stores will powder the poria for you), 1/2 teaspoon of black sesame powder (optional), 2 teaspoons of wild honey, an egg, and 2 teaspoons of olive oil. Knead into dough, form into cookies, and bake on a cookie sheet. Eat two per day.

Prime-Time 30-Day Eye-Beautifying Program

Follow the first seven recommendations in the Prime Time 30-day anti-wrinkle program given above. Also do the following:

- Keep taking the eye-beautifying herbs you have chosen from Chapter 9.
- Keep eating the eye-beautifying foods you have chosen from Chapter 12. Work them in to the recommended meals in this 30-day program.
- Follow the anti-wrinkle facial massage protocols from Chapter 6 every day this month.
- Make the eye-beautifying masks from Chapter 9 or 12 and use them every other day this month.
- Practice the eye-beautifying Qi Gong exercises from Chapter 11 every day this month.

Breakfast: Make a juice from equal amounts of the following fresh vegetables and fruits: Chinese cabbage, carrots, spinach, and blackberries. Make your omelet with chopped spinach, black mushrooms, onions and red pepper. For tea, add wolfberry and two dried chrysanthemum petals to a cup of green tea.

Lunch: Mix a salad with dark green vegetables and fruits: seaweed, sea grass, apricots (dried or fresh), mulberry fruit, and grilled fish. Serve with fresh squeezed ginger juice. Grill lean meats seasoned with ginger and cayenne pepper.

Dinner: Choose recipes from Chapter 12. Include lean meat, chicken, or beef or chicken liver with black fungus, Chinese dates, and wolfberries. You can use all of things in a casserole, adding 3 grams of poria and a teaspoon of crushed cinnamon.

Tips From Ping

A good between-meal snack for Prime-Time adults concerned about eye bags is a handful of dried wolfberries mixed with a cup of blackberries.

Mature Prime Time (50 and up)

This period of the life cycle is marked by a steep decline in your metabolism rate. Many are likely to see deep wrinkles and sagging of the chin and the eyes. This is due to a decline in kidney essence.

Aging is a natural process, but by adopting this healthy program and continuing your efforts with herbs, acupressure, Qi Gong and food therapy, you can slow down physical and mental aging. This program will help you maintain facial beauty by tonifying the body's essence.

Follow the first seven-lifestyle recommendations in the Prime Time 30-day program above. As a mature Prime-Timer, it's also important for you to adopt the following lifestyle recommendations:

- Exercise every day. The best choice is walking. Remember, life depends on movement.
- Keep calm and maintain a happy emotional state
- Eat healthy, easy-to-digest food
- Do facial massages daily, especially those from Chapter 6.

Tips From Ping

It is very important at this age period to use a nutritional based massage cream when performing your facial massages. In my clinic, I always use a facial cream with pearls and gin-seng and it always brings wonderful results.

- Keep up your favorite Qi Gong exercises from Chapter 7, 11 or 15.
- Use the facial masks from Chapter 5, 8, 9 12, 13 or 16 depending what your concerns are.
- Keep taking the herbs you've chosen from Chapter 5, 9 or 13 depending on your specific need.
- Use nourishing natural skin care products.

Tips From Ping

More facts about pearl powder. Especially for aged skin, pearl powder plays a big role in delaying skin from getting wrinkled and protecting it against age spots and a dull complexion. Not only does it contain many essential amino acids (the ones your body doesn't make itself), it also helps with the skin renewal process. Also high in calcium, which serves as a good calcium source for the increased calcium needs of older people.

Your diet program for these 30 days can basically follow the same guidelines as those given above for Prime-Timers. Choose the option that addresses your major concern — wrinkles, eyes bags, puffiness and dark circles or discoloration/age spots.

> **Tips From Ping**
> Everybody should drink at least six 8-ounce glasses of boiled warm water each day. This is especially important if you are in the Mature Prime-Time age group. But adjust the diet program to include the following recommendations for Mature Prime-Timers.

Breakfast: Always drink one cup of warm water before breafast. Also include one or more of the following four warm soups or drinks.

1. A cup of bird's nest soup or one cup of tremella soup each morning (See Chapter 8 for instructions.)
2. Prepare a decoction of caterpillar fungus by boiling 4 grams of the fungus (ask for it at Chinese herb stores) in water for 1-2 hours. Drink just 2 ounces a day. Or take 1 gram of caterpillar fungus powder with water per day.
3. Cook on medium, 3 grams of Chinese ginseng root in 2 cups of water for 30 minutes, drink 2 ounces of the tea daily. If you have high blood pressure, use American ginseng.
4. Drink one cup of green tea with 1 gram of pearl powder sweetened with 1/2 teaspoon of honey.

Also include the following with most meals:

- One cup of soymilk boiled with 1 ounce of black sesame seeds, 7 pieces of walnuts and 1/2 cup of oats. For the soymilk you can substitute organic 2% milk.
- One piece of whole grain bread
- One cup of mixed berries, especially cherries, blackberries, and mulberries.

> **Tips From Ping**
> For between-meal snacks make yourself a mix of pine nuts, sesame seeds, sunflower seeds, peanuts, and walnuts. Eat sparingly. Or prepare a bird's nest soup, it's a big plus for aging skin! You'll find instructions in Chapter 8.

Lunch: Most lunches should include:

1. Steamed or gilled fish, or less than 6 ounces of lean meat.
2. Dark green leafy vegetables (steamed or in a salad).

3. Black mushrooms, soybean sprouts, black and red beans, carrots. See chapters 8, 12 and 16 for ideas including these in dishes. Can be put in pig's feet or pig's skin soup.

4. Pig's feet or pig's skin soup. Make sure to skim the fat away by waiting until it cools down for the fat to form a layer on the surface.

Dinner: Including the following most days:

1. One big bowl of seafood soup made with fish, sea cucumber, mushrooms, black fungus, tofu, egg white, seaweed, and tomatoes. See Chapter 8 for instructions.

2. Mixed spring mix salad (masculine salad, raw or steamed) and 1 teaspoon of olive oil, and lemon juice.

3. 1cup of brown rice.

Your Alternatives

Again, if you can do the herbal preparations, food recipes for your skin concerns, that's great. But if you do not have time to search and prepare them, you can have an alternative way by using Nefeli supplements and skin care application, they rejuvenate the skin and body together, beautifying it from inside out.

CHAPTER 20

The Four Seasons of Life Rejuvenation

Way back in Chapter 1 we talked about a very basic Taoist principle that underlies all Chinese medicine. That principle is to follow nature's way. That's exactly what we've been doing throughout this book.

Traditional Chinese medicine teaches us another way to keep facial rejuvenation program in tune with nature.

Here you will learn to coordinate your anti-wrinkle and facial beauty treatments with one of nature's most marvelous and fundamental phenomena — the changing of the seasons.

With each season of the year, our body systems manifest themselves differently. These changes are reflected in our facial skin. Use the following season-based strategies to fine-tune the treatments you've been using. They will help you look even younger and healthier.

SPRING

In springtime, the Yin energy in nature decreases as the Yang energy increases. mother nature is waking up from the cold of winter, so the general direction of energy is upward.

The same is true with our bodies in spring. There is more blood and energy flow outward toward the extremities. Springtime facilitates the transportation of Qi (life energy), blood and body fluids.

So we need to replenish essence to our all body systems for maximum health in springtime. We need to maintain Yang energy. One way to do that is to get to sleep earlier and wake up earlier. Another is to start the day with refreshing exercise to augment your body's Yang energy.

According to TCM theory, the liver system is associated with the wood element, which in turn pertains to the spring season. Spring energy wants to flow upward and outward, and liver energy tends to do the same. That's why in spring it's important to avoid any emotional constraint. Such constraint will impede the free flow of liver energy. The resulting stagnation creates organ imbalance, suppressing the immune system and inviting disease that will show in your face.

So remember that in springtime you need to make a special effort to keep your mind clear and your mood happy. That will help the all-important liver energy to move smoothly throughout your body, helping keep your skin young looking.

Spring Food

The food you eat for beauty and health in springtime should be warm and tonifying. Such foods arouse Yang energy. Tonifying the spleen Yang is especially beneficial for health and beauty.

Make a special effort to avoid sweet and oily food in the springtime. You want your food prepared in an easy-to-digest fashion to help nourish that Spleen Yang energy. So soup and porridge are good choices for springtime.

Top springtime foods include chicken and lamb, fish, fruits (especially apples and bananas), walnuts, black sesame seeds, orange, lemon, hawthorn berry, carrots, broccoli, cilantro, green bell peppers, mushrooms (especially black), cherries, lotus root, black beans, coix seed, oats, and brown rice.

Spring Acupressure

Here's a 10-minute routine you should consider using in the springtime, in addition to whatever other routines from previous chapters you've chosen. Using both thumbs, press the following points to boost your body's ability to fend off disease and increase your facial beauty from the inside out: ST 36, LI 4, UB 23, UB 20, LI 5, DU 14, DU 20. Repeat once a day. Find these points in Chapters 6, 11 and 16.

Spring Qi Gong

In the springtime, choose Qi Gong exercises that emphasize breathing. They'll help your body take in the fresh spring energy from nature and get rid of winter's unclean energy. Also try to include physical exercise, such as walking. The combination will help support your body's healthy immune system and promote adequate Qi and blood flow to the facial area.

SUMMER

Summer brings peak Yang energy just when the natural life cycle reaches its peak, flourishing in full. With so much Yang pushing outward, the body's skin pores open easily to release perspiration in the hot weather. The Yin energy stays inside the body.

TCM theory holds that summer belongs to the fire element, which corresponds to heart energy. Since the heart also houses the spirit (Shen), king of all emotions, spirit rejuvenation is a priority. Light outdoor activities help keep your mind clear and spirit high in summertime.

At the same time, though, the bright summer sun is harmful to the skin, leading to spots and facial wrinkles. So be sure to protect your skin from the sun's UV rays by using a sun block with an SPF of at least 30.

Sweat is a body fluid associated with the heart system. Losing too much will weaken the heart's Qi. Since we tend to sweat a lot in summer, it's important to re-hydrate to keep your skin from wrinkling. Drink plenty of water (at least six 8-ounce glasses a day) and other fluids.

The long days and high Yang energy of summer calls for preserving some of that Yang energy for later in the year. Daily exercise is a good way to do that. Another is to sleep slightly less, going to bed a bit later (but still before 11 pm) and waking up slightly earlier.

Take extra care to keep your face clean all summer long. Wash several times a day, using the herbal washes described in Chapters 5, 10 and 15. Use light facial creams and the herbal masks you've chosen from those same chapters.

Summer Food

Heart fire is in excess during the summer while kidney water (Yin) is often deficient. Summertime herbal teas (cooled if you like) help correct this imbalance. Good choices are chrysanthemum flower tea, Chinese asparagus tea, and green tea with lemon and American ginseng.

Summertime food choices for health and beauty are based on the principle of clearing away internal heat, replenishing body fluids, and building up the digestive system by boosting spleen energy. Avoid extra cold food, which actually adds to the fire (heart) element. Also stay away from bitter or oily food. Pungent and slightly warm (in the TCM sense, not necessarily in temperature) food will help nourish the lung and Yang energy, which will help heart and kidney energy as well.

Best summer choices: Dark green leafy vegetables, watermelon, figs, cucumber, cherries, fresh luffa, winter melon, soy bean sprouts, mung bean sprouts, tomatoes, carrots, grapes, turnips, Chinese cabbage, kiwi fruit, fresh berries and quail eggs.

Summer Qi Gong

An excellent summertime Qi Gong choice is the "Ke" sound exercise described in Chapter 17, because it nourishes heart energy. Swimming and walking are also good activities for summertime.

Summer Acupressure

Add this special summertime routine to whatever acupressure protocols you've chosen. Work on the following points for a total of 10 minutes: REN 12, ST 36, KI 3, Ht 3, and UB 23. Find the points in Chapter 6, 11 or 16.

The idea behind this routine is to retain heart energy and replenish Kidney essence.

AUTUMN

When the hot summer ends, the body's Yang energy finally disperses itself outward. It's time to pull back, to retain. Mother nature helps us do this by letting the Yin energy grow in autumn as the Yang subsides.

Your body and life preservation strategies, as well as your facial beauty efforts, should focus on protecting and nourishing internal Yin. You want to help your body retain inward energy. Accumulating Yang energy for the upcoming winter is even more important now.

The autumn air in most regions gets drier and cooler. That affects your body and your emotions. In TCM theory, autumn corresponds to the element of metal, which is associated with the lung system. The emotional state of the lung system and metal element is sadness and grief.

So despite the high and clear skies we often see in autumn, it's a restraining period in nature as well as your body. Emotionally, we can easily become sad and even depressed. These emotions can affect our physical state.

To balance the body and mind, we need to keep our spirits calm and minimize the harmful effect of this Metal season. Long ago, ancient Chinese sages recognized the need to retain spirit and energy in autumn, especially lung energy, to keep it from "leaking" outward. Besides the food and other recommendations, there are two good ways to keep your body and mind in balance.

One is to take advantage of the fresh, crisp autumn air by going on leisurely hikes in areas of natural beauty. The other is to increase your sleep time, after shortening it slightly in summer. As the days get shorter, get to bed earlier.

Special Autumn Skin Treatments

The cool dry air of autumn injures lung Qi, as it dries up lung Yin and body fluids. Since the lung system functions to nourish and moisten skin and hair, you need to take measures to offset the dehydration.

Besides drinking your six 8-ounce glasses of water daily, drink three cups or an 8-ounce glass of warm water each morning. Boil the water first, then let it cool to a nice warm temperature.

Do what you can to keep your indoor environment appropriately moist. Use a good hydrating skin cream that contains nutrients for your face. Use the hydrating masks described in Chapters 5, 10 and 15.

Choose herbs that nourish the Lung system. Tremella, bird's nest, and American ginseng are wonderful food/herb choices for the autumn season.

Autumn Food

Make sure you eat less pungent food in autumn time, since the pungent flavor is related to lung Qi, which your body already has plenty of in the autumn metal season.

Instead, eat more sour-tasting food to add liver energy for lung and liver balance.

The following foods are most helpful in your autumn quest to protect body fluids, nourish body Yin and calm the heart spirit: honey, walnuts, sesame seeds, tremella, lily root, lotus seeds (and root), fish, chicken, duck, lamb, beef, sea cucumber, water chestnuts, rice, Chinese dates, hawthorn berries, blackberries, blueberries, strawberries, lemon, green apples, soy milk, organic milk, oats, and millet. Consult Chapters 8, 13, and 18 for ideas on how to prepare these foods.

Autumn Acupressure

To calm the spirit, release stress, strengthen the lung system and beautify your facial skin, add this routine to whatever acupressure protocols you have chosen. Simply work the following points for a total of 10 minutes: LIV 3, LI 4, LU 11, and KI 3. Consult Chapters 6, 11 or 16 for information about these points.

Autumn Qi Gong

Good Qi Gong exercises are crucial to autumn health and beauty, especially since they help you achieve the happy mind that's so important in autumn. Your best choices are the "Xi"-sound breathing exercise described in Chapter 17.

WINTER

In winter, nature's Yin energy reaches its peak while the life force hibernates and Yang decreases. To follow nature's course, we should go to bed very early in winter and wake up slightly late. This will save Yang and nourish Qi. The days are much shorter, so the Yang energy stays deep inside the body.

Also, avoiding exposure to the winter cold helps your body retain Yang and protect the elevated Yin.

Winter corresponds to the element of Water, which pertains to the Kidney system. Emotions tend to run low due to the seasonal weather conditions. Give them a boost. Go out when weather permits, communicate with family and friends, listen to music you like (very healing) and do exercise.

Winter Herb Strategies

Chinese physicians stress body tonification during wintertime, when Qi and blood flow is slower, as is the metabolism. The goal is to support the healthy immune system that helps you fight off disease. By taking tonic herbs, you're nourishing these systems, helping them survive the winter and get ready for next year.

Tonic herbs recommended for wintertime rejuvenation for body and skin are ginseng (if you have high blood pressure, substitute it with American ginseng), deer antler, astragalus, E Jiao, rehmannia, and wolfberries.

Special Winter Skin Treatments

The oil secretion rate in your skin is slower in winter. A dry heating system in the house will make it even more difficult for your skin to retain moisture. So it's very important to use a mild facial cleanser daily, and to follow up with a nourishing skin cream. Do anti-wrinkle skin masks (refer the instruction from Chapter 5 and 8)

Even in winter, use an SPF 30 sun block on sunny days, make sure you drink plenty of water. Take care to limit your skin's exposure to cold, dry and windy weather conditions.

Winter Food

Wintertime food should be warm in nature. The following foods are the most beneficial for facial beauty in wintertime: Pig's feet/skin (in a soup), fatty fish like salmon and mackerel, lamb, venison, chicken (especially black chicken), duck, mung bean sprouts, loganberries, walnuts, yam, eggs, soy products, dark green leafy vegetables (like Chinese broccoli, spinach, and kale), carrots, sunflower seeds, pine nuts, mushrooms (especially reishi) , black fungus, black sesame seeds, sesame oil, seaweed, sea grass, chestnuts, and Chinese dates.

Winter Acupressure

To strengthen your organ systems and maintain facial beauty in winter, add the following Qi Gong exercise to your usual routines: Work the following points for a total of 10 minutes: ST 36, REN 6, REN 12, REN 4, SP 10, KI 3. Refer to Chapters 6, 11 and 16 to locate the points.

Winter Qi Gong exercise:

Winter Qi Gong exercises help increase Qi and blood flow, and improve the body's slowed metabolism. Your best choice for nourishing kidney energy in winter is the "Chu" breathing exercise from Chapter 17. If you've thought about taking up T'ai Chi (a great idea), it's an especially beneficial exercise in winter.

Tips From Ping

As you follow the food and exercise guidelines for each season, remember to continue using the herbs you've chosen. As always, a complete program including herbal treatments, Qi Gong exercises, acupressure routines and food therapy. This is the key to achieving a wrinkle-free, smooth and youthful-looking face.

CHAPTER 21

Ping's Nefeli™ Herbal Formulas, Creams and Masks to Complement Your Anti-Wrinkle Program

The 30-day programs we've just reviewed will serve as the basic units of your anti-wrinkle and facial beauty program. Follow these programs as you practice the herbal treatments, acupressure routines, Qi Gong exercises and therapeutic food suggestions described in this book. You have plenty to choose from.

There's even more you can do to enhance your program. You can add commercially available herbal supplements, topical creams and masks.

Again, it is not usually recommended to use do-it-yourself herbal formulas (as opposed to one-at-a-time herbs) for internal use. You're better off consulting a TCM professional for personal advice.

But there are some herbal formulas, as well as some special skin creams and masks that will enhance your 30-day programs including the Nefeli product line developed by my years of experience. They are safe and natural to use.

The products are all based on Traditional Chinese Medicine theory. They are all natural herbal based, holistic and promote facial beauty from the inside out. They fit nicely into your 30-day programs, boosting the herbal aspect of your strategy, and provide the right kind of natural skin care as an alternative for other comestic topicals when they are called for.

Before I describe them to you, I would like to share with you my personal story of how I came to design my own line of herbal skin care products.

I Grew Up With Natural Chinese Medicine

I remember summers as a child, when my mom and grandma would teach me how to grow summer plants so we would have fresh vegetables at harvest time. Among them was fresh luffa, a plant that's familiar to you too by now as an herb and food (as well as cleansing tool) in your anti-wrinkle program.

Luffa grows curling up trees and fences, its beautiful yellow flowers eventually giving way to the fruit. My mom would collect, fresh off the vines, the juice from the luffa fruit.

The next morning we'd all wash our face with the juice and notice the new glow to our skin. We'd also give the juice to a neighbor with stomach problems, and saw his condition improve.

Very early, then, I began to appreciate the natural power of Chinese medicine. I also heard the stories of women from the old times — such as the famous "Last Empress" — who used such amazing substances as pearl powder to keep her face radiant and wrinkle-free as the years went by.

I heard about how energy herbals, like ginsing kept even farmers' hands youthful as they got older.

I was fascinated by these stories as a child, and even more amazed as I began trying them out for myself, experiencing first-hand the dramatic results.

Why I Make My Own Products

Baby boomers today are in their 40s and 50s, with the very oldest just entering their 60s. As they began aging, they look for natural products that would make them look and feel more fit and vibrant. They would ask me for natural, simple anti-aging formulas or topical treatments.

I would give them pure herbal formulas to take internally to regulate and balance the organ systems according to TCM principles. They and I could both see that as a result their eyes were getting brighter, and their overall skin condition improved, becoming more supple and radiant. Dark spots faded. Their entire face glowed instantly even their hair was rejuvenated.

In addition to internal herbal formulas, I saw a need in my patients to use more natural ingredients in their skin care products. There was no line of products on the market that truly implemented the TCM concept of facial beauty — that is, of taking care of wrinkles and other facial concerns by promoting inner balance. So I set to work in coming up with ways for baby boomers to combine their skin care regime with healing herbals.

For instance, I would give them pearl powder to add to boiled mung beans, and have them drink half the mixture and wash their face with the other half. The results were always dramatic.

I would also give professional seminars for acupuncturists and herbalists, and use the occasions to train my peers in the use of hall-natural herbal skincare cosmetics.

From these many years research, teaching and practical experience, I accumulated enough experience to formulate my own line of anti-aging herbal supplements and topical treatments called Nefeli™. They specifically address the concerns of my patients and people like them — people like you. My aim was to make available skin-care products based on my philosophy of promoting beauty from the inside out.

I took the ancient Chinese miracles that I had been discovering throughout my life since childhood, and especially during my years of research and practice, and handcrafted them into each bottle of my health and beauty products. My products are derived solely from nature, fulfilling my life goal of bringing to my patients and customers the best that TCM has to offer for health, beauty and a rejuvenated life.

> **Tips From Ping**
> One of the most frequently asked questions by my patients and colleagues is this: What's the difference between Nefeli's herbal skin-care products and other skin-care products that include herbal extracts? While other producet lines use individual botanicals, I combine Chinese herbs into specially designed formulas based on TCM healing principles. The herbs in the formulas work together synergistically for a more effective healing to balance body, mind, and spirit.

Heavenly Beauty from the Earth

Each product I came up with is a specific blend of time-honored Chinese herbs. Every formula is packed with ancient healing herbs whose power derives directly from nature. Each helps you achieve that harmony by restoring the delicate balance of the root treasures of our beings that are so familiar to you by now — essence (Jing), spirit (Shen) and life energy (Qi).

All the herbal components in Nefeli's skin-care products (whether supplements to be taken internally or topicals to be applied externally) use100 percent natural herbs. The herbs are carefully blended into a full range of topical and internal formulas. Most of the herbs used have been shown by modern Western-style medical research to contain specific healing agents that achieve the purposes intended by Chinese medicine. But, as you well know by now, that's of secondary importance. The skin-rejuvenating effects of these herbs have been proven for literally thousands of years. Their healing action lies not exclusively in any physiological process recognized by Western medicine, but in their long-established balancing effect on your internal essence, spirit and energy.

One of the most important herbs in my formulas is one you haven't heard much about in this book. It's called Rhodiola root. I was inspired both by the legendary stories about this special herb and by the modern scientific findings that support its efficacy.

The Legend of Rhodiola - During the Qing Dynasty, a general and his army were battling barbarians in the desert. After fighting for several days, the exhausted men were given rhodiola to restore their energy. It worked. The refreshed men went out and won the battle. When the emperor heard of this miraculous herb, he named it "Xian Shi Cao," which means "heaven-sent medicine." Nefeli uses rhodiola in skin-care products to replenish the skin's vitality and restore its youthful glow.

Rhodiola root is loaded with free-radical fighting antioxidant nutrients, essential amino acids, trace elements, and vitamins. When I began to put it into my daily creams combined with other herbs — the prototypes for the Nefeli products — I saw a difference in my face that became more pronounced every day.

Eventually, one of these prototypes became the "Skin Brighten Day Cream" that not only brings about a healthy internal balance restoring your complexion to its natural brightness and evenness, it also empowers your skin to fight the environmental "evils" that damage your complexion.

Most of the other herbs that work together in Nefeli skin care formulas are already familiar to you. Here are some of the most important ones: They are used in different kind of skin care and herbal care formulas. These specially formulated formulas are only available in Nefeli's line of product.

- **Chinese Reishi Mushroom**. Known as the "skin magic herb," this powerful antioxidant source is an anti-aging herb par excellence, with especially strong effects (for supporting the body's healthy systems) for face brightening and helping to improve wrinkled-skin conditions, discoloration and age spots. It contains amino acids, vitamins and high molecular-weight polysaccharides.

- **Ginseng**. The king of Chinese herbs, ginseng is a superior energy (Qi) tonic that addresses your wrinkle concerns by rejuvenating skin cells, relieving skin fatigue and promoting microcirculation in the skin.

The Legend of Ginseng - In a small mountain village in China, ginseng was harvested daily. Workers did not take the herb, but carried it to nearby villages to be sold. As the years went by, the villagers' bodies and faces would age normally, but their hands remained youthful and supple. Just by touching the ginseng plants, their hands benefited from ginseng's rejuvenating properties. Today, Nefeli uses ginseng to rejuvenate your face and entire body, not just your hands.

- **Astragalus.** A major Qi tonic and antioxidant, astragalus firms up sagging facial skin by energizing the skin itself while ridding it of toxins.

- **Pearl.** A mineral considered an herb in the Chinese tradition. Packed with 17 different kind of amino acids, and minerals, including: calcium, magnesium, zinc, iron, strontium, copper, selenium, silicon, titanium, ferric oxide, and silica. Many of pearl's components are involved in DNA and RNA metabolic activity, helping promote and accelerate cell renewal.

  This "superior treasure" also has a strong anti-wrinkle effect. Pearls are a gift from the natural water world where the first life on the earth formed hundreds of millions of years ago. When I combine pearls with other skin healing superior herbs in the correct ratio, the results go far beyond what pearl can accomplish on its own.

  The Legend of Pearl - Perhaps one of the most famous people who used pearls as a beauty aid is the "Last Empress," who was renowned for her youthful radiance. Her secret: Every day she would take a freshly crushed pearl and place the powder on her wrinkles. Using a stick of jade, she would massage the pearl powder into her skin, essentially rubbing away her wrinkles. Today Nefeli uses pearl powder in much the same way for maintaining beautiful, wrinkle-free skin.

- **Angelica**. Nourishes the blood to improve skin circulation, helps bring nutrients to the skin layer.

- **Fu-Ling**. An anti-aging herb that collects life-force energy from the root of an evergreen tree, helps brighten the complexion and fight age spots and discoloration.

- **Coix Seed**. It contains minerals such as calcium, phosphorus, iron, and vitamins such as thiamine, riboflavin and niacin. Coix seed also helps to block harmful UV Rays.

- **Atractylodes.** Known as Bai Zhu in China, it contains essential oils and amino acids, which are beneficial to your skin's tone and brightness.

- **Luffa.** It has a high concentration of essential fatty acids that helps to replenish the skin's surface.

Eating for Beauty:
Nefeli's Anti-Aging Herbal Supplements

Here are some of the natural herbal nutritional supplements you can consider to incorporate with your 30-day programs.

"Wrinkle Smoother" This is an herbal formula that bears special properties to support and maintain the body's natural ability and healthy skin's function to reverse signs of aging, smooth existing wrinkles and delay the appearance of new ones.

"Wrinkle Smoother" helps a healthy body to fight wrinkles by following traditional Chinese medical principles. It's an herbal blend specially formulated to strengthen the healthy liver, lung and kidney systems.

Here's a sample of the kinds of herbs "Wrinkle Smoother" uses to smooth your face: E Jiao (Donkey-hide Gelatin), Ginseng (Panax Ginseng). "Wrinkle Smoother" is for you if you want to:

■ Prevent wrinkles due to internal body deficiencies or aging process.

■ Smooth wrinkles due to external factors such as sun and wind exposure.

■ Smooth wrinkles due to an unhealthy lifestyle.

■ Smooth wrinkles due to deficient body conditions or aging process.

■ Try an alternative and natural way to smooth your wrinkles.

"Bright Complexion" This formula brightens a dull and withered complexion while addressing discolorations and dark spots due to internal body deficiencies and the aging process. The choice of herbals in "Bright Complexion" is based directly on China's classical herbal texts and offers an herbal composition specifically designed for maximum effect. These herbs' special properties support the body's natural ability to harmonize and cleanse your entire internal environment — not just the face — to create a body balance that deals with dark spots and brightens your face.

Four of the herbs in this powerful herbal blend are especially well known for their ability to your complexion needs. They are Dong Gua Ren (Winter melon seed), Bai Zhu (Atractylodes root), Fu Ling (Poria) and Sheng Di Huang (Dried rehmannia root).

"Brighten Complexion" is for you if you have:

■ Age or dark spots from internal body deficiencies or aging process.

■ Facial discolorations from internal body deficiencies or aging process.

■ Dark spots due to sun exposure. You want to brighten your dull, lifeless complexion.

"Complete Balance" This one is designed to nourish and balance the Three Treasures so that you may realize our whole potential and optimum health. Nefeli's "Complete Balance" consists of 14 time-honored herbs carefully selected and blended to achieve ultimate synergy and maximum potency. All are rich in precious nutrients, which are essential to your health. More important, all embody ancient Chinese healing wisdom.

Some outstanding examples of the herbs in this formula are Ling Zhi (Reishi mushroom), Ginseng (Panax ginseng), and Rhodiola (known as Hong Jin Tain in China).

"Complete Balance" is for you if you want to:
- Improve your overall health and well being.
- Occasional sleep problems, low spirit, constipation, stress, fatigue, and indigestion or poor memory.
- Erase the signs of aging, such as appearance of dull complexion, tired eyes, and sagging of the face.

"Eye Refresh" This is a formula to refresh and brighten your eyes. "Eye Refresh" is designed to maintain the total well being of your eyes, so that dark circles, puffiness and vision concerns can be addressed.

The herbals in "Eye Refresh" are specially chosen according to their traditional use in Traditional Chinese Medicine to maintain the normal function and appearance of the eyes. Some of the more important ones are Huang Qi (Astragalus), Gou Qi Zi (Wolfberry fruit), and Mu Zei (Shave grass)

"Eye Refresh" is for you if:
- You have ark eye circles, puffy and swollen eye bags due to internal body deficiencies or natural aging process.
- You have blurred or cloudy vision due to internal body deficiencies or natural aging process.
- You want a more beautiful and sparkling eyes.

Tips From Ping
Internal imbalances cause many other health and beauty problems besides those related to the face. Those problems can include unreasonable weight gain, hair loss, menopause symptoms, frequent colds, aging body skin, and many more. I see these concerns in my clinic every day. So, again, combining knowledge from thousands of years of TCM healing and my own experience, I developed 100 percent natural formulas for addressing these problems. These Nefeli products include "Weight Management," "Healthy Hair," "Menopause Soother", and "Cold and Allergy Care." For more information on understanding how they work, refer to the appendix located at the end of the book or log on www.nefeli.com.

Nefeli's Natural Topical Creams for Youthful Complexion

Your 30-day programs call for using topical creams often. You might want to consider some of these creams I created and are available from Nefeli. In creating these topicals, I used not just TCM principles and my own experience, but also the very latest environmental research and studies of possible harmful effects of certain substances. As a result, my topicals are free of parabens and potentially harmful ingredients as well as mineral oils, as suggested by the Environmental Work Group (www.ewg.org).

Tips From Ping

The emphasis in Nefeli products is always on safety and purity. Each ingredient in Nefeli's internal herbal supplements is processed by GMP and TGA world-certified manufacturers, and produced in GMP manufacturing plants in the United States. Complete lab tests are done for all individual ingredients, both at the initial production stage and once again before final packing. Manufacture lab randomly tests the final products for heavy metal contents and macrobiotics to insure they surpass the FDA requirements as nutritional supplements. A Certificate of Analysis (COA) is available by request.

1. Anti-Wrinkle/Sagging Skin Healing Series

Traditional Chinese Medicine, especially the Taoism has long offered a healing approach to facial wrinkling. Over the years of research and clinic experience, I formed this line of anti-aging skin care to bring you that wisdom. The secret lies in powerful herbs that help you overcome the roughness and sagging that lead to fine lines and deep wrinkles.

In the process of designing this line of anti-aging skin care products, I combined traditional Chinese herbal medicine's healing power with more recently recognized natural plant components, such as antioxidants that neutralize skin-cell-damaging free radicals. The special herbs that are used are blended precisely so they can work synergistically to fight aging. They also fight the wrinkles that go with aging by helping with the re-energizing and replenishing process of your skin at the cellular level. Such herbs are found in each of the anti-wrinkle creams for smooth, supple facial skin and a stress-free face that radiates natural beauty.

"Intensive Wrinkle Care Day Cream"
This is the first cream I created using Pearl, Rhodiola and Ginseng together. According to TCM theory, the cooling function of Pearls, the detoxification function of Rhodiola, the rejuvenating function of Ginseng, all synergies together to protect the skin, calms the skin, and release the toxicity form the skin. In order to promote blood circulation in facial area, I added gingko biloba. And to further fortify the formula, I chose white peony root and green tea.

"Intensive Wrinkle Care Night Cream" Elite herbals work together with a precise ratio to fight winkles and firm up the face for you while you sleep. Astragulas strongly promote the defensive energy according to TCM, it helps to strengthen the skin. Luffa cleanses skin, at the same time nourishes skin, Ginseng and Reishi Mushroom energize the skin, while pearl calms the skin, Ginkgo Biloba promotes the blood flow to the face. When they work together, skin's natural rejuvenation process is greatly strengthened, that means, they not only replenish cells with nutrients, but also promoting skin healing and repair by aiding the renewal process.

"Intensive Wrinkle Care Mask" This herbal mask is designed to de-stress the skin by using Chinese herbal extracts of Astragalus Root, Angelica, Sinenis, Luffa, Coix Seed, and Papaya. These potent herbs nourish, hydrate, firm, and protect the skin while diminishing the appearance of fine lines and wrinkles.
The above set of creams and mask fight wrinkles and are also excellent for sagging of face.

2. Skin Brightening Series for Radiant and Flawless Complexion

The inspiration for me to design this line of product comes from my patients' request. They often ask me if there are any Chinese herbal miracles that can taking of their facial discolorations and dark/age spots. They went through chemical acid peelings, sometime, laser treatments, but they want something that is less harsh and more nourishing.

Fortunately, there are answers to these requests from Traditional Chinese Medicine. According to Traditional Chinese medicine, dull, discolored, or spotted complexion is due to internal body disharmony, stagnation, or deficiency. External factors, such as excess sun exposure, also contribute to an uneven, spotted complexion.

These skin complexion-brightening creams are designed to deal with precisely the factors identified by the medical sages of ancient China.

The "Brighten Complexion" series blends carefully selected Chinese herbs to bring a healthy balance to restore the complexion to its natural brightness and evenness. The herbs also empower your skin to fight the environmental "evils" that damage your complexion.

"Intensive Day-Time Skin Brightening Cream" Featuring rhodiola, this cream guards your skin and energizes it to give it a radiant glow as it helps get rid of wrinkles. As I have mentioned before, dull, spotted or discolored skin results from internal body disharmony such as stagnation or certain deficiencies, as well as external factors such as sun exposure. Guided by TCM healing theory, I chose the herbs in this formula for their ability not only to fight the existing spots and discoloration, but also because they protect the skin against toxins and other environmental factors. The skin must be energized to get that protection.

After many trials with many herbs, I finally came up with the balance of herbs needed to make "Intensive Daytime Skin Brightening Cream" effective. And the key herbs turned out to be pearls and rhodiola. Inspired by both their legend and scientific findings, I began to put them into my own daily creams. Amazingly I found my face got a natural healthy glow almost immediately after applying the cream. Day by day I found my skin kept the healthy rosy complexion and was getting firmer yet felt softer. Now they are the featured herbs in "Intensive Daytime Skin Brightening Cream," which will bring a healthy balance to the body and restore the complexion to its natural brightness and evenness.

"Intensive Night-Time Skin Brightening Cream" As its name indicates, this is the nighttime version of the cream we just described.

For thousands of years, Chinese physicians have lauded the superior herbs poria, pearl, licorice and atractylodis for their ability to heal dull complexions and facial dark spots. Simple and natural ways to use these herbs in facial creams have been well documented throughout history. Today, after carefully studying their components, functions and medical indications, I was able to put them together at an ideal ratio. Now your face can benefit from this special formula, achieving a radiant and flawless complexion from Intensive Night-Time Skin Brightening Cream while you sleep.

3. Rescue Remedies

Sometimes looking your best can be an emergency situation. Your wedding day, high school reunion, a must-get job interview are examples of the many times when you need to put on your best look. That's why I put together a "Rescue Remedies" series of Nefeli products, to provide instant anti-aging miracles when you need them the most.

As always, the products follow Traditional Chinese Medicine teachings and use time-honored Chinese herbs that work at the cellular level to bring out your youth and beauty for all to see. Ginseng, designated king of the superior herbals by the Chinese medical texts, is my first choice for this line of product. Other important ones are pearls, Angelica root and Safflower (Carthamus).

"Eye Rejuvenating Mask" With a combination of Ginseng, Ivy, Green tea, Reishi Mushroom, Safflower and other herbals, this fast-acting formula rejuvenates the eye area by freeing energy flow, transforming dampness, and unblocking stagnation. A synchronized effect of these superior herbs help to decrease the appearance of fine lines around the eyes, fade dark circles, and smooth eye bags and puffiness, leaving the eyes feeling refreshed and soothed.

"Facial Rejuvenating Mask" Applying TCM healing principle, this mask combines the super Qi tonic Ginseng with Angelica and Licorice roots, Pearl, Rhodiola and Atractylodis. The special blend provides time-released hydration and vital essential nutrients to the skin. As you can see this multifunctional herbal formula readily send it's healing to the skin by energizing it, detoxifying it and promoting more blood flow to nourish the skin from inside out. It works to help brighten and revitalize the skin tone, and at the same time helps to reduce the appearance of fine lines and wrinkles. I also frequently use it for my patients as after- sun- damage mask. It works great due to the rejuvenation healing powers especially the anti-toxic properties of the herbal ingredients. It often serves as face rescuer for my patients who worship the sun , love the beach or play a lot of out door sport.

4. An All-In-One Eye Care

"Essential Eye Care Cream" This cream is packed with ancient natural healing herbs. Combining Ginseng, Ivy, Reishi Mushroom, Safflower, Persimmon Leaf, and White peony, it energizes the eye area and promotes blood flow. The Ivy is used here to transform the dampness, according to TCM, that's a cause of puffy eyes and eye bags. Safflower not only promotes blood flow to the eyes, it also nourishes the skin around them. The Persimmon Leaf has an astringent effect, fighting puffiness.

5. Cellulite Reduction/Weight Management

"Cellulite Cream" Acupuncture for cellulite reduction is effective. But herbal cellulite reduction cream can be just as effective. This formula is based on the TCM healing theory that considers cellulite to be phlegm accumulation. So I use natural Chinese herbs such as ivy that function as phlegm transformers. Others, such as Ginkgo Biloba, move the blood.

Keep in mind that quick weight loss can lead to sagging skin. I designed this herbal formula with skin firming herbs, which includes evening primrose (Ye Jian Cao) and Chinese Black Tea.

CHAPTER 22

Proof Perfect

A Picture is worth a thousand words. These photographs have been taken of people (some of them are my patients) participating the 30-day program.

The herbs, food, acupressure, massage protocols and Qi Gong exercises used in the 30-day program are all based on what I have introduced in this book. All of them used my herbal-based Nefeli line of skin care as mentioned in Chapter 19 for their topical skin application.

Please take special notice of the dramatic changes in eye bags, dark under eye circles, discolorations, wrinkles, skin laxity and tone before and after the 30-day program. Share these pictures and share the participants' feedbacks. I believe the results to be remarkable, you be the judge! *(see attached before and after pictures)*

Feedback From 30-day Program Participants

"My skin has never felt better since I was a teenager, despite using many, very expensive products, both from the department stores as well as from Dermatologists. Before coming to Ping's Office, I was using top of the line skin care products. None of those compare to Ping's products, from which my skin has become more moist, firm and with a noted diminution of wrinkle and fine lines.Additionally, from the herbal supplements I feel more energized, less depressed, and have overall a more positive outlook on life.

I have recommended Ping's products to many friends with pride and certainty that their lives, and their skin will be much improved."

A. S.

"I am delighted with the Nefeli skin products...I had been using other high-end products previously. They helped at first to even my skin tone and to tighten large pores as well as smooth out and tighten wrinkles. However, results were minimal and not cumulative. Results were apparent only just after I applied the products.

The picture is very different with Nefeli. Results are dramatic and cumulative and are immediately apparent. My pores are tighter and the texture of my skin is much finer. This is the result of using the masks. Results last for days. When I use the creams I see an immediate glow and wrinkles get tighter immediately, and they stay tighter. The creams also appear to lift my skin so that sagging is lessened. Again results don't diminish once the products have been used, they increase. My skin has never looked so beautiful. I get many compliments."

J.L.

"I feel the skin treatments I received from Ping Zhang have had very positive results. The herbs were quite calming and the food (including collagen from pigskin) was delicious. With the food, masks, creams, massages, pills etc., my skin became tighter, smoother, plushier and more radiant and my jaw line better defined. The skin tightener that I had to refrigerate worked immediately; with the lifting of my face, my eyes became more open, larger. My more youthful appearance was definitely noticed by others as well as myself.

These improvements are especially significant because before I began the treatments I was taking collagen pills and using DMAE cream and a very famous anti-acne product. All of these I discontinued while under Ping's care, my skin is very sensitive and I am prone to rosacea and acne, I had no incidence of either of these during the treatment. I also noticed my vagina became more moist during the time. I am 61 years old and very pleased."

S.K.

"I am so happy and so pleased with the result I am getting since I started your skin care program. Every Nefeli product I have been using has made a significant difference in the texture and brightness of my skin. My fine lines have disappeared and my skin has a natural glow.

One evening I met some friends whom I had not seen for six months. When I approached them in the restaurant, I couldn't believe the expression on all of their faces. They immediately wanted to know what I had done. Suspecting that it was a surgical procedure.

Two weeks ago I ran into an old friend of mine who happens to be the #1 Cosmetic Surgeon in the world. He did not stop praising me... "you have never looked so good" is what he kept saying to me.

I have an inner and outer glow thanks to you and your skin care program. Your unique treatment.....treating the skin from inside out has proven to be most effective. Most people cannot believe my age.

I am so blessed to have met you and I look forward to a continued success with your products and treatments. I want to share my experience with the world!"

L.G.

"During the period of Ping Zhang's 30-day program, I was going through a very difficult time in my life. I was unable to sleep and woke up every morning very tired. And all these could be seen in my look (face).

When I began to use Ping Zhang's method, my look and how I felt inside immediately changed for the better.

The food in general supported me with energy and this energy lasted all day. The Nefeli products I put on my face and neck immediately worked and changed the feel and look of my face and neck. I looked more radiant and younger, and several people commented on it. My chin immediately lifted after using the face mask and stayed beautifully toned. I have noticed an immediate change that the products deliver and after using them for a period of time. The change becomes permanent –so they worked over a period of time too. What also surprised me was, that I tend to have very sensitive skin, but these products did not irritate me. Even the fragrance was mild and pleasant.

I am a western trained physician, and I don't know exactly how this system works, but it definitely does and I am intending to use it every time I need a look tune-up."

M.T.

"I have had a wonderful experience with Nefeli products during the 30-day program. Every time that I wash my face and use the Skin Brightening Face wash my face glares and becomes rosy. I love the way it leaves my face; I can feel the blood flow through. I have seen great improvement since using these products, my wrinkles have smoothened out, my jaw has been lifted, and my eyes bags are less noticeable. I have also been eating food that Ping Zhang has recommended; it has given me more energy.

My daughter has noticed the great change on my face. She has told me that the lines around my eyes are less apparent. My brother who hasn't seen me in a few months also had comments; he told me that I look younger than my age.

I just absolutely love the Nefeli products. I would recommend them to anyone. Because of them I have a more beautiful and healthier appearance."

N.R.

"I am very satisfied with the great results I got from your 30-day program. My skin now is perfectly polished, soft, smooth and luminous after using Nefeli products.

I noticed an instant difference in the texture and my skin was glowing. Gradually, I noticed my pores shrinking and the appearance of lines diminishing! I had several people notice my complexion when not wearing makeup. They commended that I didn't need to wear make-up.

My skin just feels and looks young!

The Facial Rejuvenation Mask is simply amazing. It seems to erase the lines around my eyes!! I can't wait for my mom to try it!!"

B.D.

"C.P . is a 35 year old African American, suffering from a myriad of health conditions including irritable bowel syndrome, slow metabolism, sleep deprivation, anxiety, stress, low energy, dull and lifeless skin, water retention and cellulite on thighs and buttocks.

By not paying attention to my body, everyday stress has wreaked havoc, leading me down a road to destruction. By refusing to be attached to synthetic medication to treat my health conditions, did I decide to make a lifestyle change.

That is when I was introduced to Ping Zhang, recommended by a friend, did my health completely turn around for the better, after years of suffering.Ping Zhang discussed my overall health issues and was able to implement a long-term goal that would improve my health overtime, without synthetic medication, which was a major concern because of side effects.

Combining a once a week commitment to acupuncture and using the herbal products, I have seen many changes with my overall health. Within a month's time, I have lost weight and water retention, my skin is firmer, the cellulite has nearly diminished and my skin now glows like a ray of sunlight.

I haven't felt this good in years and it shows. Family, friends and complete strangers have commented. You have such a glow about you, what are you doing? Ping Zhang, I reply with a smile.

During the thirty-day trial, the following products were incorporated into my daily lifestyle.

Nefeli Products used to treat anti-aging with respect to wrinkles, dull skin and dark circles around eye area.

- *Nefeli Cellulite Cream   (Used every other day, focusing on thigh area)*
- *Nefeli Wrinkle Smoother   (dietary supplement)*
- *Nefeli Essential Eye Care Cream   (Used daily morning and evening)*
- *Nefeli Day cream for face*
- *Nefeli Night Cream for face*
- *Eye Rejuvenation Mask   (Used once a week or as needed)*
- *Facial Rejuvenation Mask   (Used once a week)*
- *Chinese Herbal Foods. Used in conjunction with the above anti-aging products*
- *Tremella – Boil in soup (Eaten twice a day)*
- *Bean & Nut Soup – To use as is or to mix in a soup."*

C.P.

"I have been working with Ping for about 4 or 5 weeks now.
I've been taking supplements, using a wash, a morning cream, and an evening cream. For the past 4 weeks, I feel that my face is smoother.
I've used the eye mask every other day and a face mask every 3rd day.
As I've taken the supplements I feel more balanced and with more energy.
I'm a smoker and now I don't have the lines around my mouth and lips like I use to. It just feels that my wrinkles are gone and that my skin is smooth.
I will continue to use Nefeli products."

R.S.

Remarks from Practitioners

As the first Traditional Chinese Medicine practitioner brought the whole TCM rejuvenation concept to the TCM college in the US, and continue to give professional level trainings to TCM practitioners, I also consistently get positive feedbacs from the students who graduated from my class and practitioners who have taking my training sessions about their successful stories from their patients.

The professional training I offer to the practitioners is the same in terms of utilizing Traditional Chinese herbal Medicine, acupressure, food and Qi Gong exercises mentioned in this book. Of course, the only difference is that they also get trained from me for how to do facial acupuncture. (Refer my book "A Comprehensive Handbook for TCM Facial Rejuvenation). However, in their practice, they all utilize the protocols including you've learnt here from this book.

The following are findings that fellow practitioners have seen in their practices utilizing the healing powers of traditional Chinese medicine:

"Ping Zhang's product line of both herbal and skin care products are far superior to any other product line that I have used. By the mere virtue of their purity and ability to out perform all other products in their class they should be heralded as the new wonder-child of facial rejuvenation for this decade.

I have used the Nefeli line for at least three years on my patients and myself with outstanding results. Eye bags, lines and dark circles disappeared for some, including myself, in a few days, for others within one month. Dark spots, sagging, large pores and texture of the skin have also been met with the same success.

For me, I delight at watching the complexions of my patients turn from shallow to bright and from dull to a glowing radiance. My own face took on a translucent porcelain quality in only a few weeks. Having been witness to the benefits of these remarkable products, I am quite sure that if one adds Ping's 30-day dietary plan, acupuncture, massage and Qi Gong exercise to their regiment, the results will be nothing short of phenomenal."

D.B., M.S. L.Ac.

"Ping Zhang has invaluable information in her seminar that has changed the lives of my patients. Her technique and herbal products have proven their effiency over and over again. She has the wonderful ability and willingness to share her knowledge through her informational seminar. The best seminar and herbal products yet".

A.R., L.Ac

"Ping Zhang's facial rejuvenation protocol has enabled me to expand my business immensely. I have had only very satisfied clients who look refreshed and healthy when they leave my studio.

The course Mrs. Zhang presents is a comprehensive overview of the modalities and products used to achieve these amazing results. My hat is off to her for sharing her great knowledge and expertise to help me attain great results with my clients."

K.M., Managing Director

"The facial rejuvenation seminar with Ping Zhang was very useful in my practice. The needling techniques along with the point selections and theory really helped me get the results I was expecting. The use of her herbal formulas along with the massaging techniques, she demonstrated, really help the acupuncture treatments perform more effectively. My patients are looking 5 to 10 years younger!"

A.G., M.S. L.Ac

Before and After Pictures
The 30-Day Program

30 DAY PROGRAM

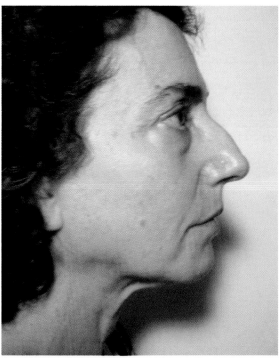

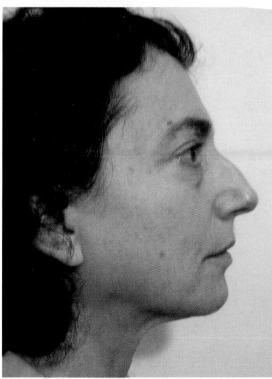

- What a great lift and over-all improved look for this woman's face.

- The appearance of sagging in her face, chin, and neck has significantly improved.

- Her jaw line appears to be more defined.

- The appearance of lines around her lips and nasolabial fold seems to be much reduced.

- Eye bags look smaller and puffiness is less.

- The appearance of the lines around her neck is also less deep.

30 DAY PROGRAM

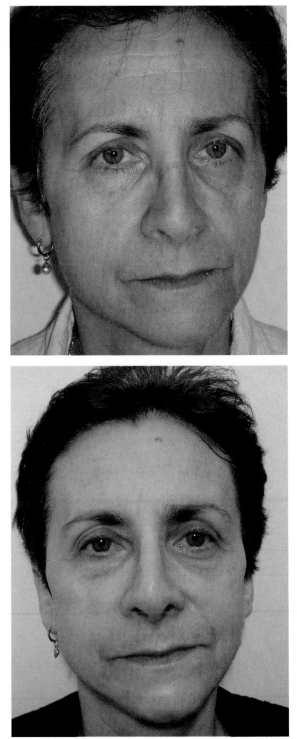

30 DAY PROGRAM

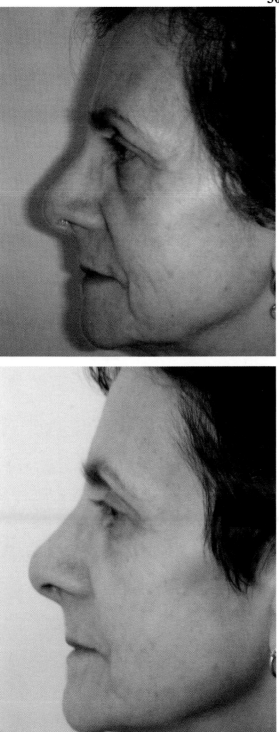

- What a significant lift from this woman's face.

- Her skin becomes more radiant and firm.

- Her jaw line is more defined.

- The appearance of forehead and frown wrinkles as well as nasolabial folds has been improved.

- Eyes seem to be more lifted.

- Eye bags appear to be smaller and less puffy.

30 DAY PROGRAM

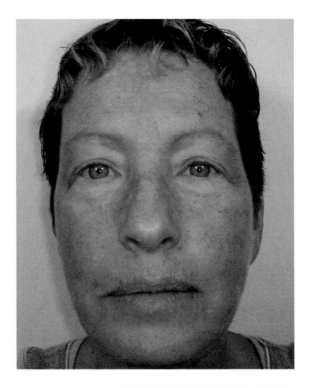

30 DAY PROGRAM

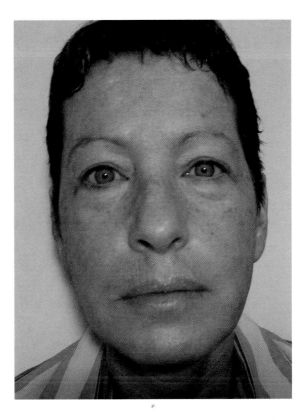

- The rough appearance of her skin has greatly improved.

- The appearance of wrinkles on her upper lip (smokers line) is greatly improved.

- Contours of her face are more defined.

- Eye bags appear to be smaller and flatter.

- The appearance of wrinkles (crows feet) around the eyes seem to be diminished.

- Complexion is more even and radiant.

30 DAY PROGRAM

30 DAY PROGRAM

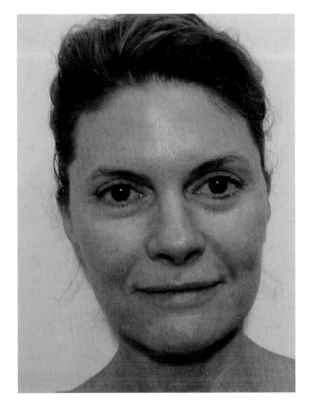

- Skin tone is much improved

- The appearance of the wrinkles around her eyes has been greatly improved.

30 DAY PROGRAM

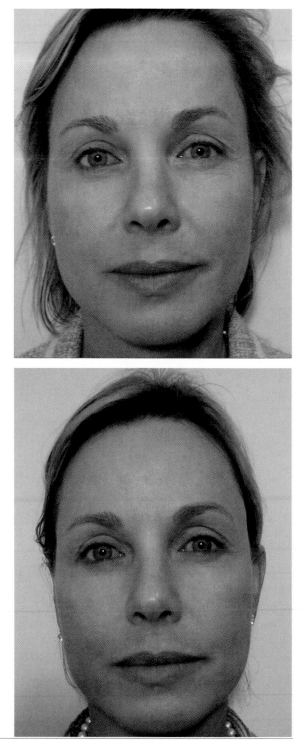

30 DAY PROGRAM

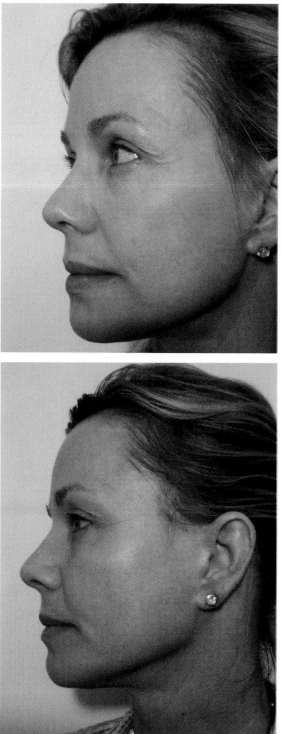

- Great improvement in the appearance of her face contours.

- Skin is more radiant.

- Eyes look more defined.

- Appearance of wrinkles around eyes has been reduced, especially the crow's feet around the right eye.

30 DAY PROGRAM

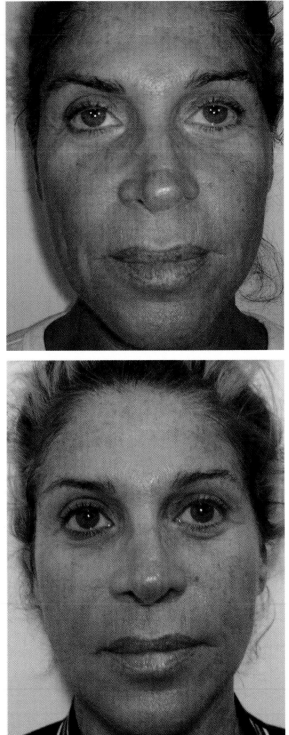

30 DAY PROGRAM

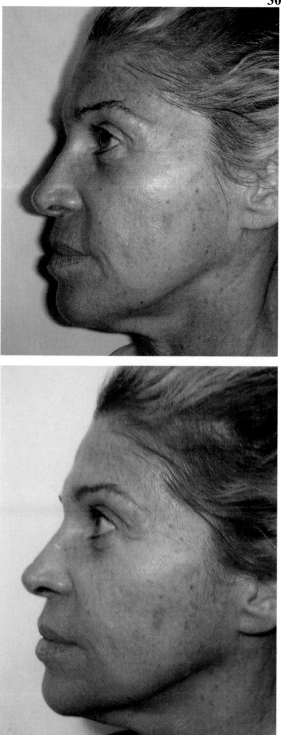

- The appearance of the roughness and uneven tone has been transformed into a smoother and younger look.

- The appearance of the lines around her upper lip, side of lips, and nasolabial fold is much improved.

- Her jaw line seems to be more defined.

30 DAY PROGRAM

30 DAY PROGRAM

- Her nasolabial folds appear to be less deep, especially on the left side.

- Her skin tone around the lips looks more even and firmer.

30 DAY PROGRAM

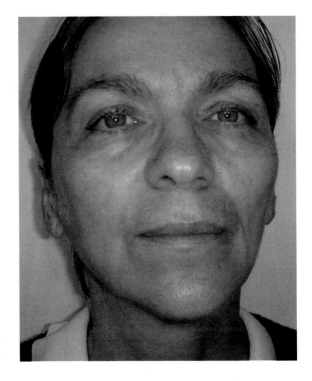

30 DAY PROGRAM

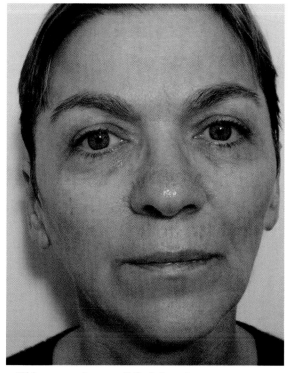

- This woman's overall facial contour appears to be much lifted.

- The unevenness and sagging look of her face has been improved.

- Her skin looks firmer.

- Her jaw line appears to be more defined.

- Her eyes seem lifted and less puffiness is noticed under her eyes.

INDEX

APPENDIX
Nefeli Herbal Supplements for Health, Beauty and Rejuvenation

HEALTHY HAIR

HERBAL SECRETS OF BEAUTIFUL, HEALTHY HAIR

Traditional Chinese Medicine sees healthy hair as a symbol not just of youth and beauty, but physical and spiritual health as well. So does Nefeli's "Healthy Hair." This product follows the Chinese medical theory that hair is closely connected with the blood, and its health and beauty depends on an abundance of liver and kidney essence.

HERBS MAKE THE DIFFERENCE WITH "HEALTHY HAIR"

The herbal botanicals in this formula are carefully studied and selected to make sure that the ingredients work together synergistically for maximum effectiveness against hair loss. Working together, the herbs in "Healthy Hair" balance the body's internal system so the hair and scalp are nourished. The herbs in "Healthy Hair" support the body's normal function to promote healthy hair growth, maintain normal and healthy blood and energy circulation to the scalp, and cleanse the scalp to maintain clean conditions for the hair follicles.

Here are some of those herbs have to offer:

HE SHOU WU (Fleeceflower Root)
• A vital herb for graying hair and beautiful face.
• Nourishes the life energy (Qi), and the blood while replenishing liver and kidney essence.
• An anti-aging, longevity-promoting Chinese herb.
• Rich in antioxidants.

SHOU DI HUANG (Cooked Rehmannia Root)
• Rejuvenates body's internal system to prevent hair loss and graying due to aging. Supports the body's normal function to replenish the blood to the hair follicles, ensuring a rich supply of the basic nutrients needed for hair growth.
• Replenishes kidney and liver essence, so vital for healthy hair.
• Contains 15 amino acids and more than 29 trace minerals.

CE BAI YE (Biota Leaves)
• Major herb used by Traditional Chinese Medicine to promote healthy hair conditions.
• Nourishes "source" Qi and the internal organs.
• Contains flavonoids, vitamin C, and trace minerals.

JU HUA (Chrysanthemum Flower)
• Works as a "guiding" herb to bring the rest of the formula to the scalp area.
• An excellent herb in its own power for helping maintain healthy hair functions to promote hair growth and prevent premature graying hair.

- Beautifies skin by clearing heat, expelling wind, and detoxifying the body (including the face and head).
- Contains powerful antioxidants and vitamins that improve hair health.

"HEALTHY HAIR" IS FOR YOU IF . . .

- You are losing any of your hair due to internal body deficiencies or aging process.
- You have premature graying hair due to internal body deficiencies or aging process.
- You don't suffer from hair loss or premature graying but you want to rejuvenate and beautify your hair and skin.
- You've tried other hair health products without satisfying results, or with uncomfortable side effects.

MENOPAUSE SOOTHER

A SAFE AND SMOOTH MENOPAUSE . . .NATURALLY

Nefeli's "Menopause Soother" is a natural herbal formula specifically designed to reduce normal menopause symptoms. Because it's based on ancient Chinese principles that have treated menopausal symptoms for thousands of years, "Menopause Soother", combining with a healthy life style and diet, serves as an all- natural and safe alternative for risky hormonal replacement therapy.

Unique among current products, "Menopause Soother" is based on the Chinese healing principle that traces menopause symptoms to insufficiencies in kidney energy (Qi) and in the body's "essence". The herbs in "Menopause Soother" are specially selected and precisely blended to address those underlying problems by nourishing the internal body systems, particularly the kidney system, including yin, yang and essence according to Traditional Chinese Medicine. The result: noticeable relief from hot flashes, day sweats, night sweats, mood swings, anxiety, dry mouth and skin, decreased vision and hearing, poor memory and other discomforts associated with normal change of life during menopause.

HERBS TO HELP YOU THROUGH THE CHANGE

Here are just some of the powerful traditional Chinese herbs that go to work when you take "Menopause Soother":

DI HUANG (Fresh and Prepared Rehmanniae Root)

- Supports the body's natural ability to deal with hot flashes, dizziness, night sweats, palpitations, insomnia, premature gray hair and dry, wrinkled skin due to the natural aging process related to menopause.
- Both forms of Di Huang replenish the vital essence to support healthy liver and kidney functions.
- The fresh version clears heat, nourishes yin, generates needed fluids, tonifies the five internal organs, and supports healthy bones.
- Contains polysaccharides, vitamins, 15 amino acids, more than 29 trace minerals.

XIAN LING PI (Epimedium Leaf)

- Helps to maintain healthy body function to address low energy and poor memory, which are associated with normal menopause process.
- Tonifies both kidney yin and kidney yang.
- Long lauded for its ability to maintain a healthy body function to regulate menses and raise low libido.
- Contains nutrients such as flavone-type compounds, saponins, linolenic acid, oleic acid, and vitamin E.

"MENOPAUSE SOOTHER" IS FOR YOU IF . . .

- You have occasional episodes of the following situations due to deficiency conditions of the body or aging process related to menopause:
    - Irritability, anxiety or mood swings
    - Hot flashes, night sweats, dry mouth or dry skin, palpitations, insomnia.
    - Memory loss.
    - Decreased vision or hearing.
    - Decreased libido.
    - Vaginal dryness or irritation.

WEIGHT MANAGEMENT

LOSE WEIGHT, GAIN BEAUTY

"Weight Management" is not only a superior formula for weight loss, but also superior for your body's overall health and for promoting longevity. What's more, "Weight Management" supports and maintains your healthy skin function to promote a beautiful and firm skin, so you won't have to worry about weight loss leading to sagging or loose skin.

GETTING AT THE ROOT OF YOUR WEIGHT PROBLEM

Being overweight is a common condition in our society, where processed foods are the norm. Chinese physicians recognized thousands of years ago that being overweight is a serious health risk, and they devised highly effective herbal remedies to help people reach their healthy weight.

"Weight management" uses those same herbs to address the internal causes of weight gain. That includes unhealthy conditions such as toxic buildup and compromised organ function.

SUPERIOR CHINESE HERBS FOR "WEIGHT MANAGEMENT"

Nefeli's weight-loss formula treats your problem safely according to Chinese principles. The specially selected herbs include absolutely no ma huang or ephedra, but they do help you lose pounds by maintaining your body's healthy metabolism, controlling your appetite, supporting normal body energy and blood circulation, and at the same time, they assist your body's normal function to detoxify itself.

Here are some of the essential herbs in "Weight Management":

SHAN ZHA (Hawthorn Fruit)

- A natural body cleanser, it's famous for its ability to overcome food stagnation from meat or greasy foods.
- Helps to maintain healthy heart function, and supports the body's natural ability to maintain normal cholesterol levels.
- Contains citric acid, flavones, and vitamins C and B.

HE YE (Lotus Leaf)

- An ideal herb for promoting healthy weight loss and suppress the appetite.
- Clears heat and promotes urination while strengthening digestive function.

HUANG JING (Polygonati Root)

- This body-lightening herb keeps you from feeling hungry.
- For centuries it's been used to nourish the body, benefit the Qi of all five internal organs, and promote longevity.

• Improves digestion and nourishes the skin.

"WEIGHT MANAGEMENT" IS FOR YOU IF . . .

• You have weight problems due to the following:
  • excessive appetite
  • low energy
  • low metabolism
  • constipation

COLD AND ALLERGY CARE

NO MORE MISERY FROM COLDS, FLU AND ALLERGIES

Every year, millions of dollars are spent on commercial products that promise to relieve runny noses, calm allergies and soothe sinus cold conditions. Many of these products are great for relieving bothersome symptoms, but they pay little attention to maintaining a healthy immune function so your body can better deal with the crisis.

Nefeli has a better way. "Cold and Allergy Care" delivers natural symptom relief by actually supporting your body's healthy immune system response instead of weakening it. You feel better and won't get sick as often in the future. Most important, this natural herbal supplement helps the body to address seasonal allergies and flu effectively.

"Cold and Allergy Care" uses herbs directly from the Chinese tradition of treating colds, flu and seasonal allergies. Unlike typical "cold medicine," "Cold and Allergy Care" works with your body's natural defensive system to address the root causes of the condition while soothing symptoms.

THE SPECIAL HERBS IN "COLD AND ALLERGY CARE"

Chinese herbs in this potent formula are specifically selected and blended to:
• Supports body's healthy immune function.
• Supports and maintains the body's healthy function to create a balanced condition so your body gains enough strength to fight the invaders, such as flu.
• Expel wind and clear the heat or cold.

Meet some of the top natural herbs in "Cold and Allergy Care":
BAN LIAN GEN (Isatis Root)
• Clears heat and detoxifies the body.
• Helps to support the healthy body's ability to fight off seasonal flu, bacteria and parasites.
JIN YIN HUA(Honeysuckl Flower) and LIAN QIAO (Forsythia Fruit)
• Both these herbs clear heat, relieve toxicity and address signs of sore throat related to seasonal cold and flu.
XIN YI HUA (Magnolia flower) and CHANG ER ZI (Cocklebur Fruit)
• They work together to help the body's natural ability to unblock nasal passages and relieve allergy symptoms.

DA ZAO (Jujube Fruit) and BAI SHAO (White Peony Root)

• These herbs harmonize ying (nutritive aspect of the body) and wei (defensive energy) to help maintain a healthy body function.

YOU NEED NEFELI'S "COLD AND ALLERGY CARE" IF . . .

*You want to maintain your healthy immune function so you can fight and prevent sinus colds and flu in a safe, natural and effective way.

About the Author

Ping Zhang is a New York State Licensed Acupuncturist, and a national certified herbalist with a master's degree in Traditional Chinese Medicine, has more than 10 years of clinical experience specializing in facial rejuvenation acupuncture, acupressure and Chinese Herbal Medicine.

She is a pioneer in the field of anti-aging and facial and body rejuvenation on Traditional Chinese Medicine. She designed and taught the first-ever graduate-level course in the U.S. on Traditional Chinese Medicine facial and body rejuvenation for the New York College for the Health Professions.

She is the President and Founder of Nefeli Corporation. She designed and develops the Nefeli anti-aging product line specializing in nutritional herbal supplements and natural herbal skin care products for health, beauty and rejuvenation.

She represents the fourth generation of her family to practice Traditional Chinese Medicine. She was interviewed by *WABC-TV (Eyewitness News), WB11, PBS Television, Reuters News Agency*, as well as the *Element Magazine* on how to use Anti-Aging Traditional Chinese Medicine to promote natural skin healing from body, mind and spirit with acupuncture, acupressure, natural Chinese herbs, as well as Qi Gong exercise. She is the author of the book "*A Comprehensive Handbook for Traditional Chinese Medicine Facial Rejuvenation*" and the author of series educational CDs for anti-aging therapy and prevention for healthcare professionals .

She continues to teach and lecture internationally and give advanced TCM facial and body rejuvenation certification seminars for professionals in NY, while maintaining a private practice in Port Washington, NY.